FOXING
WITH THE EXPERTS

PETER CARR

CO-AUTHORED, COMPILED AND ARRANGED BY

Peter Carr

CONTRIBUTING AUTHORS

Robert Bucknell, Gary Green, Howard Heywood, Andy Lovel,
Andy Malcolm, Mark Nicholson, Byron Pace

DESIGN

Chris Sweeney

EDITOR

Nick Robbins

PHOTOGRAPHY

Unless otherwise stated, photography is courtesy of the authors, iStock,
Shutterstock or Brian Phipps

British Library Cataloguing-in-Publication Data
A catalogue record for this book is available from the British Library

ISBN 978-1-910247-12-9

Printed in Europe by Cliffe Enterprise Print Partnership

Blaze Publishing Ltd
Lawrence House, Morrell Street, Leamington Spa, Warwickshire
CV32 5SZ
T: 01926 339808
F: 01926 470400
E: info@blazepublishing.co.uk
W: www.blazepublishing.co.uk

CONTENTS

INTRODUCTION

It has given me great pleasure to compile and co-author this dedicated foxing book that distils a collective 400 years of combined foxing knowledge. The likes of 'Sir' Robert Bucknell – knighted by his followers rather than the regent, though there is hope in next year's honours list for his services to the Essex countryside and efficient predator control – and that other foxing stalwart Mike Powell really do need no introduction. They are the undisputed leading foxing experts in Britain, and already established authors on their subject, with thousands of foxes under their belts.

These two premier foxing sages' knowledge is complemented by the experiences of professional gamekeepers and writers Andy Malcolm and Mark Nicholson, who offer us two distinctly different angles of fox control: Andy from a hill keeper's perspective and Mark as the lowland keeper counterpart. Their familiarity with the fox and how to bring him to book knows no bounds as their jobs depend on it, and both have received some acclaim for their writings on the subject. Howard Heywood is another long-standing authority on fox control and regularly follows the fox around the country, hunting him on hill, fell, farm and forest with lamp and rifle – his passion really is their pursuit. Howard's dedication and subsequent articles have always been well received across the sporting press and shooting journals.

Gary Green and Andy Lovel are the new breed of amateur foxers, or varminters to use an Americanism that is gaining some favour in English sporting parlance. They spend much of their spare time in pursuit of the fox and have developed their interest into a fine art form, using different techniques and the latest kit to bring marauding foxes to task. Both have found some fame with the pen based on practical experience providing a protection service for local farmers, shoots, and other countryside stakeholders. Finally we have young Byron Pace, who, despite still being in his youth, has amassed a lot of foxing hours both behind the rifle and as a sporting journalist covering foxing experts across the country for *Sporting Rifle* magazine, and internet TV channels The Shooting Show and Fieldsports Britain. He has won his place in these pages for his practical no-nonsense coverage on the subject and his dedication to duty.

That, then, is a brief résumé of the writers I have compiled to make this book what it is. What we were keen to do with this book was to let the experts speak for themselves. This isn't a book where we'll dictate what to do, what rifle to buy or what scope and moderator to marry it to, or indeed what tactic to use; it's a book where the collective wisdom of the finest fox shooters in the UK can be compiled and dispersed in one tome. Some of the advice from one author may contradict that of another, but the beauty of foxing is that the sport is so unpredictable, and what works for you may not for someone else. Different locations, availability of food sources and myriad other variables must be considered for each and every possible scenario on one's own ground. The fox is one of nature's survivors and Britain's most successful mesopredator – he has no natural enemies now living in our Isles apart from man and the occasional crazy eagle. So rather than arm you with a prescriptive guide on how to be the best foxer – because there is no

Above:
The author after a
successful fox hunt

such thing – we're arming you with knowledge, anecdotes, advice and stories that will, I'm sure, help you to shoot more foxes. However, it will be down to the reader to judge how to best turn the wealth of guidance contained in these pages into practical use.

Once the sole pursuit of gamekeepers and shepherds alone, fox shooting has developed into a sport in its own right. As I mentioned earlier this sport is increasingly being labelled 'varminting', a term imported from the States. It does have similar parallels to stateside coyote calling and shooting, and the encompassing term includes prairie dogs. This side of the Atlantic pond we include rabbits and rats when varminting, but being an Imperial traditionalist I like to stick to the simple split terms of foxing, rabbiting and ratting. I do hope the reader will forgive me for that.

In my five-year tenure as editor of *Sporting Rifle* I have been amazed at the increase of this dedicated branch of fieldsports and the rapid advance of dedicated fox control technology – and long may it continue. This augurs well for all of Britain's shooting sports and the game and wildlife of our islands.

The fox, of course, is a serious predator of game and domestic livestock. It is also a serious threat to most of our wildlife – much of it already threatened – and a vector of serious diseases such as erysipelas, brucellosis, leptospirosis, tick-borne encephalitis, and others. Fortunately we do not have rabies in the UK, but it shouldn't be forgotten that the fox is the main vector for spreading this scourge in mainland Europe. It is a chilling consideration if rabies ever crossed the channel. Good hygiene practice should never be forgotten when handling foxes. They harbour not only diseases that could seriously affect one's health, but they carry a number of parasites both internally and externally that can cause significant discomfort to the unwary hunter

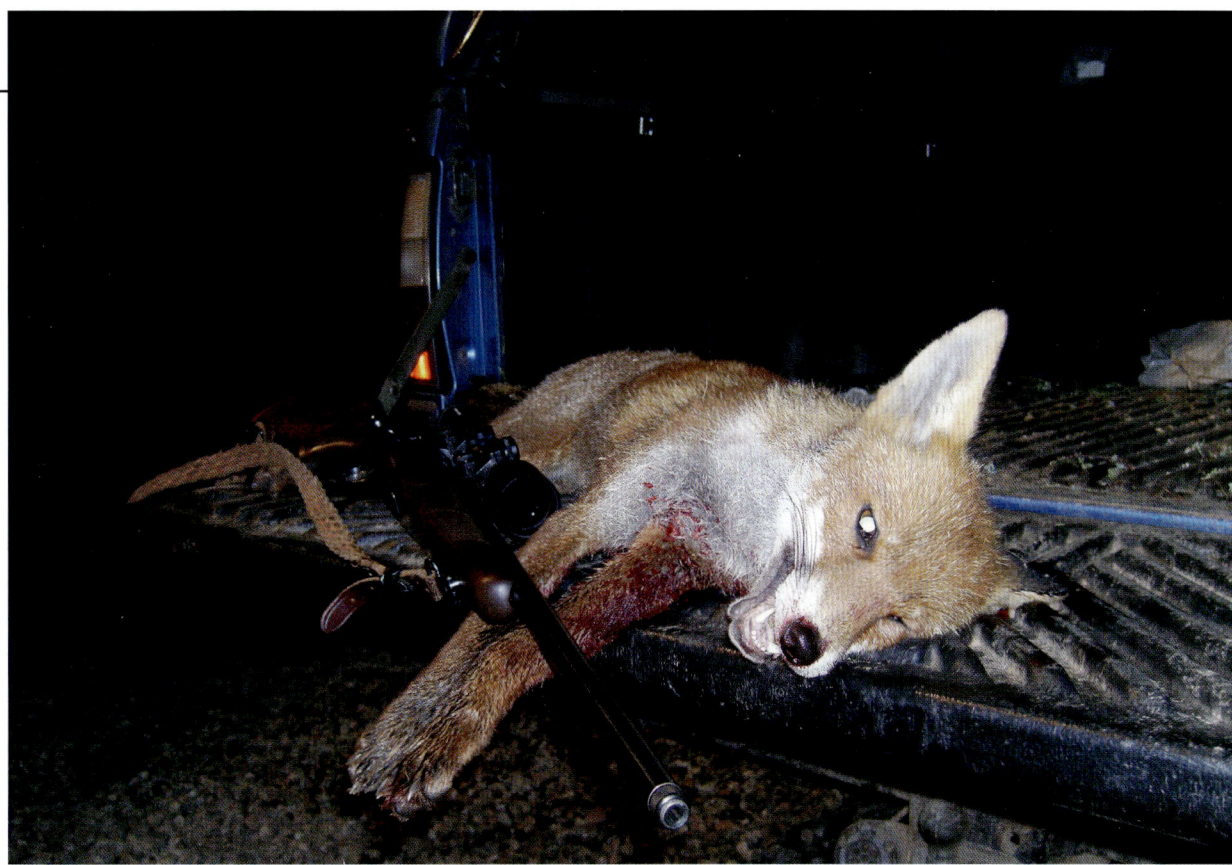

and which could be passed on to their family. Sarcoptic mange is caused by the same mite as the human scabies mite, and most foxes are infected with worms of one kind or another, all of which have varying degrees of adverse health on human beings if contracted.

I wince when I see shooters carrying foxes barehanded by their brush. Faeces and urine will obviously contaminate the brush on a daily basis so please be aware. It is better to carry foxes by their front legs with the head pinched in between pointing downwards to avoid contact with their teeth – another area of concern. It goes without saying that one should always use gloves for handling them.

Over 25,000 foxes are taken in Britain annually, which is of enormous benefit to our wildlife, game and farming interests. The greater degree of these foxes will be shot at night with lamp and rifle. Shooting in the dark hours of course brings its own set of safety concerns.

More and more people are coming into the sport and our impressive safety record must never slip. To do so would bring about legislative consequences that would seriously curtail or even ban what we do. Each and every one of us is an ambassador for our sport and firearm ownership. The following words tell of two stories that will hopefully make one think and remember that taking a chancy shot is the mark of a moron.

During my duties at the CLA Game Fair a few years ago I had the pleasure to fall into conversation with one of the country's leading fox controllers. The man in question related to me an urban legend he had recently been told, which I will pass on to you here: A couple of shooters ventured out one evening with lamp and rifle in search of foxes on their local estate. During the evening the pair picked out a pair of eyes nicely clear of a hedge bottom at the foot of some rising ground. The two foxers confirmed to one another that the eye shine was indeed a

Above:
Over 25,000 foxes are taken in Britain annually, which is of enormous benefit to our wildlife, game and farming interests

fox, its facial features well defined in their scope and binos. The shot had a safe backdrop and the animal was killed with an accurate shot. But as they approached the newly deceased fox, a moaning sound emanating from the nearby hedge bottom caused their blood to run cold. Two torch beams frantically pierced the inky blackness, and the shot fox was soon found. It turned out to be a corgi. The dead dog was complete with tartan collar attached to one of those 30-metre retractable dog leads with which one regularly sees an excitable dog towing its urban owner around town. Following the leash with hearts in mouths, the hapless pair soon found the source of the moaning. The moaning was, in fact, the rough snoring of a drunken chap who had become lost since leaving his latest watering hole on his way home.

After what must have been quite an emotional debate, the two geniuses decided on leaving the inebriated fellow to sleep it off where he was, and stole away with the corgi's corpse after rebuckling the now empty tartan collar and carefully cleaning the area of any evidence. Nothing was ever heard about the pub-goer or corgi. Although, if the story is to be believed, I guess the poor guy had one hell of a hangover and a lot of explaining to do after returning home to the missus… minus the family pet.

This particular story was probably – and hopefully – a legend based on a modicum of fact. However, tongue-in-cheek humour aside, it has some unnerving parallels to a similar situation that I was involved in some years ago. I was manning the rifle on a foxing foray while a senior colleague worked the lamp. Some time into the excursion my partner picked up the possible eye-shine of a fox working its way along the top of a wall. Eager and excited as he was for me to extinguish Charlie's existence, I was not happy to take the shot. I had picked up the face of the fox but something wasn't right – firstly with the facial image and secondly with its motion along the wall. I quite rightly refused to fire, despite the expletives and threats to my health from my superior.

Severely disgruntled, my co-pilot punched the 4x4 into gear, exiting the field at a rapid rate of knots, and turned left before pulling up where the wall in question met the road. He shone the lamp along the wall, where an elderly lady was walking down hill beside the wall with a chestnut-headed Jack Russell under her nearside arm. That experience has stuck with me ever since. We have an excellent sporting firearm safety record in our Isles and we need to keep it that way. The key to fox shooting during the evening is positive quarry identification – 99.9 per cent is simply not good enough when centrefire rifles are involved. It's not a case of beyond reasonable doubt, but rather a definite, unequivocal identification that the creature about to be killed is a fox. Remember, any fool can send a bullet on its way, but not even a genius can stop it during its flight.

Stick with positive quarry identification and you'll stay safe. I am sure that this book will help expand your knowledge and respect for the fox, and that with it you will hopefully shoot more foxes efficiently and safely. At the very least *Foxing With The Experts* will inspire you to spend more time in pursuit of this adaptable species that is only just kept in check by dedicated professionals and enthusiasts. I would hate to see the fox increase to pest proportions has it has in some European countries due to legislation that has given it limited or, in some cases, full protection. The fallout from this has been the catastrophic depletion of ground nesting birds and hares. We can all help to ensure this never happens in Britain by supporting all of our shooting organisations that lobby politically against those who would try to import European legislation to Britain. And by following safe, efficient, and ethical best practice, this book will help you to do that.

Shoot straight and be safe,

Peter Carr
Yorkshire
June 2014

FOXING RIFLES

Years ago, when I first started shooting foxes, it was really only the preserve of gamekeepers and a few like myself who sold fox pelts to the fur trade. More often than not we used shotguns, as the damage to skins was minimal. Since then,

things have moved on rapidly and today foxing is looked upon much more as a sport in its own right and, with the fur trade's demise, rifles are now the preferred weapon of choice. There are myriad suitable rifles to choose from, and the multitude of accessories available are good

evidence that fox shooting has now become big business.

There has been a great deal of debate regarding which rifle is best suited to fox shooting. A run through the vast number of threads on the various shooting websites will demonstrate that this subject is hotly debated, with many shooters having a firm favourite that obviously works for them. These personal views may well be helpful in steering you toward your particular rifle purchase.

All centrefire rifles are more than capable of killing a fox, but normally the calibre choice lies between the diminutive .17 Remington, up to the 6.5x55 Swedish – for the newcomer, choosing a calibre can be bewildering to say the least. Between these two extremes is a vast range of credible calibre possibilities to choose from.

Many sportsmen, especially keepers, will also use their foxing rifle for corvid control. Members of the crow family are very wary indeed and often require a long range shooting solution. Under these circumstances, the high-velocity, flat-shooting, lighter calibres come into their own. The .17 centrefire has its admirers, but the extremely light (usually 25-grain) bullet travelling at around 4,000fps is extremely frangible, and will fragment far too easily, rather than having the ability to penetrate and inflict deep-seated trauma – essential for quick, clean kills on larger quarry. Rifles in .204 Ruger, .220 Swift, .222 Remington, and the very popular .22-250 Remington are lethal on small vermin and foxes alike. For those who require a foxing rifle alone, the .223 has been the rifle of choice for many shooters for some time now, and a number of Scottish stalking enthusiasts use this calibre for roe. However, in England, a move up to and above .243 is necessary to stay within the law for roe, although recent legislation allows .22 centrefires to be used on muntjac and Chinese water deer. The .25-06 also has many enthusiasts, as does the 6mm, but personally I am inclined to look upon these two

options more as a deer rifle than an out and out foxing tool.

Recently the old .22 Hornet has seen a bit of a resurgence, it is a proven fox round out to about 200 yards, cheap to reload, and appeals to many who remember it from years gone by. Interestingly it now has a smaller sibling, the .17 Hornet, which is very fast (3,600fps) and good for all vermin, including fox out to around the 200 yard mark, and rather more for smaller vermin. The downside to this calibre is if you are using it for both fox and rabbit you would have to consider the cost of the ammunition. Reloading, though perfectly possible, is debateable if large numbers of rounds are used for rabbit control.

My personal calibre of choice for foxing has long been the .223. As with all conversations about calibre there are a multitude of choices and preferences. I settled a long time ago for the 223 as I found it did the job required perfectly, there was a wide choice of factory ammunition available and reloading was easy for this round. My fox rifle of choice is a Sauer 202, which shoots 55-grain Hornady V-Max extremely well. I have to say it is a really excellent rifle, highly accurate and beautifully made. I still take pleasure in the appearance of a rifle and the woodwork and overall design are very good indeed. I would like to add that the service I got from Steve Beaty at Ivythorn Sporting Guns in Somerset, a Sauer Master Dealer, was second to none.

For about eight months of the year I have it set up for night shooting with the Longbow night vision unit. This piece of equipment has the advantage of being a true day/night scope, which removes the need for scope switching. For the midsummer months this is usually replaced by a Leupold or Swarovski scope.

The Sauer has a light fluted barrel as I now need a much lighter rifle – age dictated that my faithful H-S Precision had to stand aside – and the Sauer has already proved its worth. There is little doubt that heavy barrelled rifles have

I seldom take shots over 250 yards. This is down to both safety factors and ethical considerations – I know my limits. Although there are a few shooters out there who are capable of taking safe, accurate shots over 300 yards, the vast majority of us will look to take our shots at much less than this.

The experienced fox shooter reading this will doubtless have already formed his or her own ideas on which type of rifle, ammunition and other equipment they should use. Much of this will have been by trial and error, which can be a costly exercise. The idea of this introduction is, in the main, to guide the newcomer as inexpensively as possible to their choice of calibre and rifle. There are, as previously stated, a bewildering array of choices and an equally massive amount of advice as to what is best. Remember this – an expert's particular point of view will not necessarily be taken so by others, but with careful consideration you will be able to choose with confidence – the old adage

Above:
.17 HMR rounds are extremely frangible, so care must be taken to avoid hitting an obstruction en route to your target

the edge over their lighter brethren when it comes to accuracy, particularly when one has the opportunity to use it from a secure rest. However, carrying such a heavy rifle when a large area needs to be covered on foot, by day or night, can reduce the pleasure of the outing considerably. And, in truth, the gain in accuracy can, in many cases, be academic at most. Modern rifles, irrespective of their weight, are more than capable of hitting a target the size of a beer mat at the ranges the majority of shots will be taken.

Talking about range, the average distance I have shot the majority of my foxes over the years has been approximately 120 yards.

Right:
Home loading helps ensure consistency in your shooting

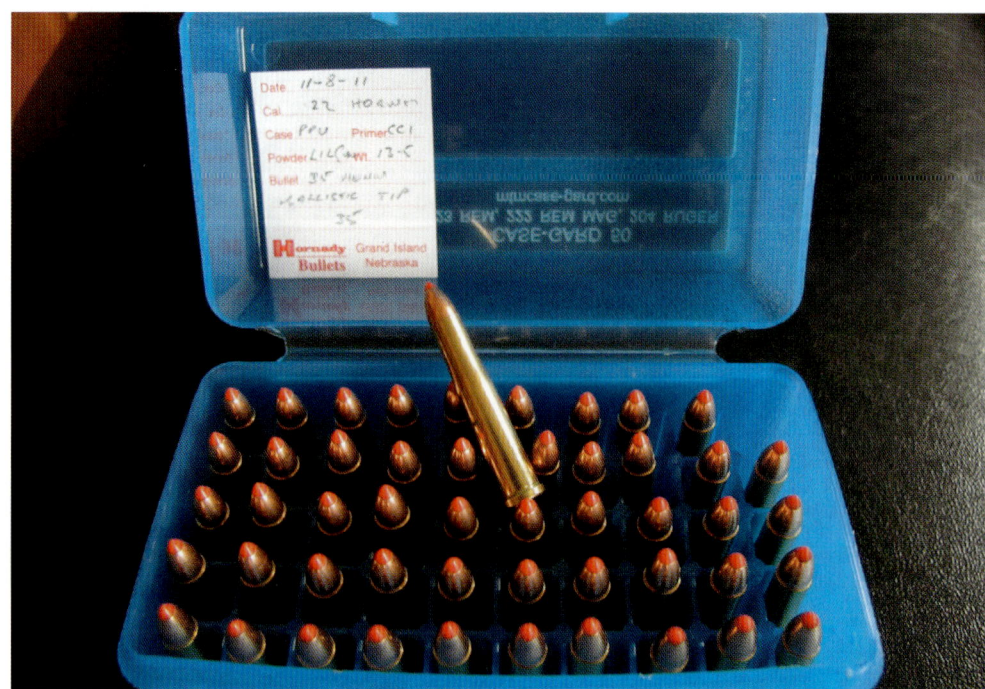

'buy in haste and repent at leisure' is extremely relevant.

During my shooting career, I have tried all sorts of rifles and have come to the conclusion that it really does come down to personal choice. We are all built very differently, so what fits one well may be a different story for someone else. It is imperative that you are comfortable with your rifle. Aesthetic qualities may not be a practical priority, but if you don't like the look of your rifle in the first place, you will be unlikely to do well with it. Fine walnut looks nice and would be my choice, but it is vulnerable to scratches and can occasionally warp, causing problems with your zero. If the rifle is going to be used from a quad, pick up, or 4x4, synthetic is the way to go as its resistance to damage ensures it will still look good after years of use and will never warp or shrink.

My personal choice is for the .223 – if for foxes and long range vermin shooting only. This calibre choice is freely available in most models of modern factory-built rifles as is the ammunition. Police authorities usually do not have a problem with this calibre when applying for a firearm certificate variation for foxing. That said, if deer are also on the shooting menu on the land on which you have permission, then the .243 Winchester would have to be my rifle of choice. Again, it is freely available in wood or synthetic in most brands and there is a range of ammunition from 55-105 grains, covering all eventualities from fox to stag.

Most modern rifles are well made and accurate, providing you select a brand of ammunition that suits your particular choice. Of course, home loading has become a hobby in its own right and does help the enthusiast wring the very best out of the rifle accuracy-wise. But quality factory ammunition bought in the same batch numbers are equally as effective at killing foxes. A three-shot cloverleaf group will kill a fox just as well as a one-hole group. ∎

MIKE POWELL

OPTICS AND MODERATORS

Possibly more is talked and written about scopes and moderators than almost anything else in fox shooting circles. A visit to almost any of the best shooting websites will reveal long and sometimes heated discussions on the merits or otherwise of which scope or which moderator is the best.

The problem in coming to a decision on either of these two items is that everyone's view is clouded by their own experience and perception of what is expected from them.

Below:
A scope with proven light gathering qualities is a must

Let's look at telescopic sights. The choice is absolutely enormous and the price variation is too. Take a firm like Schmidt & Bender: its products are top shelf and prices can range from almost £2,000 down to £400. Another firm in the same price bracket is Swarovski. Again, scopes at the top of their range are around the £2,000 mark. Zeiss too is in this bracket, as is Nightforce, a well-loved brand among experienced fox shooters.

What is it that puts these makes at the top of the tree and is money well spent acquiring one of these optical gems?

I personally think that there is absolutely no doubt that where scopes are concerned you get what you pay for. Looking in the sort of price range outlined above shows excellent build quality, top of the range optics and in most cases after sales back-up. However there are many less expensive brands that would rightly claim that they too offer such products and service to go with them.

Leupold is a make I rather like, producing excellent scopes below the price points of those listed earlier. Kahles is one of the oldest European makes, and produces optics on a level with Leupold price-wise. IOR and Meopta too are also held in high esteem at this price point.

In this piece I am referring to optics to be used on centrefire rifles used for fox shooting

rather than rim fires or air rifles. Moving a little further down the price scale opens up an even bigger selection of goodies to look at. Deben with their Hawke range are one of the best known, and many of their scopes are for air guns many are eminently suitable for centrefire use. Some of their special reticles are extremely good at giving the user pre-determined aiming points at a variety of ranges. I have used one of these for some time now and find them very good indeed.

I could go on and on listing names of manufacturers, all of whom are providing good quality useable scopes. In truth there are few bad ones on the market today, such is the quality of modern CNC machinery.

So where does this leave the prospective purchaser, in particular, first time buyers and those wishing to upgrade? Well what I have to say is purely my point of view, and will not necessarily be endorsed by all. I own several

scopes and have had several more through my hands – some very expensive ones too – and what I've found is that they all do the job. It's many years since I had a scope that in itself caused problems, so don't fret if you're on a limited budget – your scope will do the job for you whatever the make. But, like most things in life, some of the most expensive items not only do the job... they do the job with style. In the case of optics, top quality glass will give clarity unsurpassed by lower-priced models.

Also there is of course the ever-present lure of the big name. I suppose in the shotgun world it would be like the man with a Webley 700 aspiring to own a Purdey. When he gets one he will love it and he'll be the envy of all his friends, but he'll probably only shoot the same number of birds as he did with the cheaper gun.

I would love to be able to own a really top of the range scope, but in the meantime the ones I have do the job very well.

Above:

Nightforce scopes are well thought of by experienced foxers

Right:
Few scopes will let
you down, but it pays
to go for the best you
can afford

Finally the choice you make will be influenced by exactly what you want to use the scope for, the late night deer stalker will look for superior light gathering abilities, whereas the casual rabbit and fox shooter will be able to settle for something a little less.

Enjoy looking at what's on offer and go for the best you can afford, they will all do the job – some just a little better than others.

Much of what I have written about telescopic sights applies to sound moderators. Sound is very much like beauty: in the eye, or in this case the ear, of the beholder.

Many and varied are the views on which is the best centrefire moderator. One thing is certain: arguments will rage on for as long as people use moderators.

Sporting Rifle magazine has conducted in-depth tests using sophisticated sound measuring equipment to come up with tables showing decibel levels and proclaiming one make or another to be quieter than others. Yet when actually in use in the field it is extraordinarily

difficult to tell the difference using the human ear – if possible at all.

As an example I have a Wildcat moderator on one of my rifles. In one of the tests I read it showed well down the list, but I really like it and have no reason to change what is a very efficient unit.

Peter Jackson of Jackson rifles is one of the leading retailers of moderators in the country offering BR, ASE Utra and Sak models – all very good and retailed by a man always ready to share his knowledge freely. Then there is the PES range distributed through JMS Arms; and JLS stalker silencers also have their followers.

A moderator that has seen a lot of favourable press is the A-Tec, an over-barrel design, which gives good sound reduction according to its users.

Gerry Lapwood's Husher moderators are unusual in that they have no internal baffles and can have extra chambers added to improve efficiency. UK Custom Shop produces the Wildcat range – nicely made in stainless steel

– that are strippable and lightweight. Another one well worth a mention is the LEI, a good example of a muzzle-mounted moderator, which is aluminium-cased with stainless baffles. Finally for anyone looking for the most up-to-date model, Alan Rhone is importing Aim Sport moderators. I have one myself and am more than pleased with it.

So where does this leave us? Basically the choice comes down to two types, muzzle mounted and over-the-barrel versions. Both have benefits and disadvantages, relating to price, user-friendliness, ease of maintenance and longevity. The benefits have to be weighed against variations in length, weight, price and materials used.

What really doesn't help someone choosing a moderator for the first time is that you can't just take out a selection and try them. All you can do is to read the test reports on as many as you can and find one in your price range.

One thing you can rely upon, though, is that they will all do the job well enough. Using a moderator not only cuts down disturbance to others, it protects your hearing as well.

In the field, the use of a moderator diffuses the sound so that the quarry cannot usually detect the source – particularly useful when out after foxes.

Whatever type you decide upon, always remove the moderator when returning home after shooting. Some advocate a quick spray with something like WD40 for the types that do not come apart, whereas the types that can be dismantled should be given a regular clean.

I started off this piece on scopes and moderators by saying the choice is difficult and that it can be bewildering, as there are so many points of view. Vision and sound are interpreted by each of us in different ways. Choose the accessories that suit your pocket and personal physical preferences. Modern technology means there are few scopes or silencers out there that don't work well enough to contribute to the job of fox control when mated to a decent centrefire rifle. ■

BYRON PACE

FOXING CALIBRES

Foxing is the fastest growing sector of the shooting sports, with the amount of kit available increasing on a near daily basis. Though I have always enjoyed foxing, my hunting antics have traditionally been weighted towards stalking deer and hunting big game. However, through my duties for The Shooting Show, this balance has dramatically shifted and my nocturnal activities increase exponentially. I have been fortunate enough to spend time with some great foxers as well, and learned far more than I ever knew to begin with.

This has led me to a number of my own conclusions on kit and tactics, but the most emotive issue is always one's choice of calibre. Instead of imposing my own views on the matter, I have pulled in friends and hunters on each foxing calibre, along with providing the raw facts myself.

The list of suitable foxing calibres is vast, even if not always particularly practical. Everything from the bunny-stopping .17 HMR to the militarily selected 7.62 sees use chasing down Basil, but there are some that do the job better than others. If we tackle the subject from day one, there are a few questions most hunters will ask:

- What is the cost of ammunition?
- What is the availability of ammunition?
- Are rifles readily chambered in the calibre?
- What are the down-range ballistics and performance like?
- How long will my barrel last?

With this in mind, there is no point, for example, suggesting that an 85-grain .22-250 Rem is the answer, as finding a factory rifle with a twist to support it would be all but impossible. That is the realm of custom rifles.

So now we get to the list. The first couple were easy enough: .243 Win, .22-250 Rem, .223 Rem. I doubt there is a big brand manufacturer who doesn't chamber them, and they are widely used across the country. Then we get to some of the newer calibres, .17 Hornet and .204 Ruger. A quick call around my foxing buddies provided one further addition: the mighty .220 Swift.

Plenty of hunters reading this will shake their head at the fact I have missed their calibre of choice, but we need to keep the criteria in mind and accept that we need a short list to start with. The most notable absence is the .17 HMR, and I and many of my hunting companions have cleanly killed foxes with this little calibre. However, most will concede that it is simply not a foxing calibre. It has the capabilities, in the right circumstances and conditions to take foxes, but few professionals would embark on a night's foxing with only a .17 HMR in hand.

.22-250 Rem

Having handed over the rest of the calibres to my colleagues, I thought I would take the .22-250 Rem on board myself – indeed, this is what my Howa 1500 foxing rig is chambered in. The treble-two-fifty can definitely be described as a sweet shooter. It's not as gentle as a .222 Rem or the smaller cased calibres, but a moderated rifle fitted with a varmint barrel will hardly recoil, with sight picture easily maintained between shots. It's a soft shooter, but you are very aware that a lot of energy is hurtling down-range.

In terms of terminal performance, the .22-250 Rem is superb. I am yet to have a fox do anything other than drop on the spot when the person behind the trigger does their bit. Shooting homeloads of 55-grain Nosler Ballistic tips, there is only occasionally an exit wound, with the internals blended into a claret soup. It tends not to be a particularly fussy calibre either, with loads fairly easy to tune, and most accepting an array of factory fodder. It is also inherently accurate, with my own rifle putting pretty much any ammo into ¾in, and homeloads into a five-pence piece at 100 yards.

Ballistically, it's not the most impressive, but then it's not far off either. There are some benefits to this, though, with barrel life better

than the short-lived Swift. Loaded to sensible levels of around 3,600fps, you're looking at a 300-yard drop of just 5in when zeroed 0.88in high at 100 yards. With that you will tackle almost any situation you will encounter at night. Obviously wind has to be taken into account, and that will be the limiting factor of the .22-250 Rem.

In terms of our list, it is one of the more expensive calibres, but choice certainly won't be a problem. Neither will finding the rifle you want, as every manufacturer worth their salt will chamber at least one model in .22-250 Rem. I can't see me ever replacing my foxing set-up in .22-250 Rem.
Byron Pace

.204 Ruger

The .204 Ruger launched itself as the new foxing champion, boasting the title of 'the fastest factory centrefire in the world'. The hype has long since died down, and after a few years

Above:
Danny Lawson night foxing with the .204 Ruger

Left:
Spent .22-250 Rem cartridges

bullet. As with all light calibres, wind is a big consideration, and the lightweight 32-grain load will shift as much as six inches at 200 yards with a 10mph wind. However, if you up the weight to 39 grains, you will have much more satisfactory results, on par with the rest of the foxing calibres. Barrel life is better than the over-bore .22-250 Rem and .220 Swifts, but the high speeds can chew throats quicker than a .223 Rem.

I would compare down-range terminal performance to shooting a 55-grain .223 Rem. It's hard to separate them really, and this is evident in their 300-yard energies. Again, dropping to 32 grains almost halves the 300-yard performance in this department.

The .204 Ruger is a lot of fun to shoot, and once tuned, very accurate, but I am not convinced it really lived up to the hype. It would make a superb round for long-range varmints, but as a foxing calibre I still rate my old .22-250 Rem as being superior.
Danny Lawson, head keeper

.220 Swift

I had gathered the information and views on the Swift in preparation for this test, but I will have to cut the analysis as there is very little between the 50-grain Swift and 55-grain .22-250 in terms of energy and trajectory.

Of course, the lighter 40-grain Swift shoots a lot flatter, with less than four-inches of drop, but you will have more than 100ft/lb less energy than the 50-grain bullet at 300 yards, and at more than 4,200fps it will be a serious barrel burner. Ammo is expensive and rifles are less readily available than the .22-250 Rem, which in terms of hunting capabilities for foxes does everything the Swift does with a heavier bullet and a longer-lasting barrel. So although it is an excellent killer, shooter and grouper, by comparison the Swift has to be counted out.

.223 Rem

It is probably fair to say that the .223 Rem wouldn't be as popular as it is today without it being a military calibre. Like the .308 Win,

of infield testing, we can finally see if the calibre has lived up to what it promised.

The first thing to note is that most hunters aren't loading the light 32-grain bullet, which crossed the 4,000fps mark. The benefits gained in flat trajectory just don't compensate for the wind drift, or the loss of down-range energy when compared to the heavier 39-grain load.

Although many manufacturers chamber the calibre today, when I first had the urge to get my hands on a .204 the choice was limited, so I went the custom route, with a tactical, Remy-based rifle put together by Callum Ferguson of Precision Rifles. As you would expect, the rifle is extremely accurate, but I have found the .204 Ruger quite finicky to tune loads for, and by far the fussiest of any calibre I have owned. The other issue is ammo availability if you don't load your own.

You would definitely describe the .204 Ruger as a gentle shooter. Recoil is negligible when moderated, and you would almost think you are firing a .22WMR. As already alluded to, trajectory is super flat, and out to 400 yards is almost identical to a .220 Swift pushing a 55-grain

the availability of cheap ammunition and rifles certainly helped establish the calibre in the sporting world.

There is no doubt that the .223 Rem is very popular as a foxing calibre. As you would expect, there is a vast selection of rifles chambered in .223. Off the shelf ammunition selection is good, and, of course, you can obtain very cheap military surplus ammo as well. Being non-expanding, it can't be used for hunting, however it does provide a cheap way of getting a lot of practice in. Having said that, of the mil spec ammo I have fired, I have never found any to group particularly well in a hunting rifle. This is most likely due to the clash between rifle twist rate and the loaded bullet weight.

Shooting the .223 Rem is a very calm and understated affair. When moderated, there really is very little fuss, and I have never had any trouble getting factory ammo to shoot well. Shooting with a very modest muzzle velocity, barrel life is generous. It's unlikely most hunters will ever shoot out a rifle in their lifetime, unless doing a serious amount of range work. The same cannot be said for some of the other calibres. It's not the flattest shooter, and a 55-grain bullet will need a full inch and a half at 100 yards to drop on target at 200 yards. Once you're comfortable with that, it becomes second nature. At night, most shots will be up to 200 yards, with a much smaller proportion past this, so the drop beyond isn't too much of an issue as long as you're aware.

Possibly one of the most convenient points of this smaller calibre is that you can get away with having a much shorter barrel than, say, a .22-250. Cut a .22-250 down to 18-inches and you will be wasting a lot of performance. You can get away with it when it comes to the .223 Rem, and that makes shooting in and out of a vehicle much more convenient.

I would say finally that, although the calibre kills the vast majority of foxes outright, every now and then you will get them running on a way. Obviously this could happen with any calibre, but it is more noticeable with the .223

Left:
The 70-grain .243 held more energy than any other round tested at 300 yards

Rem than a .243 Win or .22-250 Rem.
Phil Chapman, grouse keeper

.243 Win

Although most people think of the .243 Win as a stalking calibre, its origins lie in the pursuit of varmints. A 100-grain bullet may be the default choice for many, but most rifles will shoot better with some lighter fodder. Indeed, most hunters never really get to see the true capabilities of a .243 Win until they downsize to 70 grains or less. It is here that you will see what a tremendous calibre it is for foxing.

Without a decent moderator, the .243 Win does induce enough muzzle flip on recoiling to cause loss of sight picture. This is not at all ideal, but clamp a moderator on the end of your rifle and it's a different animal entirely. Although it may be the heaviest recoiling of the shortlist, moderation makes it only marginally more noticeably than a .22-250 Rem.

Rifle choice and ammunition selection will never be a problem for what is probably the UK's most popular calibre, and for the

bullet placement is a bit off, it will knock a fox off its feet where it stands. The same cannot be said for some of the smaller calibres. Even at 300 yards, the energy is more than 1,000ft/lb, whereas a .223 Rem is almost half that.

The weather on Skye can be unpredictable, with winds whipping up in seconds. The broken, rough terrain makes locating a dropped fox hard enough even when you know where it is. I am not shooting super long ranges, and nor do I want to think about complex ballistics before pulling the trigger – that's for prairie dog hunters and target shooters. With relatively cheap ammo on offer, the .243 Win does everything I want it to do and is my number one choice.

It is possible to load a .243 Win very hot indeed, especially with 55-grain bullets. Even with factory loads, these return more than 3,800fps MV, and will vastly reduce the life of your barrel. However, from 70 grains upwards bullet velocities are more modest. If you're worried about flat shooting, the 70-grain bullet offers an excellent compromise. Only dropping 5.5-inches at 300 yards with a one-inch high zero at 100 yards, it still delivers more energy than any of the other calibres listed here.
Scott Mackenzie, professional fox controller

.17 Hornet

This is the newest calibre to tickle the foxing world. As a result of this, few people seem to have done extensive foxing with it. Obviously the lightest bullet weight of the short list, it is the softest to shoot. From my experience, it is a very accurate factory round. Trajectory replicates the .223 Rem shooting a 55-grain bullet, as discussed above, while down range energy is only about a third. At 300 yards, the .17 Hornet has slightly less energy than the ME of a .17 HMR. As you would expect, wind is probably the biggest consideration. It drifts the most, with more than a foot of compensation needed at 300 yards with a 10mph wind.

So as a foxing round, where does this leave the baby of our calibre line up? Of those listed

handloader there are plenty of excellent bullets available for experimentation. It doesn't normally take much to find ammunition to suit a .243 Win, and even factory rifles with factory ammo can return less than ¾in groups with a bit of trial and error.

Most importantly, though, it's a very forgiving calibre when hunting. For me as a gamekeeper/stalker and a paid fox controller in the Hebrides, I need a calibre that is going to put a fox down and keep it down. Like many, I have rotated my gun cabinet through the 'in' calibres of the day, but I keep coming back to the .243 Win. Loaded with 100- or 105-grain bullets, even if

above, the .17 Hornet has been used the least as it is the newest. It is quite apparent that the .17 Hornet will drop foxes quite convincingly many times in a row, but the margin for error is much smaller than the bigger foxing calibres. It is far more suited than a .17 HMR, but lacks the knock down and anchor power of the other calibres. I am sure rifle choice will continue to grow, although at the moment it is limited (as is ammunition choice). That said, the Hornady Super Performance 20-grain ammo is superb.

One of the big bonuses is that rifles are light, feeling more like a rimfire than a centrefire. Although I don't know anyone who has shot a barrel out yet, calculations show you should get more than from a .223 Rem due to minimal powder burn. I think the .17 Hornet probably sits more comfortably as a long range varmint round, and no doubt finds considerable favour in the States after prairie dogs and rock chucks. With only 11 grains of powder required, re-loading is cheap by comparison, too. ∎

BALLISTIC COMPARISON TABLE

Bullet	MV (fps)	ME (ft/lbs)	300yd energy	Bullet drop 300 yds	Wind drift 300 yds/ 10mph
.220 Swift 50gr	3850	1646	757	-4.7	9
.22-250 Rem 55gr	3625	1605	780	-5.2	8.8
.243 Win 55gr	3850	1811	904	-4.4	7.9
.243 Win 70gr	3450	1851	980	-5.5	8
.223 Rem 40gr	3700	1216	500	-5.5	10.8
.223 Rem 50gr	3240	1282	598	-6.8	10.4
.204 Ruger 39gr	3750	1218	623	-4.7	7.8
.17 Hornet 20gr	3650	592	200	-6.4	13.5

A YEAR OF FOXING

MIKE
POWELL

In these days of instant access to pretty well everything you ever wanted to know on the internet, I find it interesting to read the various questions newcomers to foxing ask about the best time and place to shoot them. Does weather have an effect? What circumstances move the odds in your favour?

All my life I have sought out the fox for various reasons, such as control, prevention of damage, and skins. There have been times when, as far as I was concerned, the only good fox was a dead one. Times change, though, and although I still take care of reasonably large numbers, my interest in this creature has grown over the years.

So what would be my answer to the first question: when is the best time to come across Charlie? Clearly there are times of year when their activities are governed by the natural urge to procreate. Mating time, generally in full flow at the start of the new year, is an opportunity to locate dogs and vixens by day and by night. Obviously they are far more active during the hours of darkness, but when the mating urge lies heavy on them, they will not only be seen during the day, but heard as well. In January 2014 when I was out with the ferrets, I heard a dog fox barking. This continued for well over an hour, with him covering a considerable distance in pursuit of a vixen.

This, however, is only a small part of the year. What of the winter and summer periods

– will weather conditions play a part in how many foxes are shot? Speaking from my own experiences, I learned long ago when shooting foxes for a living that weather can certainly affect their behavioural patterns. Most animals, I suspect, react to conditions much as we would if we had to be out and about no matter what. They, like us, would tailor their movements to alleviate the unpleasantness of torrential rain, biting winds, or snow. In other words, they would seek shelter to minimise the discomfort.

But foxes have to eat, and on a regular basis, so even on nights of foul weather their stomachs dictate they have to be out hunting.

However, they will make the most of any circumstances that will keep the worst weather off their backs. Those circumstances will vary depending on the country they are living in. In more open country, field hedges and the natural folds of the ground will offer a little respite from the weather, while in more heavily wooded areas foxes will keep to the shelter afforded by trees and bushes. Prey species, too, will be far more likely to be in areas giving protection so the two systems work well together.

Rest assured: even on bad nights, they will be out there somewhere. It's about knowing your ground and putting yourself in the fox's place.

Much is said about 'snow foxes', and when the land is covered in the white stuff, many go out to seek the fox. I suspect that foxes view

MIKE'S TOP TIP

Stealth cameras are useful for charting the wildlife on your permission

snow similarly to how we do: once the original novelty has worn off, it is a pain in the brush. If snowfall is heavy and settles, foxes will often be found out in the open hunting for mice and voles, which continue to go about their business beneath the white covering.

Many people will have seen foxes pouncing on rodents in grass. This behaviour will often be replicated when snow is on the ground, where the colouring of the fox is in stark contrast to the pristine whiteness. For those who don't have night vision, a decent scope will show up foxes against the white stuff out to 150 yards or even more depending on the moon phase.

When winter has its grip on the land, bitter winds will definitely affect fox behaviour. I can't think of any creature, including us, that likes to be out in a bitter wind – it dulls the senses and masks sounds, and at the same time everything is moving. I think every predator, us included, would probably say cold, strong winds are probably the worst conditions to hunt in. As with rain, the foxes will be there, but seeking areas sheltered from the blast.

Leaving winter behind, summer arrives with a host of different problems. Fields suddenly become no-go areas when standing crops of grass or cereals mask what is going on. Again, our behaviour will give a clue as to where foxes will be found – we will skirt standing crops and avoid heavy cover. Most animals, including foxes, tend to do the same.

Established runs will stay open – constant footfall prevents crop growth. Bait put out where the runs meet open ground can give success, as can fields where stock grazes. I have found that whenever foxes are on the hunt for food, they will nearly always visit stocked fields in preference to empty ones. Clearly there is food of one sort or another where cattle and sheep are disturbing the ground.

As summer progresses, fields that have been laid down to crops will eventually be cleared. This will free up much more territory for foraging. One particular farming practice will often give results, and that is topping off weeds. I have shot many foxes that were just sitting around waiting for the tractor to finish this task. Many of the fox's favourite food items can be picked up after the topper's blades have skimmed across the field. Rodents, beetles and the like will be there in abundance, and Charlie will more often that not take advantage of this.

As the summer season nears its end, sitting out on warm evenings, particularly if you have a high seat, will give you a good chance of apprehending foraging parents or cubs out hunting for the first time. Pick out rides in woodland or spots you know are frequented by foxes. Although they will forage pretty much anywhere, the margins of fields, particularly

where the headlands have been left under a stewardship scheme, offer rich pickings.

I have seen a substantial rise in the number of foxes using these headlands. My local farmer friend has headlands around almost the entire farm, most about 15 metres wide. Their inception was only a few years ago, but they are now well established. The difference they have made to the local insect and wildlife in general is becoming increasingly apparent. While I think it is a shocking waste of good arable land, my friend gets well rewarded financially for taking this ground out of production, and it has certainly encouraged not only the aforementioned insects but also the larger species such as roe, rabbits and foxes, not forgetting our friend the badger.

As summer drifts into autumn, the unmistakable hint that winter will soon be with us shows in leaf drop. The evenings will start drawing in and the lamping and night vision equipment will come into its own once more. The countryside opens up and most of the land will once more be clear.

This is without doubt the most prolific time for fox culling. The new season's cubs will be causing trouble, particularly with the poultry and game. Focusing on these should pay off, but once more foxes will be out and about everywhere. If you live, as I do, in an area that carries a high population of the top predator, you can be pretty sure that almost all the land you shoot over will be visited by foxes during the night

The trick is, of course, to work out the most likely areas. You can make this a bit more predictable by baiting, or if you have the time, studying where your foxes are travelling. Judicious use of stealth cameras can certainly help – I use these at all times of year, and they really do give a good indication of where and when wildlife of all sorts is about.

Finally, we arrive back at winter, and another year spent tackling the fox has passed.

To sum up: foxes are around far more than most people think, and the more you get out on your land, the more chance you will have of catching up with one. Certainly kind conditions are better, but remember they have to eat, and like us, in truly bad conditions their movements will be more restricted. Whatever the conditions, they will be out there. ■

Above:
Foxing is year-round pursuit, and a thorough knowledge of Charlie can make all 12 months bountiful

CALLING THEM IN

For several years I have been using a variety of night vision equipment. I find this is an intriguing insight into the way nocturnal wildlife carries on when it is undisturbed. To increase one's knowledge, it is sometimes better to watch than shoot. For most of my life I did the latter, particularly where foxes were concerned, and while this worked well in the circumstances and in doing so I did learn a bit about the quarry, in retrospect the knowledge was pretty shallow.

For example, when using conventional lamping methods, in most cases by the time the fox is in the lamp it is well aware that something is up. From then on in there are two ways of dealing with it: hot pursuit or fieldcraft. As far as I can see there is little connection between the two. Belting across the fields with a driver, a lamp man and a shooter does take a certain amount of knowledge as to where

obstacles may be and the best way to gain access to the next field. But the fox is a target, one that hopefully will stop long enough for a safe shot with the rifle.

Don't misunderstand me – I have done a lot of this myself over the years. But I also remember shooting foxes for their skins commercially with a shotgun, where fieldcraft was essential. My knowledge of a fox's behaviour after dark was extremely limited – I knew how it would react to a lamp and how to get close enough to be sure of a kill with the 12-bore and BBs, but of the animal's general behaviour, my knowledge was skimpy at best.

This state of affairs continued right up to the point when I was first asked to test some night vision equipment. It soon became apparent that what foxes, and to a degree rabbits, did when they felt comfortable in their own environment had little to do with what

MIKE'S TOP TIP

Calling is an imperfect science; time and patience are needed to make the most of it

I had occasionally imagined. To start with I operated much as I had when lamping in the conventional manner, walking the fields and spotting with the NV. This worked to a degree, but I learned early on that more often than not the fox I spotted was aware I was around. This is something that became more and more apparent the more I used the new technology. Gradually I found I could change tactics and get the same results – with more financial expenditure (much more) but with less effort.

There are so many little things you pick up about foxes when you resist the temptation to pull the trigger, at least for a while. For example, in the past I always aimed to start out with the lamp during the winter months about nine or 10 at night – by then, foxes would be up and about. By using static positions and waiting, I soon learned that this is a fallacy. In winter, most troublesome foxes I deal with are shot before 7pm. As soon as darkness falls, they are off – after all it is their breakfast time

and it has been a good 12 hours since their last meal.

The 'static' method of foxing requires two things to be really successful: patience and knowledge of fox movement. Patience, I suspect, is something that comes with age. When I was young I spent countless nights out, walking equally countless miles after foxes. We shot a lot but used up vast quantities of energy – willingly I admit – doing what we loved. I still do what I love, but I spend a lot less time doing it and get much the same results. Waiting, though, does require patience and a lot of it. I mentioned knowledge of your ground. Time spent just walking your land looking for runs, scats, or signs of kills will give you a feel of where you would go if you were a fox. Eventually you will see areas a little nearer to how a fox possibly sees them.

One other factor that receives a great deal of comment is calling the fox. There are a few people endowed with an innate skill to call foxes

Above:
Using night vision gives the foxer an opportunity to study their quarry's behaviour 'after hours'

Right:
Look out for tell-tale
signs of foxes – like
fox scat...

Below:
...and this well
used run

in almost at will. But these are rare birds indeed; most mere mortals rely on learned skills, mostly trial and error with the emphasis on the latter. Why should calling in foxes be so problematic? My take on this is that foxes, like us, are individuals and are influenced by factors, many of which are not understood by us humans.

To emphasise this, I remember going after a particular fox on a foul night with intermittent rain and a bit of mist about – not ideal for night vision use. Parking up the 4x4 against the top hedge of a field I knew the predator used,

I settled down to wait. At about 7pm a fox appeared as if from nowhere and crossed the field below me a fair distance away. I tried the ever faithful WAM caller, watching all the time through the NV. Absolutely no reaction. Next was the Best Fox Call – same result. I also had my reliable Mini Colibri and let fly with three different calls: rabbit distress, vixen scream and mating vixen. Through all this the fox never once looked up, concentrating on picking up worms and other invertebrates.

I tired of the test and, putting the crosshairs on the chest, dropped what turned out to be a stocky vixen (no wonder the vixen calls didn't work). She was just over 200 yards out and the .223 Hornady Superformance 53-grain ammo did its usual grand job.

So what did I learn from this particular exercise? Precious little to be honest, except showing that calling foxes is an imprecise science. All the calls I tried on the vixen have worked for me in the past, but on this occasion the fox just wasn't interested. Like all fox shooters I have had them come in to a call of one sort or another flat out and had to pull them up with a whistle or shout. Equally, I have had foxes come to a particular call and pay the price, but on the same night, with the same call, another has turned tail and fled.

Calling, particularly at mating time and when cubs are first out hunting, can be lethal, although the first of these situations needs far more experimentation with fox calls. Sometimes foxes react very differently from the way we would expect. With digital callers, I suspect that the reproduction in the way the speaker actually delivers the sound has a bearing on how the fox reacts. It is not uncommon, when watching foxes going about their business, to see their reaction when a real rabbit is caught either by a fox or a stoat. The ensuing scream gets an instant reaction from any fox within earshot. No hesitating – they are there in seconds, so clearly they can detect differences in the sounds they hear.

We have little idea of what a fox's ears transmit to its brain. Certainly any animal that can hear a mouse squeak from around 100 yards away doesn't hear sounds the same as we do. All I suggest is that if you have the opportunity to watch foxes for a while, particularly at night, try a few calls and just watch the reaction they get. Be warned, though, you need to be prepared as sooner or later one will come in full tilt and observing will have to be put on the back burner.

After many years of pursuing the fox, I would say I do know more now than I did all those years ago when shooting them as a means of income. However, it is only since the advent of night vision (and a certain lack of energy) that I have really been able to learn more about the fox. Fifty years ago I wouldn't have spent hours in a high seat, or anywhere else for that matter, waiting for a fox. There was no NV and I certainly didn't have a 4x4 then, so waiting was only an occasional option. Now this is generally the way I do it – I survey the land quite carefully to see the fox signs, try to put myself in their situation and exploit this knowledge to make life easier for me. ■

Below:
It's best not to put all your faith in one call – there's no predicting when one may or may not work

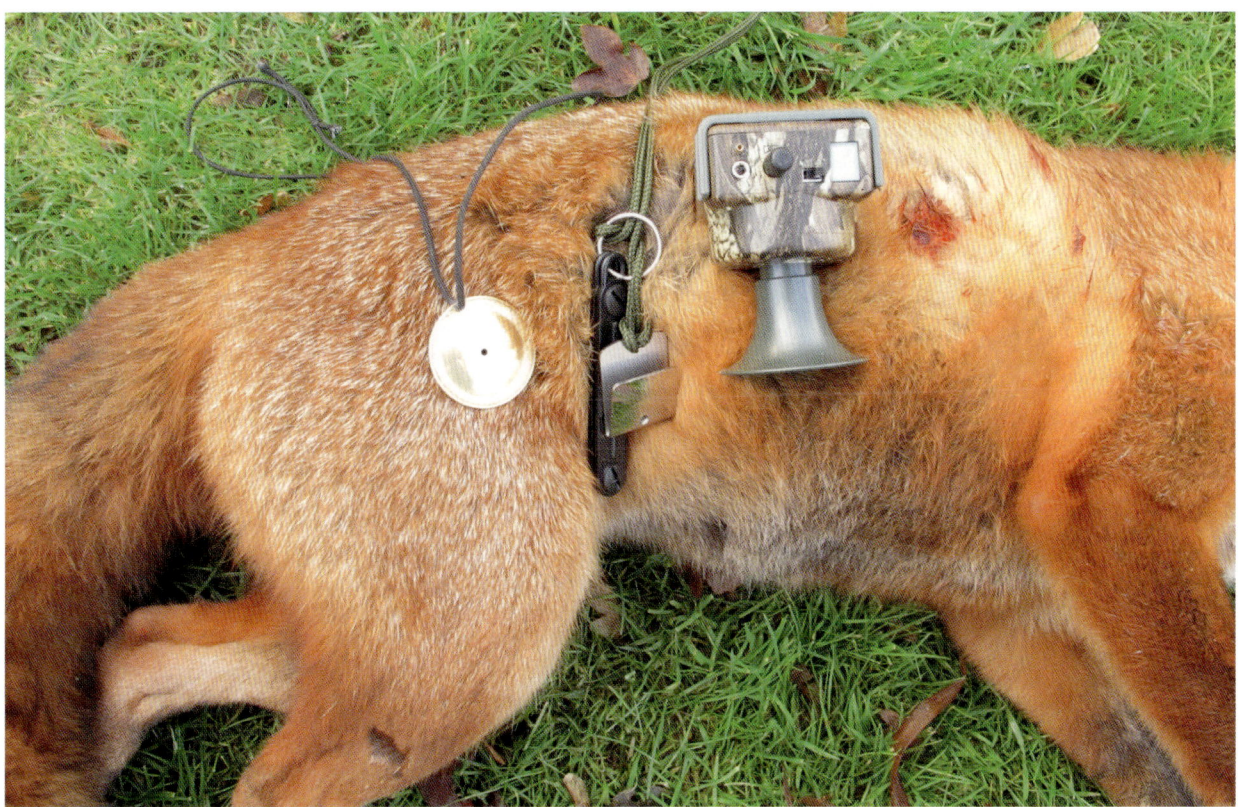

CLASSIC CALIBRE

The .22LR is not my first choice for taking out foxes – though it is capable of doing so at sensible ranges, a lot of care has to be taken when placing the shot. Most .22s are extremely accurate, and most users should be capable of a one-inch group out to 75 yards. If they can't do that, a bit of practice could be needed, particularly if the fox is the target.

Over the years I have shot a fair number of foxes with this calibre. In my opinion, although many are shot at greater distances, I reckon 60 yards must be about the maximum. Although they will often die eventually from a long range .22 hit, foxes do not drop on the spot at 70 yards unless hit in one or two choice spots (brain, heart). At sub-60 yard ranges, most shooters should be able to deliver an accurate

enough shot to either drop Charlie on the spot or at worst traumatise it enough for a swift second shot to finish the job.

My choice of rifle for normal fox control is a .223 Anschütz fitted with the Longbow night vision scope – or, during the summer months when longer-range shots are on the cards during daylight, the H-S Precision .243 WSSM or the lighter barreled Sauer.

Yet there are times when the .22LR is the best option. One such occasion was when I received a call from a client asking for some help with a fox that had taken a dozen of his best (it's always the best ones) chickens. I arranged to get up and see him later in the day, and when I did, the usual scenes of carnage were plain to see. The usual puffs of feathers and sad remains of the slain, together with

MIKE'S TOP TIP

The .22LR is a humane tool for fox control in the right hands

the traumatised and injured victims, were everywhere. Having had the same problems myself in the past, I could only sympathise, and promised to do what I could.

In situations like this I always ask the owners to leave everything as it is until I've been to have a look, as I can often pick up clues as to where the fox has come from and whether he has taken anything with him. The first thing to look for was signs of a carcase being taken off. This will often be found within 100 yards, usually in an open space where the raider can keep an eye out for possible interruptions to the meal by humans or other foxes. If not the open, then it might use a secluded spot in woodland or brambles.

I knew this ground and had a pretty good idea whence the fox had come. Sure enough, the chewed remains were found well out in the neighbouring field, which lay between the smallholding and the nearby woods.

Walking round the perimeter of the smallholding, which only covered about an acre, I spotted several runs, both badger and fox. The main problem was a footpath that ran outside the boundary. Although this is a relatively quiet spot, people do use it, and clearly I wasn't about to put myself in a conflict situation with Joe Public.

There was one spot where a bank about four feet high presented a safe backstop stretching about six or seven yards down the hedge – it was the only place a shot could be taken. From here, the land dropped away to the hamlet below, so there was no way a centrefire rifle could be used. Silence, too, was important, so the only option was the good old .22LR.

The weather was cold and there was a frost forecast. Throw in a full moon and you have the perfect scenario of when not to go out after a fox. Fortunately the owners' bungalow was situated at the top of the field and he had one or two vehicles parked about the area. This was to my advantage as although foxes quickly recognise changes where vehicles are concerned nowadays, they are so used to

them coming and going that one more doesn't seem to make a difference.

Sorting out the spot where I would park, I pegged out a couple of the dead hens in a direct line between me and the backstop. Rangefinding the hens showed them to be about 40 yards away – ideal.

Having warned the owner I would be there as the light started to fade and asking him to carry on as normal, I arrived at about 5.30pm and settled down. Within half an hour the moon rose directly in front of me, illuminating both the target area and myself. In situations like this I wear a dark veil and gloves, as foxes will instantly see any movement from uncovered hands and faces. I had also discarded the night vision as it was quite easy to see through the MTC Genesis scope I was trying out.

After about half a freezing hour, a fox showed briefly at the far end of the field and was gone. I suspected from its behaviour that it was a casual visitor. The grass was by now white as the frost tightened its grip and the moon was almost dazzling me. The thought of getting home by the fire was pretty appealing, but I knew that the best chance of getting the killer was that night.

Suddenly it was there. Coming in from the right, it never hesitated as it trotted up to the first carcase. This behaviour was typical of a fox that knew exactly where the next meal was coming from. The first visitor had not picked up any scent in the cold, windless night, but this one clearly was returning to the crime scene. I have to say, I was surprised just how clearly the fox stood out. A moment later the fox was down and motionless, the bullet catching it just behind the ear.

Above:
Foxes can cause devastation for poultry farmers

I decided to hang on for another half an hour. In that time saw another three, none of which approached the safe shooting zone. It was pretty clear evidence that I had got the right one.

Speaking to the landowner, who was more than happy, I mentioned that I had seen four others, and asked if he want me to deal with them. Both he and his mother were amazed that I had seen so many, both of them saying they had only seen two in the 30 years or so they had lived there.

The other thing they both said was that wasn't it such a coincidence that the fox had got into the hen house on the one night they had forgotten to shut it? I gently explained to them that foxes are there every night, and if you make a mistake, they will exploit it. During the next few icy nights I picked up another three foxes with my Anschütz 1710 .22LR, now with the Genesis on board. The son told me he had seen several more with his torch – it's amazing what you can see when you look for it. I had no doubt that I would be called back.

This little episode shows how useful the .22LR can be in the right situations. Of the four foxes I shot, only one needed a follow-up shot to finish the job. I am no 'wonder shot', but as I said earlier, if you can get a one-inch group at 50 or 60 yards, you should be able to humanely dispatch any fox out to that sort of range. ■

Right:
Mike's years of experience, coupled with the right kit, help him bag two brace

SCENT OF A VIXEN

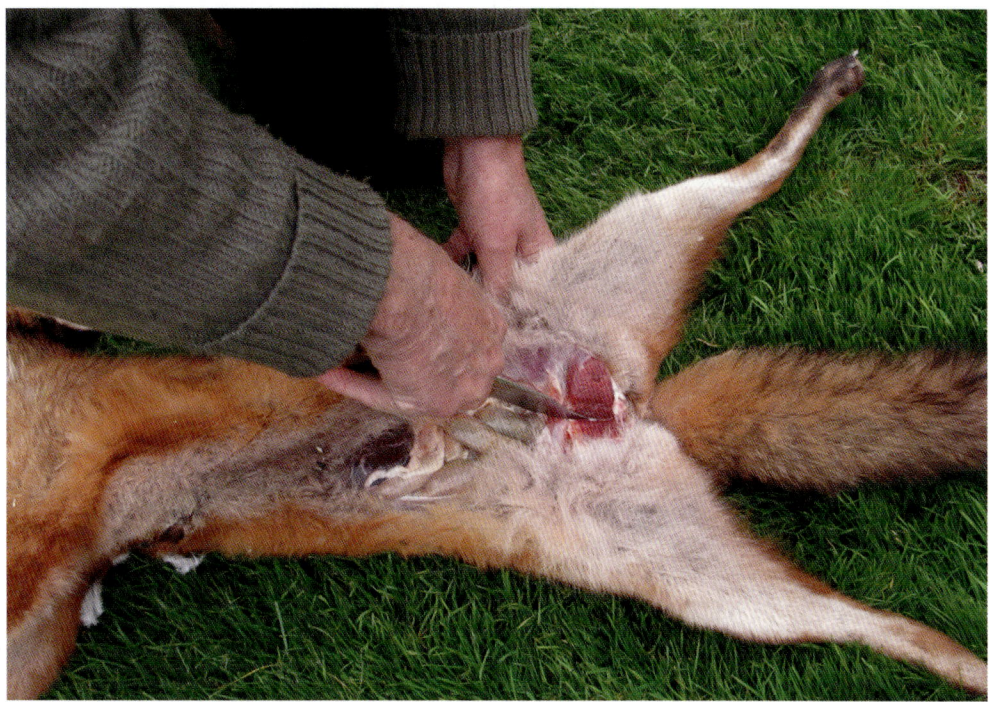

The recent influx of magazines, books, and videos giving advice on how to be a successful shooter has got me thinking about my own knowledge. The advice in these books mostly relates to two areas: deer stalking, of which I have limited knowledge, and foxing, which I know quite a bit about – or I am supposed to, anyway. I can remember quite a lot of the foxes I have shot – and forgotten a whole lot more, as there have been thousands – but today, do I know much about the fox itself? The honest answer would be no. I still shoot a lot of foxes using experience gained over 60 years, but I have learned how to deal with them in my own way and have never really worked out what makes them tick. Whenever I think I have sussed something about them, they will do something that blows the idea out of the water.

Where foxes are concerned, much is based on hearsay rather than evidence. This is understandable – with a few notable exceptions, when shooters see a fox they are inclined to shoot it rather than study it. It's a practical approach, I agree, but it doesn't really further one's knowledge of the creature.

Many sweeping statements are made as to foxes' behaviour, particularly when they cause humans problems. One generalisation is that they travel the same routes at the same time each night. Until recently I would have gone along with this, but the advent of 'stealth' cameras has now shown that there is virtually no pattern to their movement. Of course, the track from where they lie up will always be used, but when they are away and on the hunt there seems to be little regularity in their travels within a pretty wide area.

Size and gender is another area where I suspect guesswork plays a significant role. True, the very large (over 20lb) specimens are more often than not dogs, and vixens by and large weigh some 15 per cent less than the dogs. However, anyone who has shot a lot of foxes will know that there are some very large vixens and very small dog foxes.

MIKE'S TOP TIP

Don't ever think that you know everything about the fox... your education is ongoing

Size just isn't a reliable indicator – that's why our first action on coming up to a shot fox is to find out what sex it is.

How far does your average fox travel in a night's hunting? Again it is hard to say – the stamina these animals have is incredible. In the days before the hunting ban, there were many tales of foxes running at about 15mph for hours. Many years ago, there was a bob-tailed fox living three miles from my home. It was instantly recognisable, being very light and sandy in colour. I saw it no less than four times around my home area, and a keeper friend who also knew this fox (and, remarkably for those days, tolerated it) reported that he saw it most days. This animal was clearly prepared to do a round trip of about six miles in a night. There are many reports of foxes travelling much further than this.

Although they are dog-like in appearance, foxes' behaviour is rather more catlike. Their eyes, their gait and their methods of hunting are more akin to cats than dogs. Their haunting, eerie calls, particularly at mating time, are often described as a vixen's scream or a dog fox's bark, but both sexes are capable of replicating these sounds.

One thing is never in doubt: foxes are highly resourceful creatures, taking advantage of whatever is presented. The number of people who shoot foxes has seen a tremendous surge, yet the number of foxes never seems to diminish. They can obviously cope with many of the measures we take to get rid of them.

There are, of course, several sources of in-depth information on foxes. Among them are books by Robert Bucknell (*Foxing with Lamp and Rifle* and *Going Foxing*) and David Macdonald (*Running with the Fox*). Everyone interested in shooting foxes should read these. However, even though I have read these excellent publications, the fox in the field always seems a bit of an enigma to me.

A year or so ago, I was asked to see if I could get rid of a fox that had been taking poultry and a couple of small cats. This was a large animal with a fine brush, and although it frequented an area on the edge of a town, it was extremely wary. Like many of its kind, it was very aware of its surroundings and could sense anything different.

The area concerned backed on to fields, so I assumed it would be relatively easy to deal with this one. Not so! I saw it in the distance on several occasions, and it would be gone at the merest hint of a lamp. I brought night vision into play, but when using it I never saw the fox. It was obviously used to human scent, as humans were always nearby when

it travelled, but it seemed to have the ability to separate safety from danger. Of course, this could have just been coincidence – but it certainly seemed like the fox knew something I didn't. On and off for several weeks, I tried to get on terms with it, and failed dismally. Baiting a certain spot drew in others, but not the chosen one. Calls of all sorts were tried with no luck.

Finally, as the old year passed into the new I had an idea. Mating was in full swing, and I had little doubt that my elusive fox was joining in the yearly love-in.

A vixen had been active in one of the fields that back on to my house, and after spending several cold nights waiting out I finally shot her. As I suspected from her general behaviour, she was in season. I opened her up and removed her bladder, which was reasonably full. I also removed her anal glands and the brush that houses the supracaudal gland. I put the bladder

Left:
Sometimes going solo is the only way forward, and with the right mounting accessory most lamps can be secured to the rifle

and glands in a plastic bag, together with a piece of cloth, which would soak up the malodorous mess.

A day later, I armed myself with the cloth and the brush and set off for the area where my elusive dog fox had last been seen. In the area there was a gateway where foxes travel on a regular basis and where I have shot several in the past. I dragged the rag and the brush around the field and through the gateway. I must admit, this messy and extremely smelly plan was a first for me – and a somewhat desperate effort – but as I was getting nowhere with conventional methods, I had nothing to lose.

That evening, I set up both the UCaller and the Fox Pro Spitfire, and retired to a spot where I could see the gateway some 60 yards away. I would be using the .17 HMR – at this sort of range, and being near to houses, I find it the ideal choice.

Using the two callers, I planned to have a vixen and dog calling at close intervals. The Spitfire was away to my left, about 100 yards out, and the UCaller was just inside the gate. The idea was that a fox – hopefully the one I was after – would be drawn through the gate by both the sound and scent of a vixen, and most of all by the call of a rival.

I waited for about an hour and saw nothing resembling a fox, so I started playing fox duets on the callers. Within a few minutes, the night vision picked up eyes approaching at a rapid rate across the big field next door. After one more shout from the dog fox call, I got ready. A moment later, the fox appeared in the gateway and started sniffing the scent point. 'Eau de vixen' was the last thing he smelled. I was 95 per cent sure it was the one I was after.

In the end, my messy strategy had made things easy. However, to accomplish this you do need an in-season vixen and an extremely strong stomach. Cutting up scent glands and mixing them with fox urine is not for everyone. The scent of fox that followed me the next day was not a problem as I live with my son and there is no lady of the house, but that won't be the case for everyone.

I would never normally choose this method, but it was all I could think of to deal with a very difficult and elusive predator. The poultry and cat killings ceased soon after – I had hit the jackpot. Once again, I will never really know what the fox was drawn to. Was it the scent, or the call, or was I just in the right place at the right time? Never mind – what matters most is that I got him. ∎

AFRAID OF THE LIGHT

When the midsummer growth obscures much of the countryside, I spend a substantial amount of time sitting out and waiting for the quarry species to come to me. Not only is this a rather pleasant way to spend long summer evenings, but it usually pays off where both rabbits and the odd troublesome fox are concerned. It suits the ageing shooter, and gives me time to think about what I can do to improve my techniques using the lessons I have learned over very many years of pursuing foxes.

Although it is the middle of summer, my thoughts almost always stray to night shooting because this is what I have done continuously throughout my life. The one question that crops up time and time again in magazines, on the web and whenever fox shooters meet, is the old perennial about that 'lamp shy' fox.

From my earliest days going after foxes using rudimentary equipment, I too used to go on about foxes that would turn tail and run at the first glimpse of a lamp. Back then I had no doubt in my mind that they were lamp shy. But as the years have passed and so much has changed in the way of life in the countryside and the growing numbers of people who shoot foxes, my views on lamp shyness have undergone radical changes.

It goes without saying that with anything to do with wildlife, and possibly foxes in particular, there will always be exceptions to the rule. There will be foxes that are scared by a lamp, particularly in areas where lights at night are few and far between. However, these areas are dwindling at an alarming rate and I am leaving out these havens as I suspect they are in a minority.

Firstly, why should a fox be scared of lights at night? In this day and age, lights are everywhere. Some areas are even setting up reserves where no lights are allowed so that we humans can look at the stars. A fox on his nocturnal travels is beset with human-induced lights: street lights (even in villages), security lights, vehicular lights. These are not only

MIKE'S TOP TIP

Foxes aren't scared of lamp light... they're scared of you!

constant on the roads, but in the countryside itself as farm equipment works late into the night with headlamps blazing, and, of course, the odd shooter out there in the 4x4 or pickup with lamp flashing here, there and everywhere.

Why, then, should the average fox worry about something that has become a normal part of his nocturnal wanderings? I rather tenuously link this to pigeon shooting. I normally park about 150 yards away, as it saves walking, and am often asked, "Why don't you move your 4x4 further away from the hide and decoys?" My response to this is that pigeons fly over and see infinitely more vehicles every day of their lives than we do, many of which are parked very close to them when they roost or feed, so why should they worry about one more?

A few years back, I was talking to a very experienced pigeon shooter on a summer evening as we were sitting on the rear of his vehicle. Pigeons were dropping in within 30 yards of us. In a similar way, I do much of my fox control while parked up in my 4x4, and for 95 per cent of the time foxes totally ignore it.

No, I don't think that foxes are shy, wary (call it what you will) of lights – it's the thing that holds them that's the problem. Foxes are not unintelligent creatures, and one thing they are really good at is adapting to changing circumstances. I have a zoo near me with a considerable numbers of wild foxes that inhabit the grounds and enclosures. During the hours that the place is open to the public, they will totally ignore the crowds of people who pass within a few yards of them. In fact, they have become a bit of a feature.

Likewise, there are foxes in my own village that will lie out in the sun within yards of the local primary school playground with the din that only 50 or 60 small children can create. They take absolutely no notice of them at all. However, as soon as the zoo and the school close, the whole demeanour of the foxes changes and they are back on alert. It is their ability to be able to separate normal from dangerous that enables this master predator to not only to survive but to thrive.

All those years ago when we shot lots of foxes for their skins with shotgun and lamp, we got very good at working out how to get within 30 or 40 yards of our fox – we had to or there would be no money coming in. Yes, we had some foxes that were clearly brighter than others in exactly the same way as rabbits. By the end of the winter, the rabbits that were left were the crafty ones and it was the same with the foxes. The really wary ones were still out there and we had to raise our game to match theirs.

Wild animals that live on their wits to survive, let alone thrive and increase their numbers,

Below:
NV has shown Mike that foxes are usually aware of shooters even before they spot the lamp

44

develop skills that we have little conception of. Foxes are blessed with senses that we can see to a degree in our own working dogs, but even man's best friend is, in many cases, losing its senses compared to its wild brethren.

When we set out after a fox in our off road vehicles, foxes are clearly fully aware we are there. They will, until pressed, largely ignore us in much the same way rabbits in a field will apparently ignore a fox passing through. However, they will keep a watchful eye on it and, should its demeanour change, they will sheer off. Still not scattering willy nilly, they will wait until an attack is pressed home to get an idea of exactly what is going on.

This applies to large prey species too. Just watch programs on Africa where, for instance, the hunted will watch lions even at quite close range waiting to see exactly when and from where the charge will come. Sadly, for many of these the lions are one step ahead and will often wait in ambush. So it is with the fox. Although usually the hunter, it is also the prey when man is about, especially at night.

The advent of night vision, particularly thermal imagers, has given us the chance to look into the night-time world of the fox. By watching and not always shooting, I found that a great many of the things I had assumed for years to be correct were wrong. I have watched others through my NV as they track a fox with their lamps and what is abundantly clear is that in virtually every case the fox is well aware of the shooter's presence – usually long before the shooter knows the fox is there.

From then on it is very much like the rabbit/zebra scenario: the fox is aware he has company but doesn't wish to commit himself until he knows exactly where the best escape route lies. His three main senses will come into play. He may have heard the intruder, or smelt him, or even seen him, and for the fox the situation is relatively under control. If it's a very wary or nervous individual, it may well leg it immediately – possibly without the hunter ever having seen it.

However (and this is where the lamp shy thing comes in), if the fox has heard or smelt the intruder, it will wait until it gets specific confirmation of where the danger lies. Should that confirmation be visual (it sees the person, or has a light shone in its eyes), it will be off. I don't think it matters if it's been shot at before or not, although clearly that doesn't help.

How can we, if we wish to remove that fox, get on terms and avoid losing the chance? Clearly, you need to remove the fact that the fox knows you are there in the first place. This can be achieved by honing your fieldcraft skills, showing no light, working with the wind or buying some decent night vision. All are rewarding when they succeed. But do remember it is not necessarily the light the fox is scared of – it's you. As far as possible, take yourself out of the equation.

I have found many, many times that just putting a light on a fox won't make it run (not immediately, anyway). I know that, when waiting out at night and using night vision, if the first thing the selected fox becomes aware of is a light going on, it will stand for a moment to assess the situation. This will give the opportunity you are after.

If you feel uneasy about using technology to give you an edge, improve your fieldcraft skills. It takes time, but it works. Then you can really call yourself a true fox shooter. ∎

Below:
Whether you use technology or fieldcraft, the end result for a good shooter is much the same

FEELING THE HEAT

MIKE'S TOP TIP

Speak to people who live around your shooting areas to gain info on fox movements

I never think of summer as the best foxing time. Lush growth covers many runs, and they are often so overgrown that it is difficult to spot where foxes are running. Cubs are active by then – in fact I recall years when cubs in some areas were above ground as early as mid- to late-March. I have noticed that during the period the cubs are actually being born, fox activity seems to decrease noticeably. In my area, which has a high population, if nothing much is seen of any foxes I'm reminded of the phrase 'the calm before the storm'. All of a sudden foxes are on the move again, providing for the litters. Business as usual.

By June and July many of these cubs are beginning to take the first steps in their hunting lives. By now the vixen will have been taking live prey back to the den for the cubs to practise and hone the killing skills on which their lives will depend.

I remember as a lad, when out for an early morning walk around with the gun (a new Greener GP 12), I heard a lot of chicken noise coming from the nearby farmyard. I then saw a fox crossing the field with a chicken in its mouth. Keeping still in the shelter of the hedge, I watched as it came closer. When it was in range I let go at it. The fox rolled over as expected. More surprising was the fact that the chicken got up, ran straight at me and stopped at my feet. This was one lucky hen – not only had it survived the fox attack and a load of number fives, but it had avoided being slowly killed by the young cubs.

Young rabbits and voles are the usual training aids used by the vixen, with larger prey coming later as training progresses. Many of the pheasant wings and rabbit legs found in close proximity to the earths are the leftovers of the cubs learning to kill. Incidentally, that Greener taught me a lesson. I had been out with it on a wet day and had left it in the hall. For some reason I didn't use it for a week, and when I did, the inside of the barrel was rusted. After strenuous cleaning most of it came out, but sadly there were some rust marks I couldn't get rid of. I was upset, and have never since failed to clean any gun after use.

As summer progresses, the vixen will start taking the cubs with her on short hunting trips. As darkness starts to fall in the late evening, it is not uncommon to hear the cubs bickering among themselves over a kill. Very often, a quick but stealthy approach can give you a chance at them.

When the cubs reach five months, they will be hunting on their own but sticking close to home. It is at that time that they can really be a menace, particularly to the gamekeeper. Early poults will already be going 'over the top' of the release pens and are really vulnerable. Mature foxes will be after them, of course, but they are wary and will soon disappear if threatened. The adolescent cubs have not yet learned to be scared of humans, particularly if they were reared near habitation, so if given the chance they will take poults indiscriminately.

One method I have had some success with is cage trapping the cubs. I have found over the years that it is impossible to cage trap adult foxes, except around yards and buildings where they have become used to enclosed areas, wire netting and corrugated iron. Cubs, however, haven't yet learned these skills and are insatiably curious. I have known of cases where cubs have been caught in Kania traps

designed to kill squirrels. There are also reports every year of cubs getting caught in Larsen traps set for magpies.

A couple of years ago I caught a couple of cubs in live-catch rabbit traps. These are simple cage traps activated by a step-on plate. I put the traps in a black bin liner to exclude all the light except for the entrance, then covered the traps in litter, leaves and twigs so the finished set is just an inviting hole in the undergrowth. Bait these traps with dog or cat food – tuna is a good choice – or even peanut butter. The problem with the latter is that it will attract badgers, which will soon wreck the set.

Obviously all traps need to be checked every day in accordance with the law; I intend to try this system on a regular basis once the poults are in situ. The other, more obvious way of

Below:
Mike sets his traps by putting them in a black bin liner to block out the light

clearing up a few cubs is by calling. Whereas old foxes can be difficult to call, cubs in their early hunting days will come readily.

I have found there is not a lot of point in the more sophisticated callers at this time of year – straightforward squeal-type calls such as the WAM will generally give results. Young cubs hunting on their own for the first few times will respond better to 'small' calls such as mouse squeaks and young rabbit squeals, as these will be the sounds they have heard more than anything else in their early training days. Make the most of these early days, as their naïve period soon passes.

Above: Cubs will soon turn into marauding adults and are best dealt with early at the den

In the long, warm summer evenings, waiting for the cubs can show results. Ideally you need to know where the earth is located. This is not too difficult if you are familiar with your ground – watching from high ground or high seat will often reveal the travels of the old foxes. This can be done at any time of day, as the parents are constantly on the move to provide food for the hungry youngsters.

When the cubs begin to make short hunting trips on their own, I am happy to take out the vixen. At this point, the cubs will be able to make their own way in life if they get the chance. They may struggle a bit for food, but observation has shown that once they are starting to hunt on their own, they are capable of catching small items such as beetles, many of the larger insects, worms and very young rabbits. With this, they soon develop their hunting skills and become efficient predators.

If you have a good rapport with the owners of the land you shoot over, ask them to report any sightings of cubs. Every year I get information on the whereabouts of litters. One of my best 'spies' is the local postman. Last year he reported no fewer than six litters he had spotted on his rounds. Information like this is invaluable and can save huge amounts of time.

One of the postie's sightings proved particularly valuable. A good friend in the village had been plagued by a fox taking hens throughout the year. It was nothing sustained – just a visit every couple of weeks. This type of predation is probably the hardest to deal with as there is no tangible pattern to it. With patience and the help of some modern technology, in particular stealth cameras, regular foxes can usually be sorted in a short space of time. However, the random visitor is a different proposition altogether.

My informant said he had seen a couple of cubs in the corner of a field next door to the chap who had been visited by the fox. This was an overgrown plot of land with an absentee owner, presumably hoping to make a killing in development one day. As he lived in London, I assumed he would have no problem with me taking a look. Setting myself at the lowest point in the field on a warm evening, I waited with the Anschütz .22LR – ideal for the close-range cub.

This turned out to be one of my better evenings. From my position I could see the whole of the scrubby field, and I could also shoot into the hillside with complete safety. I had been in position for about an hour when I saw a cub stalking a rabbit. At about 30 yards, it was soon despatched. I stayed where I was. The other cub appeared about 10 minutes later, and I dealt with him similarly. As it was a warm evening, I decided to stay put a bit longer. Not surprisingly, the vixen showed up

and went the same way as her offspring. I went via my friend's house on the way back to the 4x4, and was rewarded with a substantial glass of malt.

This problem had been an easy one to sort out – the random visits stopped from then on. I later found where the earth had been. It was no more than 80 yards from his back door, yet he had never actually seen a fox there. A good example of how a bit of local knowledge can make the job that much easier. ∎

Below:

Kania traps will occasionally take small cubs

HERE COMES THE HARVEST

MIKE'S TOP TIP

Move your bait points back into more sheltered areas as the foliage dies back

As the year moves on, the opportunities for keeping the fox population under control alter. August is the time when vegetation of all types is at its densest. Harvest is almost here, but not quite.

For many fox shooters, harvest is looked upon as being the time when many of that year's cubs can be dealt with, and there is no doubt about it – this is a fact. However, before this time arrives there are other ways that we can deal with the ever-growing fox population. Although cover is extremely thick and from our point of view makes shooting difficult, it is not always ideal from a fox's point of view either.

Their vision is impaired by tall grass; rides, unless cleared by keepers and forestry workers, have turned into lush areas of weed and grass, again giving cover to the prey species and making a quiet approach difficult.

Under these circumstances the fox is forced into relying even more on its nose and ears for locating and catching its prey. Bearing this in mind, we can in some circumstances use this to our advantage. In my own case, I have been baiting one or two spots near me on a regular basis with anything I can find – usually rabbits and long-dead things from the freezers, but pretty much anything edible can be used as our friend the fox is not a fussy eater.

The bait points I use are not the same ones I use during the winter months. At this time of year I try to put myself in the fox's place. Animals are not that different from us in that they will choose the easy option if it is possible. Hunting through dense cover can be hard work and unproductive, while hunting open fields for mice, voles, young rabbits and so on is far easier, beaten only by scavenging around human habitation or raiding yards for poultry. So if a steady supply of food is provided in an easily accessible spot, it follows that the local fox population will visit it on a regular basis.

In my experience, it is essential that there is something edible there most days. I certainly don't leave them without bait for more than two days at a time. At this time of year the cubs are hunting freely on their own but still follow the vixen. They follow her hunting paths and ape her techniques, and by doing this they will learn the whereabouts of the bait points too.

Watching them at one of these points can be quite interesting, as the scrapping and bickering that goes on is very reminiscent of our own young. As a rule, I don't 'hammer' these spots, visiting them with the rifle once a week when the bait is being taken.

These open areas have proved very productive, but as the foliage begins to die back I will bring the bait points back into more sheltered areas. Most of this is common sense – when we go out with gun or rifle during the summer, most of us avoid heavily overgrown areas, and certainly fields covered with crop are out of bounds, so we head for more open ground. So it is with the fox. We are both hunters intent on a kill – what applies to one often applies to the other.

I am a big fan of the .22 Hornet. I have really got to like this rifle although it would be hard to explain why. It falls between the .17 HMR and the .222/.223 and really doesn't do the specific work that any of those calibres are good at. However, it does bring the range of uses that they have under one roof, as it were. It is capable of dropping a fox out to 200 yards with the right ammo and will, with the same proviso, deal with rabbits. In the latter case I started off by using 35-grain Hornady V-Max bullets and they certainly did the job, but unlike many others out there I am not capable of head shooting rabbits every time at ranges of 150 yards or so, and I found what was left was generally set aside as ferret fodder.

Seeking advice from other Hornet owners and the redoubtable Ken Gray from Henry Krank, I decided to try some other bullets. By now my re-loading was certainly improving. Whether by trial and error or through my pestering those who know much more than me, the results on paper proved that I was getting there, albeit with a few hiccups along the way.

I went for some 40- and 45-grain soft points, and I decided to give the Prvi Partizan 45-grain ammo a go as well. I have found before that this make can vary in its performance from rifle to rifle. My Anschütz .223, for example, shoots better with Prvi than anything else, but the Steyr throws it all over the place. Although increasing a little in price, it is still very affordable, and the brass is excellent for re-loading.

So how did the new batch of ammo perform? Compared with the Hornady 35-grain

Below:

The .22 Hornet: a compromise calibre between .222/.223 and 1.7 HMR

V-Max bullets, the damage to rabbits was certainly reduced with the heavier soft points, and it wasn't long before I had the opportunity to try them out on a fox. What I suspected was a dog fox had been seen hanging around the nearby poultry farm during daylight. I have found that around August foxes become quite active from midday until about 2.30pm. This may seem strange, but I have found it to be the case over and over again.

This time I was in luck: instead of me having to visit the site day after day, this fox duly turned up at about 1.30pm. I had tucked myself away in the overgrown hedge that ran round the field and watched as it worked down the opposite hedge about 150 yards away. When waiting out like this you hold the advantage as there is need for only minimal movement, and as you are stationary you will pick up any movement more easily.

Waiting until the fox was in a safe spot for a shot, I gave a squeak which stopped it in its tracks. The 45-grain soft point did the job, and at a little over 100 yards the fox dropped on the spot.

I am sure the .17 HMR would have done the job just as well at that range, but the larger bullet from the Hornet certainly has more knock-down power, and had the fox been farther away I would have felt much happier taking the shot with the Hornet rather than a lighter round.

There is something about the Hornet that makes it a little bit special. Once you have mastered re-loading for it – which can be a bit of a trial to begin with as the case is on the delicate side – it is really easy and you can play around with a variety of loads until you sort out the best for your purposes.

I am more than happy with the rifle and the more I use it the more I regret not having bought one years ago. The re-loading is proving fascinating, and again I have to thank those who have aided my early efforts. Henry Krank has been very helpful putting up with my questions and supplying all the component parts. ∎

ILLUMINATING IDEAS

For the ever-increasing number of shooters who are out after the sun sets, there seems to be an equally mounting number of items to aid them in their quest. Gone are the days when a battery and handheld lamp were the only items required to see what was out on a dark winter night. Still held by many to be the best way of dealing with foxes and rabbits, even these have become more sophisticated: lithium ion batteries are light and long-lasting, and have for some time replaced the old style lead acid types, while LEDs have largely replaced filament bulbs.

One of the latest lamps to emerge is the scope-mounted Tracer Sportlight 170 from Deben. This has upgraded wiring and is available as a scope-mounted model or a conventional handheld version. I had the opportunity to field test this lamp before it went into production and was very impressed. Capable of throwing a beam to 600 metres, it is lightweight and does everything you would want from this type of equipment. Employing one of Deben's lithium ion batteries, it should also give many seasons of good service.

The other scope-mounted lights that have really transformed the rifle/lamp combo are the torch type. Compact and self-contained with their own batteries, they really are the answer to the rabbit and fox shooter's prayers. There is a vast array of this type of lamp to choose from. All are similar in appearance, and one would suspect many come from the same manufacturer. Having said this, quality ranges greatly, particularly where the reflector is concerned – this component is vital to the quality of the light thrown, concentration of the beam and overall range. As I said, there are masses to choose from, but I have picked out some that do the job well for me. The first is Starlight's M3X and the second is Jetbeam's BC40.

The M3X is 750 lumen-rated with a Cree LED. It throws an intense, concentrated beam out to 350 yards, possibly more in ideal conditions, and this makes it ideal for fox use. I find the BC40, rated at 830 lumens, ideal for rabbit shooting out to 100 yards. The beam, although concentrated and extremely bright, has a wider spread. When shooting from a vehicle where the rabbits tend to move towards and along the hedge line, it is much

better for picking them up again when they move out of the beam. The Jetbeam again has a Cree LED. Both of these lamps are made well and have withstood a lot of hard use over the time I have had them. Battery life from the rechargeables in each of these lamps is in excess of 10 hours.

This type of light is extremely handy as the torch can be carried in a pocket during the evening. As the light fades, it takes a moment to mount it on the rifle. For those looking for an all-round hand lamp to use when out at night, either to shoot with or for picking up, you need look no further than Cluson's excellent Clu-Briter lamp. With a Cree LED and built-in rechargeable battery, it throws a beam out to over 200 yards – more than enough for rabbit work. If used on high beam it will last for about three hours, but on the low beam it's good for anything up to 20 hours. With a strobe facility, this is a practical and useful addition to anyone's night gear. In addition, Cluson is now supplying coloured filters for this lamp, Also their new pistol light is both compact and very powerful, I like this latest torch from Cluson a lot. Finally the Night Master range of lamps from TacLight is really taking the night shooting market by storm. Both available in IR and conventional white light they also have a red light torch, no filter is involved the light is produced by a red LED. Very efficient and certainly one of the best available.

That collection is my more conventional form

Above:

There's more technology available than ever to aid your foxing efforts

MIKE'S TOP TIP

Technology is no substitute for fieldcraft

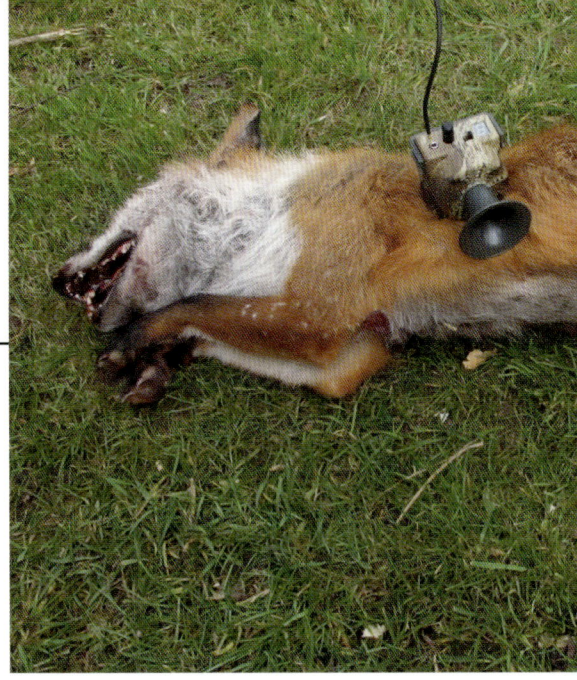

of night shooting lighting equipment. Now I move on to my more 'technical' stuff. Night vision has revolutionised shooting after dark, and there are more units available than ever before – do try to test them before you buy. It is useful to speak to someone who has tried a few as well; there can be huge gulfs in quality between different units, and it is easy to spend a lot of money on something that turns out to be a disappointment. I am fortunate in that I get to try quite a few, and the ones I have for my own use have proved themselves excellent for the fox and rabbit control that takes up most of my time.

My preferred NV unit for foxing is the Longbow dedicated night sight. Able to convert from day to night use and pick out rabbits up to 400 yards away, it is a brilliant unit. The downside of course is the price, but as is often (but not always) the case, you get what you pay for. Being able to change from day to night use, it has the advantage of being able to stay on your chosen rifle.

From the ever-increasing range of 'add-on' NV units, my own personal favourite is the Archer: usable as either a handheld spotting monocular or readily attached to the rear of your day scope, these units are practical and efficient. Thomas Jacks, importer and distributor of an array of NV units, has a front-mounted unit from Pulsar. This is one of the better options on the market. Again, it is a matter of personal choice as to which way you go. I will be testing one of these in the future, but would say this type of NV does have certain advantages over the rear scope-mounted type.

Moving into the digital world, Pulsar's DigiSight N550 has proved extremely popular, opening up a whole new world to many first-time NV users. In early darkness its performance is brilliant, and with practice it can give excellent results in near full darkness. Although still available the N550 has been superseded by the N750, in appearance it appears the same as its predecessor but it has been upgraded in many areas and without a doubt is a leader in it class.

Another recent addition to the night vision equipment range is the Photon from Pulsar. Once the initial supply problems had been ironed out and you were able to get one it turned out the wait was worthwhile. It's an excellent entry into the world of night vision, neat and as easy to fit and zero as a conventional day scope. Being digital like the N550 and N750, it can be used in daylight; although to be honest they work far better as the light starts to fade. All night vision units require an infra red light source and although the majority of them have their own without exception they will benefit enormously from additional IR. The Night Master 800 is the market leader with its three settings it will transform any NV equipment. Scott Country has brought out its Foxfire T20 IR illuminator and, while I would say it does not quite measure up to the NM800, it still represents very good value for money.

Next, a word on trail cameras. I like these a lot – not only are they highly enjoyable to use, they are invaluable for letting you know where and when your quarry species are about. The two types that I have found do the job well under all conditions are the Minox and the Spypoint. There is little to choose between them and anyone investing in a trail cam will certainly not be disappointed. Knowing the movements of the quarry species on your land not only leads to more successful hunts, but it is extremely good fun checking the camera to find what has been out and about at night. You could be in for a few surprises. There are now a bewildering number of trail cameras available, the vast majority of which do a good job

One piece of equipment I find I am using more and more is the digital caller. I have reviewed most of these in the past and at present I am giving the Mini Colibri a fair bit of work. Not only does it have an excellent range of usable calls, it is also very compact – a big advantage as in this age there seems to be more and more gear to cart around. Again there are more of these appearing, the Fox Pro range has been with us a while, I use

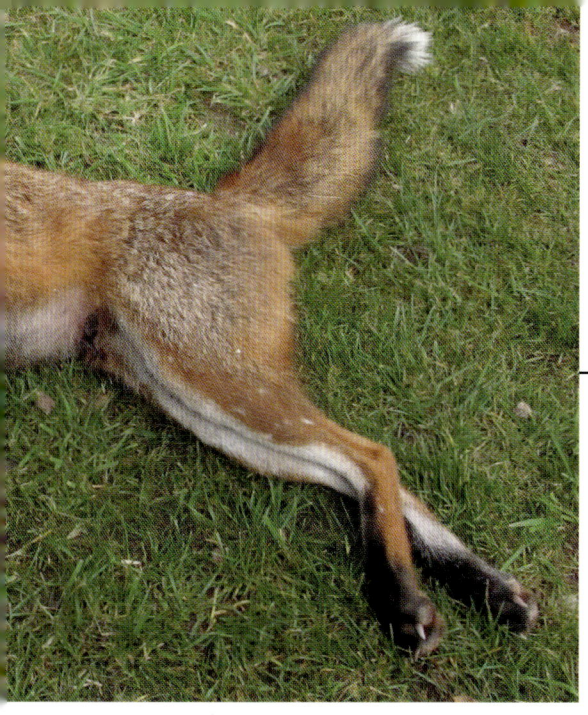

one of their products and like the Mini Colibri find it works well, like most callers they never guarantee results but nevertheless on their day they can be lethal.

An instrument I never go shooting without is my Leica rangefinder. Although most of the available rangefinders do the job equally well, the red illuminated readout on the Leica makes it ideal for low light and darkness. Again, not the cheapest, but for dedicated fox shooters it has proved ideal.

Despite the array of gear on the market, I never forget that I started with a homemade lamp set-up and a cheap rifle and shotgun. I shot a considerable number of foxes, and I guess that the items that pass through my hands have not added vastly to the number of foxes I account for (though they do allow me to come to terms more easily with specific foxes, night vision in particular). What they have done is given me far more enjoyment in my work, and for the newcomer they will probably make life that little bit easier.

At this time of year, when at last the fields are opening up, the stubbles are clean and the new season's crop of cubs are out hunting, many of the items I have mentioned will make your sport more enjoyable. There is no substitute, however, for getting to know your quarry. As I have said before, spend time studying the animal and undoubtedly your success rate will rise.

One example of how technology can benefit the fox shooter came when a customer asked me for some help. His pride and joy – his ducks – had been vanishing at a rate of two a day, causing him some distress. He had seen no signs of attack, which is not too unusual with tight-feathered birds like ducks. After looking around I set up a couple of cameras: one on the stream and one in the steep field behind. I didn't have to wait long for

a result – examining the cameras next morning, I spotted a rangy dog fox walking up the stream and leaving by the field behind the house. Finding the run was quite easy. I picked a good spot to wait and ranged various distances with the Leica.

Armed with this information, I set up an hour before dark and started the wait. Since the raid, a radio had been left playing in the hope of scaring off the fox, and not long after dark the owner came along and started to chat, at the same time lighting a cigarette. I gently pointed out that perhaps it would be better if he and his roll-up went indoors, and perhaps the radio could be turned down a bit. As he was leaving, I scanned the field with the Longbow and, despite the smells and noise, not 50 yards away was Charlie, sitting up like a collie and surveying the scene.

By the time I had moved to get a better shot, he had mooched up the field. A quick squeak stopped him for a moment, long enough for the .223 to drop him.

The Leica registered 110 yards and I climbed up the field to collect him. The old boy was delighted and came round a couple of days later to inform me that no more ducks had been taken.

I am sure I would have eventually got the fox using a lamp and rifle, but this can be a long drawn-out process: technology had given me the edge and finished the job quickly. Be it open stubble or overgrown hillsides, all of the items above will help you in your search and control of the fox.

A last word: this is not an exhaustive list of all the equipment on the market, and the latest piece of technology that is quickly becoming a "must have" is the thermal imager. I have tried three of these, the Flir, the Guide and Yukon's HD38.

All do the job well, but for the purposes I need one for I settled on the HD38. The huge advantage with thermal imagers is that you will see everything that has a heat signature, unlike conventional NV, which no matter how good it may be will always miss something if it is partially hidden or has its back to you. Thermal has revolutionised the spotting of creatures by night (and also in daylight) I would be lost without mine, and a further revolution seems inevitable as thermal scopes look set to take off, too. ■

Left:
Digital callers are able to produce a variety of sounds at the touch of a button

WINTER WEATHER WARNING

Above:
With sensible safety precautions in place, organised shoots can also take on fox control duties

MIKE'S TOP TIP
Vixens dealt with in midwinter can save a lot of trouble in later months

I live in a part of the country where snow is a rare occurrence. When it does arrive, it causes total chaos as no one is prepared for it. As I get older I have to say I have few regrets about the absence of snow. However, I read with interest about many shooters who just can't wait for a blanket of snow to cover the countryside so they can really get after the foxes.

Like many things concerning fox shooting, sometimes it becomes difficult to separate fact from fiction. I have no doubt that there are areas of the country where snow helps the fox controller – it certainly shows where they have been and where they are going, but from my own experiences most of the tracks I have followed seem to fizzle out long before I come across a fox.

There was one occasion when the snow did help me to track down a fox that had been giving me grief around the shoot where I was keeper. I had seen it on more than one occasion, but despite spending time waiting out for it in bitterly cold weather, I had no success. I am not sure it was a particularly wily creature – I am more inclined to think our paths just didn't cross at the right time.

Today, I could scan the cold fields of winter with a thermal imager and soon pick out any fox that is about. It is on these cold nights that thermal equipment really comes into its own, readily spotting any living creature that is out and about on a freezing night.

Back then, things were different. Day after day I would come across the sad remains of a pheasant that the fox had pulled down. It wasn't as if it was taking great numbers, as obviously by this time of year the birds were well scattered and roosting high up. It was just a steady drip feed of a bird a day or so, but that equated to perhaps 30 a month, and at somewhere about £25 a bird on a shoot day, this was a not inconsiderable loss of revenue.

Despite my best efforts, nothing changed and the fox continued to avoid both me and my best efforts to deal with it. Then the snow came.

As I said earlier, Devon has always been ill prepared for the white stuff, and it usually avoids this part of the world. But every now and then it really gets going, and with our steep hills and narrow lanes, carnage is guaranteed to follow.

A shoot had been arranged as usual for the Wednesday, but mild panic set in as I woke to a white world. Soon phone calls started coming in from the odd stranded gun and beater, but with arrangements as they were and with most of those involved on their way, we decided to go ahead. I set off to put out the sewelling on some of the drives, and as usual when snow covers the ground, tracks of the animals and birds that had braved the elements were there for all to see. Classic rabbit tracks mingled with those of pheasant and, it has to be admitted, more than one set of fox tracks.

Ending up with the last string of sewelling at one of the smaller woods, which happened to be where quite a few of the victims of the fox had been found, I spotted the usual puff of feathers with the main quills neatly bitten off

Credit: Steve Lawson

Left:
Snow causes more disruption to shooters than to foxes.

– the typical evidence of a fox kill – lying 100 yards from the edge of the wood. Snow was starting to fall quite heavily, but it was clear from the fast-disappearing tracks that the fox had headed for the wood and some shelter from the bitter north-easterly wind. Perhaps at last there would be a chance to get rid of this particularly difficult predator.

Returning to the shoot room for the drawing of pegs and the usual pre-shoot talk on safety, I explained to the assembled guns that instead of the usual rule of no ground game, I was hoping to enlist their help in getting rid of the fox that was not only causing me some grief but also having an effect on their shooting. To a man they were well up for it. It would be a bit of a change from the normal routine, and as several of them had never shot a fox, it caused a bit of excitement among the ranks.

Next on the list was to get a few of the beaters who had been on fox drives before to gently move through the small wood, hopefully driving Charlie in the direction of the guns. Having been involved in many

fox drives I was aware of the safety issues, particularly where inexperienced guns that had not shot on a fox drive before were concerned. Fortunately I had a box of BBs in the truck, and dished out a couple to each of the half-dozen guns who had managed to get to the shoot. Insisting on absolute quiet, we crunched our way through the snow. Heading off into the icy blast, I sent the guns off with my main beater. They were placed about 50 yards apart against a hedge that faced the wood in question.

Periodically dropping off a beater or two as we made our way round the wood, the rest of us finally arrived at the top end of the cover. The guns had been advised to let the fox, should it appear, run through them, and only shoot when it was heading for open country. As usual when driving foxes, there was no need for noise – in fact I was hoping to get through without disturbing the birds that would undoubtedly be there. No dogs were involved. Quietly, three of us entered the small area of woodland.

Already we could see pheasants doubling back past us, but they were clearly reluctant to leave the shelter of the trees and face what was by now almost a white-out. After a few minutes we heard a couple of shots, and the beater with the guns radioed in to say the job was done. The fox, just for once, had done as I had hoped and had been spotted quietly leaving the wood almost as soon as we had entered. It had laid up in some rough cover but had soon made a run for it through the line of waiting guns, where two of the guns shot simultaneously as it broke clear. The usual shoot banter broke out as to who had actually shot the fox – in fact this was never really settled.

Calling up the other beaters on the radios, we soon drove the wood in the normal fashion, and despite the earlier disturbance had a reasonable drive on the pheasants. The snow continued to fall and some warming seasonal beverages were soon the order of the day. Later, on the way back for lunch, I sent my dog Talon off to collect the fox, which he proudly brought back to the yard. All in all a good result, thanks mainly to the snow.

In terms of rifle shooting, though, I have never really found that snow is an advantage when after foxes. Yes, they show up against the landscape, but unless the cold spell lasts and the ground is frozen hard, food is not too hard to find, so they go about their business as usual.

If you maintain bait points, clearly this is a time of year when they can pay dividends. No need to overdo it – just a few bits of offal, a rabbit, perhaps a few dog biscuits, all will attract the scavenging fox. I have my winter bait spots placed in sheltered areas out of the wind, and where I am this is usually at the bottom of a hill, so I can wait on a high spot looking down. Not only does this give a good field of view, it also makes for safe shooting on hard ground.

As I started off by saying, I am sure that tough northern readers will be only too happy to be out and about in the snow. As a soft, ageing southerner, I find that, like the fox, I am increasingly reluctant to leave cover.

Midwinter can be an exciting time and can in fact can offer chances to come to terms with troublesome foxes that may not be so vulnerable at other times of year. Also remember that in many cases, vixens dealt with now can save a lot of trouble in the months to come. ■

BIGGER ISN'T ALWAYS BETTER

In these days of the internet where information can be obtained instantly, it is interesting to look back at the days when it didn't exist. I keep an eye on the shooting forums online, and one thing I notice is when a novice in the sport asks for advice. Normally there is no shortage of counsel, varying from the excellent to the downright perplexing. No more does that apply than when someone asks, "What is the best rifle for fox shooting?" That question usually brings forth a veritable deluge of advice ranging from diminutive wildcat rounds producing incredibly high velocities to rifles that would probably drop an elephant.

Years ago, anyone starting out had to learn from their own mistakes – or, as I did, tack yourself on to a friendly keeper and learn from him. But how does the newcomer decide from this welter of instant advice what the best course is?

It does not take a great deal to kill a fox with a rifle providing the bullet reaches the right place. Foxes have been shot with virtually every firearm out there including air rifles. In fact, my neighbour threw a stone at one that had been having a go at his poultry, hit it on the head and killed it – probably one of the less conventional ways.

Many shooters these days have a rifle that can deal with anything that happens along, from deer to rabbits. Here, though, I am concerned with calibres that are more fox-specific. I am not getting involved with 'wildcat' rounds, just the ones that most newcomers would be familiar with and those that I use myself.

The .243 is an excellent calibre that will drop virtually everything you are likely to encounter in this country using the correct bullet, though it is a little too much for pure foxing use. Ammunition costs are expensive and the rifles are slightly heavier than smaller calibres. I would say the best all-round rifle for out and out foxing would be the .223. Easily obtained, there are always plenty on

MIKE'S TOP TIP
Head-shooting can often injure and not kill – a fox's brain area is smaller than you think

Left:
Most calibres can humanely dispatch a fox… with a well-placed shot

59

the market, which keeps the price down a little. Ammunition is readily available and, if you decide to go down the reloading route, it is a good cartridge to start with.

It is a flat-shooting round and capable of dropping foxes out to 300 yards – this is well beyond the abilities of most shooters, and I certainly include myself in that group. As a matter of interest where range is concerned, over the years I have kept a record of the distances I have shot foxes at and the average is a little under 100 yards. A .223 zeroed one inch high at 100 yards will do the job out to 200 yards with no problems. When not using my own loads, I use 55-grain Hornady ammo. Although any of the well-known brands will do the job, some rifles are a bit choosy with ammunition, so try a few.

The .223 would be my choice as the ideal fox rifle, but what of the lesser calibres? In the course of my work as a fox controller, I have three other rifles that I use on a regular basis depending on the circumstances. They are the .22 Hornet, the .22LR and the .17 HMR.

The first of my alternatives, the .22 Hornet, is an ancient round that is experiencing a mini-revival. Again, it's relatively easy to load for yourself to start with, then dead easy once you have cracked the system. It is noticeably quieter than the .223, although not as flat shooting. It will drop foxes out to 200 yards. Incidentally, all these rifles carry moderators – essential and helpful for various reasons when after foxes. The three small-calibre rifles can also double up for small vermin. However, the Hornet is inclined to make a mess of rabbits unless you make a head shot – not always easy.

The next one down, the .22LR, has been killing foxes for donkey's years. Although not classed as a fox round, there are times when this little round can do the job perfectly. When in 'sensitive' areas – where you don't want to advertise what you are doing – I often have to shoot foxes using subsonic hollow point ammo (I use Winchester). Limiting the range to 50 yards, it seldom fails to kill outright. This is a useful round and – should certain factions get their way and lead shot is banned – there will be a multitude of .22 users who will rue the day.

Finally, the .17 HMR. This diminutive round has been with us a few years now and it has run into some problems ammunition-

Right:
Shooting foxes with the smaller calibres is challenging, but rewarding

wise. This seems to have faded away, so hopefully the manufacturers have seen to the matter. I like this calibre and have shot quite a few foxes with it. Like the preceding rifle, it is a close-range (100-yard maximum) rifle. Although the sound is a bit snappier than the Hornet, this doesn't present problems in the field. It can give rabbits quite a clout, but while others may not agree I find it marginally more accurate than the Hornet.

To get a direct comparison between the three lesser calibres (the .223 doesn't need testing), I took the rifles out on different nights over the week. They were equipped with the Archer night vision or a Klarus XT30 LED lamp.

The first candidate was the Hornet. Setting up against the top hedge of a field where I knew foxes travelled, I didn't have to wait long. A fox was patrolling the lower hedge 150 yards away. A couple of squeaks had it running up the field towards me, where a whistle stopped it in its tracks.

As it turned I released the 35-grain Hornady V-Max homebrew (13 grains of Lil Gun CCI small rifle primer), dropping it where it stood. Examination showed the shoulder shot had killed it instantly.

The following night it was the .22LR. A fox had been hanging around a neighbour's poultry and they wanted it gone. This was a different scenario as I was indoors, sitting upstairs on a chair by the open window. This turned out to be a long wait but, fortified by a scotch or two, I passed the time watching members of the local badger and rabbit fraternity. After four hours, Charlie appeared and was duly dispatched at 40 yards.

A couple of nights later I was out after rabbits with my farmer friend. We had had a dozen or so when, crossing the same stubble field where the Hornet had claimed one before, a fox moved away to our right. Swinging the pick-up round, I picked it up in the lamp (no night vision this time). It was trotting away from us but a quick blast on the WAM fox call swung it round sideways and the .17 HMR did the job.

This one was 100 yards out and the shot behind the shoulder clearly did not exit but had done severe damage within the rib cage. Incidentally, I much prefer 17-grain ammo to 20-grain – they seem to work better.

All these calibres proved themselves to be more than sufficient for a fox. Two of the ones I shot were fair-sized animals – the one with the .17 HMR weighed 24lb. I have no problem killing foxes stone dead with any of these rifles, but shot placement and range is critical. The .223 will drop them if you hit anywhere in the main body, but this is not so with the three little ones. I head-shoot foxes very rarely as it is all too easy to injure and not kill. A big fox looks like it has a big head but skinning one tells a different story: a fox's skull is small and the brain area smaller still. Particularly at night, it is very hard to guarantee a hit. I usually go for a shot behind the shoulder and this almost guarantees a quick and humane death. If they don't drop on the spot they seldom cover more than a few yards.

Shooting foxes at night is perhaps not as easy as some would have it, particularly if you want to do the job cleanly. Using small calibres is challenging but, if carried out with care, can be most effective. ∎

Above:
Taking head shots at night is a tricky business

FOXES AREN'T WHAT THEY USED TO BE

ROBERT BUCKNELL

ROBERT'S TOP TIP

Lamping remains the best way to cover vast swathes of ground quickly

Foxes have become more wary. It's something that I realised when I had a year where I noticed far fewer foxes over my land than usual. I remember speaking to Mike Powell, and he agreed – foxes were becoming harder to shoot using traditional lamp and calling techniques.

Some cubs are still relatively easy because they're young and naïve, but quite a few are harder than they used to be right from the start. I know people put this down to foxes getting an 'education' at the hands of less competent fox shooters, or the travelling fraternity with their lamps and lurchers, but I think there's more to it. I suspect we are seeing evolution in action, with us fox shooters as the driving force, breeding a new generation of trickier foxes every year.

It used to be that you'd see a fox and straight away start calling to bring it in. Nowadays I won't call as a first option. There's every chance the fox will just swap ends and disappear. Instead, I'll see if I can find a way of getting it without risking scaring it by calling. I tend to save the call for those times when I've had a good look round and can't see one. Then I might as well try the call, but it's more of a last resort. I find calls can work better in daylight, as there is no lamp to put them off.

Sometimes you can use your fieldcraft knowledge to work out where to find a fox without needing any call or bait. I recall a day when I was out trimming cricket bat willows, planted all along the side of a river meadow. The

cold, damp night had turned into a nice sunny and breezy day. I was just thinking that, if I were a fox, I'd find a sheltered spot somewhere in the warm sun to curl up for a snooze. Just after that, I spotted one not 20 yards away, fast asleep on the opposite bank of the river.

Of course that usually happens when you don't have your gun with you. It was a 20-mile round trip home to fetch it, so I just backed away and left the fox to his slumber. No point in upsetting Tod, as he may be there another day – when I come back, gun in hand!

That night another one wasn't so lucky. I was out with the gun and spotted one with the lamp, curled up in a sheltered spot in the lea of a hedge. Some heavy showers of rain had blown in and the night was a bit rough. It was not an obvious night to be out foxing. I have found many a time that if a fox is curled up somewhere warm it is reluctant to leave its bed and step out into the cold. I'm sure we are just the same when we first wake and feel the sheets cling. This one was so comfortable it didn't want to move just because someone was shining a light – and it paid the price. I got rained on, but modern clothing is so good the water doesn't get through.

The idea that we have created a more wary breed of foxes is not as far-fetched as it sounds. Science has shown that foxes can change rapidly in response to selective breeding, just like breeding farm livestock for faster growth or bigger yields.

A Russian scientist named Dmitri Belyaev set up an experimental breeding programme in 1959 with silver foxes, which are simply a grey-coloured form of the red fox, valued for their fur. He picked 130 foxes that were the most friendly towards the handlers, and bred from them. Each year after that, he picked the tamest from each litter to breed from. Within 10 generations the foxes had started to behave more like dogs, whining for attention, wagging their tails when a human approached and enjoying being petted. The opposite happened when they bred selectively from the most aggressive foxes – they

produced a strain of attack fox that wanted to tear your throat out. All that in just 10 years.

So, by applying selective pressure on foxes, we know that their behaviour can be changed. For decades shooters have been going out with lamps and calls and shooting the easiest foxes. Naturally, the ones that get shot are those that aren't lamp-shy and that come readily to a call. In effect, we are selectively breeding from the difficult foxes left behind that are wary of lamps and calls.

If that's what happens in the countryside, perhaps the opposite is happening in our cities. If people look after foxes that come into their gardens and act 'cute' – like pet dogs – then maybe urban foxes will lose their fear of humans and become more like feral dogs. It could certainly explain some of the cases we read in the newspapers where foxes become so bold they enter people's homes and end up biting children.

I witnessed another change, too. I was traveling down an urban road and a fox stood poised to cross the road as I drove past. It stood still with only its head moving as it judged the traffic and waited for a gap to safely trot over. As the motorcar is the biggest killer of urban foxes, survivors must pass on their car avoidance skills.

Foxes may be evolving, but so are we. Fox shooting methods have changed over the years. Nowadays we are much more likely to shoot from a high seat or raised shooting box over a

Above:
A change in foxes' behaviour could be the result of evolution

bait point, so the fox doesn't get to hear a vehicle or a call. And with the recent leaps made in night vision technology, more and more foxes are being shot without the aid of a lamp. Many are also increasingly targeted at dawn and dusk, which is why deerstalkers – if they will shoot a fox – can be very successful.

So all is not lost. To deal with today's more wary foxes, we only need to change our methods. I suppose it's good for the shooting industry too, because it means more sales of sophisticated kit such as night vision equipment and infrared lamps. I spoke to a fox shooter who was happy to spend upwards of £3,000 on a thermal imager so he could spot the foxes to then shoot them with his top-end night vision scope. Now that's a man who takes his shooting seriously, and luckily for him he has the money to support his habit!

It's extraordinary how equipment that was strictly military-only just a few years ago has become everyday gear – not just image intensifiers and thermal imagers, but even technology like personal global position indicators that were Andy McNab territory during the Gulf war. If the trend continues, we can look forward to some fabulous aids in years to come. Current military night vision is becoming miniaturised, so you can wear it easily on your face, like ski goggles. It will soon combine IR and TI so you see not only the heat signature of your target, but also a realistic picture of the surroundings. It is super-sensitive, so it can see in starlight with no need for IR illumination. To take a shot, you simply raise the gun and look through your day scope in the usual way – the goggles multiply whatever tiny amount of light is already passing through the scope. I can't see the foxes evolving fast enough to deal with kit like that!

After all of that, you may be asking why do I still bother to go out with a lamp? The fact is, it still remains the best way to cover the ground fast and see what's out there. ■

Below:
Shooters' methods have evolved too, with more time spent in shooting boxes than in years gone by

LEARNING FROM MISTAKES

The way some shooters talk, you'd think they've never made a mistake in their lives. In fact the only way to become an expert at anything is to learn from mistakes – both your own and other people's. I am the first to admit that I have made hundreds of mistakes, and learning from those has made me a better fox shooter. I have also been lucky enough to learn from other people who have written to me, or come to chat at various shows and events.

The real schoolboy error that most rifle shooters make sooner or later is leaving the rifle bolt behind. It's easily done. We are all so safety-conscious these days that we are careful to keep the rifle and bolt separate. It takes only a small distraction as you're setting off to leave the bolt on the kitchen table. It's not too bad if you're only going down the road, but imagine if you were travelling to the other end of the country.

Your kit is a minefield of potential mistakes. Batteries you forgot to charge, spare bulbs and fuses you didn't bring with you – the possibilities are endless. When you're

travelling by air the mantra is: "Passport, money, tickets." The equivalent three-item list for foxing is: "Lamp, rifle, ammunition." If you've got those three, you're off to a good start.

I try to keep a full kit in the vehicle, or in a pack or belt that I can grab on my way out of the door. That way I always have the vital kit and spares with me. It's a good idea to put your equipment in order straight after a trip, while it's fresh in your mind – replace any items you used, recharge the batteries and so on. If you wait until you're about to set off, it's too late.

Out in the field, even with all the right equipment, we are constantly making mistakes. There are plenty of errors you can make when you're trying to attract a fox and manoeuvre it into a position where it is shootable safely and humanely. Perhaps you misjudge the wind and the fox catches your scent, or you call too loudly or spook it with the lamp. We've all made mistakes like that over and over again – it's part of the learning process that makes us better at the job.

ROBERT'S TOP TIP

If shooting with a team, make sure that everyone's role is clearly defined

One mistake that's harder to forgive yourself for is forgetting to put a round in the breech. It can be embarrassing – after all that skill and effort getting the shot set up, you pull the trigger and... click! When you are familiar with your rifle you learn to feel when the bolt has picked up a round from the magazine on the way forward – or more to the point, you can feel when it hasn't. With practice, you can ease back the bolt and find out, even by moonlight, whether there's a round 'up the spout'.

All the mistakes we've looked at so far are annoying, but not downright dangerous. The biggest mistake any shooter can make is to take a dangerous shot – or worse still, hit something they didn't mean to. That's the sort of mistake you need to avoid by listening to expert advice, not by learning the hard way.

Two key points here are always to be sure of your background, and to positively identify the quarry before taking the shot. When you're lamping as a two- or three-man team, it helps to have a clear understanding of each person's responsibilities. When I go out three-up on my land, the driver is in sole charge of driving safely, avoiding obstacles and the like. If he doesn't like the look of it, no amount of coaxing from the other team members will make him take a risk. Typically I will be the lamper/caller, and it's my job to be sure of the background – it's my land, so I know what's where. I won't drop the lamp beam onto the animal unless I know the background is safe. Once I illuminate the quarry, it is the shooter's responsibility to make a positive identification before he takes the shot. He has the advantage of viewing it through the scope, and he has to be 100 per cent sure of what he's shooting before pulling the trigger. That means seeing not just the eyes, but positively identifying the whole animal.

It's all too easy to see what you expect to see. Many fox shooters have had a close call with a ginger cat or even a yellow dog. A roe doe in rough grass, or lying down in stubble, can look awfully like a fox face-on – especially if she is holding her ears back, which they sometimes do.

Years ago I let my guard slip, and shot a roe by mistake. I had hit a fox, and was following it up on foot in dewy grass. I followed the trail to the edge of a wood – and there in a bramble thicket was a pair of eyes staring back at me. In my eagerness to finish off the fox, I broke the cardinal rule and shot at just the eyes at about 20 yards. I found I had killed a roe that had been lying up in the cover.

The bottom line is this: never be in a rush to leave your kit behind or to make a mistake. ∎

Below:
A bad time to realise you've forgotten to bring the bolt

A CLEVER SETT UP

When is a badger sett not a badger sett? It's not a joke; it's a serious problem for people like me who need to control foxes. We have very few fox litters on the farm as a rule (I see to that). But you can never be sure you've found every one and it pays to keep your eyes open in case one moves in.

For example, there's an old badger sett in a quiet corner of the farm and I cast an eye over it from time to time. A year or so ago, I noticed a few duck feathers and the odd pheasant wing on the ground around the sett. This raised my suspicions: 'These badgers were eating remarkably well,' I thought.

The law makes it a serious offence to disturb a badger sett, although it fails to define exactly what 'disturb' means. In some people's eyes, even walking near the sett, or allowing the tractor spray boom to pass over it, amounts to disturbance. Certainly, you have to tread carefully if you suspect a fox may have taken up residence in a sett, even if you believe the badgers have all moved out.

I crept back on a warm afternoon and, sure enough, there was a litter of fox cubs playing in the sunshine. Since I couldn't be sure the badgers were gone, I decided I had better deal with it at a distance. I set up a high seat in cover. It was far enough away at 180 yards, but meant that I could take a shot at an approaching fox.

I went out mornings and evenings for two, three or even four hours at a time. Four days in a row I saw the vixen but didn't get the chance of a shot. She was wary, as they tend to be when they have cubs. You often don't see a thing, not even an eye peeping from cover. I think in this case she was using a ditch to approach and leave by. There are little signs here and there that you can spot if you know what you're looking for. The scenery changes in small ways, and the odd carcase appears by the entrance.

One evening, the vixen emerged from another hole entirely. She was obviously enjoying a break from being pulled about by the cubs. She came out, stretched and sat down. I

ROBERT'S **TOP TIP**

Get everything close to you when you first enter a high seat – you'll need to be able to find it all in the dark later on

got a bead on her but she was on the horizon. Behind her was a paddock where some local people keep their horses, so I couldn't risk a shot. It was almost as if she knew.

She sat there for 10 minutes, then set off into some cover and didn't come out the other side. I tried a few mouse squeaks but she wasn't interested and I didn't want to push it.

On the fifth evening, it was at last light that I finished my chores and almost didn't bother to go. But I chided myself: if you don't go, you'll never know. I zoomed up there, realised I had got the wind wrong and had to go round the other way to a second high seat I had set up. It was starting to look like a waste of time.

I thought about sneaking in as usual (one pace and stop, look, one pace and stop, look) in case the vixen was sitting there watching over the cubs. However, time was short as there was only 15 minutes of shooting light left. I decided to move in quietly but steadily without stopping. I reached the high seat, climbed up and gently got myself settled in to wait.

That's the time to get everything sorted out around you, so you can find it later when it gets dark. I checked the lamp and placed it within easy reach beside me. The rifle loaded and resting on the rail, I scanned the scene with my naked eye before raising the binoculars for a closer look.

There's an art to using binoculars. Anyone can hold their binoculars to their eyes and go, 'Hmm, nothing there,' but how many of us really know how to look with binoculars? For instance, you can use the binoculars' shallow depth of focus at short range to look deep into cover. Hold the binoculars still and concentrate on the piece of cover that interests you, then slowly rotate the focus wheel. You will see the focus move towards or away from you, depending on which direction you turn the wheel. By blurring the nearest cover you can see what's behind more clearly.

Most people scan from left to right with binoculars. That's the way we read and it feels more natural, but it may not be the best way to spot your quarry. I scan in the opposite direction to the way I expect my quarry to be moving. Perhaps, as on this occasion, I think the vixen will be heading back to the earth, travelling from left to right. In that case I will

Credit: dherman1145

scan from right to left. If she is moving across the terrain in front of me, she can't help coming into my field of view. If I was scanning in the same direction as her, I might be just ahead or just behind, and never see her.

Quite often I will simply hold the binoculars steady on one spot and watch, waiting for movement. Our eyes are very good at picking up something moving, even if it's not in the centre of our vision. They detect movement and flick to it almost instantly. If you are constantly swinging the binoculars this way and that, everything in your field of view is constantly moving. You're not letting your eyes do the one thing they are best at.

As it turned out, I didn't need my binoculars this time. The vixen had been laid up in some thick cover just 60 yards away, between the cubs and me. My approach hadn't disturbed her and, 10 minutes later, I saw her sitting on the edge of the cover. Once she thought the coast was clear, she set off towards the earth. She never saw me slowly swing the rifle round and, boom, that was it. After all that trouble, in the end it was dead easy.

I waited on, but nothing else moved. I finally climbed down and went over to pick her up. It was a vixen all right, but barren. I had shot a milky vixen earlier on, some way off, and had looked hard for the cubs to no avail. This was a good-sized fox and, although I had seen her approach the cubs, I was surprised they had not tried to suckle. I could now see why. The remains of game around the entrance showed she was feeding them, but the absence of any other adults left me to conclude that she had taken over the litter after I had killed their mother – but then never jump to conclusions.

Now I have a litter of cubs on my hands, but that's a straightforward task. Once you've got the vixen, the cubs tend to stay put. First, I want to see if any other adults move in. This is a good chance to catch a call or lamp shy fox. Cubs are like magnets to any foxes in the area. Even if they aren't related, they will often drop by to have a look and a sniff. I will throw the cubs roadkill rabbits and the like for the time being – they are old enough to do fine on solid food – and continue with my regular morning and evening vigils in the high seat.

As for the badgers, I haven't seen hide nor hair of one near those holes. I think I'm safe enough from being accused of interfering with a sett, and can call it an earth. ∎

Above:
There's more to using binoculars than putting them to your eyes and quickly scanning the landscape

SUCK IT AND SEE

ROBERT'S TOP TIP

Don't always listen to the experts, you have to find what works for you

Some experts will tell you there's no point calling foxes in the spring. The adults have heard it all before, and anyway they're busy looking after the cubs, which are generally born around mid-March. Wait until the youngsters are 10 weeks old and start hunting on their own, then it's time to start calling again.

Well, that's all true – but foxes don't listen to the experts. We could have given up on the grounds that it's the wrong time of year for calling.

But in my experience, foxes may come to a call at any time of year. It depends on the individual fox, what mood it's in and a whole lot of factors you can't guess. If you don't give it a go, you'll never know.

People often ask me what the best call for foxes is. The quick answer is Pat Carey, the Warrener. Pat's calling technique is something to behold. He has an uncanny ability to bring in foxes even when they obviously don't want to come – they find his insistent calling irresistible, coming in like a well-trained gundog to the whistle. In one of his videos he calls a fox so close that he can push it away with his foot, and still it comes back.

Unfortunately you can't carry Pat in your pocket – but there are some very good alternatives that you can. People have been

Foxes can come to the call at any time of year

dreaming up ingenious ways of calling in foxes for a long time, and I've gathered quite a collection over the years. A metal detector enthusiast brought me an old call that he'd found in one of my fields once. It was the wigeon whistle type, made from the brass heads of two old 12-bore cartridges with the primers punched out. It was very tarnished from being in the ground so long, but I reckoned it could be more than 100 years old.

There are many variations on the wigeon whistle call, including one of my favourites, the WAM call, which is good for a little mouse squeak to tease in a fox when it's getting close. When you need to shout out across open Scottish hillsides, though, you need something more powerful. The Tenterfield whistle, which was originally sent over here by Andre Georgescu from Australia, claims to carry for over a kilometre, for example. Bestfoxcall. co.uk has come up with a well made stainless steel version on a paracord lanyard. It makes a good, loud, raspy call that carries a long way, and is one of the easiest to use of its type.

For this particular fox, however, I used the electronic call that I had with me. It can reach out a long way, and offers a good range of calls. When a fox doesn't respond, it's so easy to swap to a different sound. I've often watched a fox carrying on oblivious of the call, then changed my tune and seen it instantly turn and head in. There must be something in the sound that we can't hear. You can have two calls that sound equally good to our ears, but foxes ignore one and find the other irresistible.

It's all about finding the sound that makes the fox think it's found an easy meal. If that fox is in the habit of popping down to the village pond for a duck, then quacking like a duck may produce the desired response. Think about what yours are feeding on.

When you're squeaking with your mouth, or even using a Tenterfield-type call, you can vary the tone just by changing the shape of your mouth, moving your tongue, or blowing

or sucking harder or softer. When you find the right tone and the fox responds, the challenge is to produce the same note again. At least with an electronic call you just have to press the right button.

This fox obviously liked the sound of my caller's young rabbit call, as the next thing we saw was its head poking out of the hedge barely 60 yards away. Unfortunately it wasn't where we'd expected. Nigel, who was on top with his gun on the cab roof, was facing entirely the wrong direction.

That's why I'm not a fan of bipods for lamping from a vehicle. If the legs are extended, it's almost impossible to change position without making a noise. If they're folded, you'll most likely gouge the paintwork too. I prefer to rest the gun on a cushion or pillow, which I can slide quickly and silently into position.

This fox wasn't totally convinced by my call, and it set off across the field. I called again and it stopped, but not long enough for a shot. Again I pressed the button, and it hesitated and went on. Then the third time, with a bit more distance between us, it felt confident enough to stand for a longer look. Nigel bowled it over. It was an old dog fox, which proved my point that when it comes to calling: every fox is different and you'll never know unless you give it a go. ■

Above:
It's hard to predict which call will work in any given situation... so it's worth having a few to hand

LOOKING AND SEEING

Above:
Learn to look beyond
the obvious to pick up
subtle clues to a fox's
presence

ROBERT'S TOP TIP

Practise the art of seeing,
not just looking

Like a lot of shooters, I spend many hours up a high seat or sitting on the ground over a commanding view, watching and waiting. I was doing that one evening when I spotted a fallow buck. To be exact, I didn't actually spot the buck. I spotted part of his hind leg.

What happened was that I looked at the wood and realised something had changed. I looked more intently and saw something that looked like a hazel stem by a clump – but it hadn't been there earlier. I raised the binoculars and studied it. From its colour, shape and texture, I worked out that it wasn't a hazel stem at all, but the leg of a fallow.

That set me off thinking about the difference between looking and seeing. It's something that people who live in the country pick up without

realising, although some become better at it than others. Those people are often the hunters.

George, a gamekeeper, told me about an incident shortly after he joined the army. A group of recruits were taken to a range, and the sergeant told them: "Right, you lot, look out across there and tell me what you see."

"Nothing," mumbled most of the recruits – but not George. "Well," said George, pointing, "there's someone hiding behind that close-in bush there – I can see his eye. And over there, in that low cover, there's a leaf or two turned over and upside down. I'd say someone has crawled through there recently, and is perhaps hidden there. And there, behind that tree, there's a trail in the dew that doesn't come out again. Whoever made it is probably still behind the tree."

George was right, and the sergeant asked the soldiers to stand up from where they had hidden themselves. Of course, you don't win any points in the army by being a smart Alec and making the sergeant look foolish. But it does illustrate how a gamekeeper's eye is tuned in to the little visual clues that most people miss. The object of the exercise was to start to train the raw recruits not to just gaze at the scene but to look and decipher the things that their eyes were showing them, but that they were not seeing. This sort of thing applies greatly to gamekeepers. Most often the keeper isn't looking for a whole deer or fox – he's looking for the little things, such as the flick of an ear or a glimpse of fur through a gap in the undergrowth.

As more people come into shooting and country sports from an urban background, they find they need to catch up on this vital but little-known skill. I couldn't tell you how many times I have heard the words 'Suddenly there was the fox/roe/fallow standing out in plain view.' Often, the practised eye would have detected the creature before it broke cover.

It's something that animals do intuitively. Whether they are a predator or prey species, they know when something doesn't look right. I'm convinced that deer have a mental picture of their local area. Perhaps you've put up a high seat, or there's a piece of farm machinery left in a different place. The first time a deer comes into view, it will stop and stare at the new thing, looking for movement.

It's the same if the deer spots you – so long as you stay totally still, it will check you out before deciding you're not a threat and continuing with its business. When that happens, I try not to make eye contact, because I'm convinced animals can sense a threat when you're looking straight into their eyes. I try to look past them.

Beware of the deer's 'double take' trick. It will look away, pretending it has lost interest – but it has taken a mental picture of the scene. A moment later its head will swing back. If the picture is different, it will often stare and perhaps stamp a front foot, telling its mates to watch out. Suddenly, they all start looking. Any more movement on

your behalf and they will rush off in alarm. You need to remain absolutely still until it has had several looks, and is properly relaxed. Then move very slowly. Remember, too, that as a prey species, the deer has its eyes on the side, and it can see you move even when it's not facing you.

It's different for the fox. As a predator, its eyes face forwards, like ours. When it looks the other way, it won't see you move – but be quick, and then freeze without making a sound. It's still easy to draw the fox's attention if you are careless.

When I'm first waiting in a high seat or watching from a vehicle, I quickly find that certain objects catch my eye. There's always a patch of darker grass, a different coloured stem or a low branch that makes you wonder, 'Could that be a fox or a deer?' You'll check these out with the binoculars, and soon learn to ignore them and look for other subtle changes in the view.

Be wary of things that draw your eye strongly – a white flint in the field, a bright flower just inside the wood, or even something very black. It's the old sniper's trick to place himself a short distance from something that draws the eye, because it makes it harder for an enemy to spot him. Your eye keeps pinging to that object, and finds it hard to scan the area near it properly.

It's very satisfying when these skills pay off. Recently I was watching a wood and saw something that hadn't been there a short while ago poking out from behind a hazel stool. Looking closer, I realised it was the tip of a fox's tail – he thought he was totally hidden.

He couldn't see me as his body was out of sight, so I carefully raised the gun to aim at the other side of the stool. Sure enough, a minute later he took a few steps forward to peer out from his hiding place. I was ready with my finger on the trigger. In a second I corrected my aim and squeezed the off the shot – and the fox was down before he realised his mistake.

Be warned. Once you start down the road of understanding, life will never be the same. As your knowledge and your skill expand, a comfortable seat in front of the telly will become a distant memory. ■

HARVEST FOXES

As I have said, once you're tuned in to the countryside, you don't need to see a fox to know it's there. You can read the signs and know what's going on behind the screen of foliage.

This was drilled home for me on an occasion when I was watching over a litter of cubs. I could have shot them many times over, but I wanted to get the vixen first.

One evening I was sitting in my mobile high seat, quietly watching. Far out to my right front, I heard a cock pheasant complaining. 'Ah, that'll be a fox moving down the track the other side of the hedge,' I thought.

A rabbit 100 yards in front of me stood up and looked away from me at the hedge. It stamped its hind legs on the ground to warn its friends. The wind blowing through the greenery had brought the smell of something unseen on the other side. If it was the same thing the cock pheasant had seen, the fox was moving across my front to my left.

A little later, I heard a vixen call quietly from the same track further to my left. It was a single call, like a triple mating call but quieter and lower. She moved into the willow bed moving round me, more to my left. Another cock pheasant started calling, "Fox, fox, fox!"

She went down the headland of a field of rape, still hidden from my view and even more left, but a blackbird on top of the hedge was

ROBERT'S TOP TIP

When shooting cubs, don't collect the shot fox immediately, others may be close by

calling "Pink, pink!" to his mate as she passed. They call differently for an owl or a cat.

At last I saw her emerge behind a house 100 yards away to my left, where someone was talking loudly on his mobile phone in the back garden. She was used to the house being occupied, and just glanced round and continued on her way, passing within 60 yards of the house.

At first I thought she was a cub as she was so small. But once I got a clear sight of her, I realised she was the vixen I'd been waiting for. She was a small fox anyway, but her coat was worn from frequently going underground and suckling the cubs.

She approached the earth, making a sweep downwind. Her caution was her undoing, however, because that presented me with a safe shot. I wasted no time putting a round in her. I had only seen her for the last 80 yards of her approach, but I had followed her progress for 500 yards or more just by reading the signs.

This is vital pre-harvest when visibility is low with the height of the crops.

Before harvest, it's often best to sit in a high seat or vehicle and wait for the foxes to come to you. Once the fields are cut, you can scoot about and find them, covering a much wider area. It only takes a minute to sweep the lamp across a field. The harvest itself provides opportunities – you can wait for a fox to bolt as the combine clears the field. It can be difficult to predict where they will run, but if you get it right, the results make it worth the effort.

I remember watching one chap get it absolutely right here on the farm. He guessed where the fox would go, and lay down with his shotgun in the middle of a 40-acre field. Sure enough, the fox broke cover and ran straight towards him. When it got close enough, he rolled upright and shot it from a sitting position.

If you do need to go after litters, remember that typically there will be four or five cubs that are starting to explore and hone their hunting skills. The litters tend to hang around together, so with persistence and patience you should get them all. A good tip is not to rush out and collect a fox you have just shot. Leave it there and wait a while. There's a chance other foxes are nearby.

Even after the harvest, it's surprising how foxes can remain hidden in a dip in the ground or a few inches of rape stubble.

Remember that in summer you have extra daylight at both ends of the day. Plenty of people go out in the evening because it fits around the other demands on their time. But if you always follow the same routine, you'll only catch the foxes that are vulnerable to that method. You'll never see the other fox that is active first thing in the morning. Vary your times and methods, and you stand a better chance of cleaning up all the foxes. ∎

Below:
A cock pheasant alerted Robert to a fox in this instance

HARVEST FOXING TIPS

ROBERT'S TOP TIP

If you're going to be out all night remember to take food and drink, otherwise you could fall asleep on he job

Your first chance to get after the foxes during the harvest is when the combine starts into the oilseed rape or any winter barley. As the combine works across the field in ever narrowing strips, a fox can find itself marooned in a shrinking island of cover. Eventually it will have to make a run for it.

In fact, the shotgun is the best tool for this job. No 1 or BB is probably the best choice out of a heavy choke. The difficulty is in picking the right spot to wait. It's not something you can do very effectively by yourself, because there are too many ways the fox might run. You could wait ages only to find the fox flees out the other side and gets away. Covering the whole field would take quite a sizeable team, and it's not easy to find that many people who have nothing else to do at harvest time.

When you get it right, however, it can be a very effective. In my book I mentioned a chap in Surrey (Mr Surridge of cricket bat fame) who had three left-and-rights at foxes, one after the other, each time the combine went round a triangular field.

One good tip is to stand just inside the uncut crop (in a tramline, so you're not flattening it) looking out, but be sure to get the wind direction right. The fox will come to the edge and look up and down, but won't see you if you are standing "round the corner". You should get a nice side-on shot as they make a dash as the combine pushes them out. The big problem is that you can wait half the day and only see one fox – or none! If you know there are a bunch of cubs in the crop it is a different matter, as you may get several of them and even their wily old mother.

Anyone with lots of grass where they shoot will have been able to keep searching their grazed land, then as the silage is taken off followed by the hay they can keep hunting. Even so, when the combines get going on the adjacent cereal land the night sky can look like London in the blitz, as weaving lamp beams shine up from so many lampers.

Once the combines have finished, foxshooters look forward to driving round after dark with a lamp, and sweeping up plenty of innocent young foxes. It can work well, but the problem is that you tend to hack round so quickly that you only skim off the easy ones. If a fox doesn't come readily to the call, or doesn't present a safe shot because it's in line with houses, roads or livestock, it's tempting to move on, knowing there will be another one down the road.

However, that's a recipe for leaving a hard core of tricky foxes on your land. I prefer to do the job properly, taking the trouble to finish one fox before moving on to the next. Often it's just a question of patience, staying with the fox you've spotted until you get your chance. It's also a time when night vision comes in handy. Digital kit like the Pulsar N750 works in all lighting conditions and is especially good at last light when the cubs often first appear. With the cleared ground it is also easier to pick them out with NV, as there is no cover in the way.

With a day scope it might mean taking a longer shot than you would choose at other times of year – but harvest is the ideal time for this. The animal stands out well against the cereal stubble,

You need to stay focused on the job in hand, and not be tempted to start banging away at rabbits. Next thing you know, the combine driver will be pointing from the cab that you've missed seeing a fox that ran out the other side.

Besides, fox shooting as the combine works needs a different approach to shooting rabbits. For rabbits, you can stand out in the open to cover the ground between the standing crop and their burrows. For foxes you must be sneakier, hiding back in the hedge or ducked down behind a bale, otherwise they will see you and go the other way.

Sometimes you have to be patient and wait for the fox to move to a clear spot, such as a tramline, where you can be sure the bullet will do its job. Alternatively you can carry a shotgun alongside your rifle. Foxes feel a lot more confident in tall stubble, so there's a good chance to call them in really close before firing.

If you can't get a shot at a particular fox for whatever reason, come back later. It will probably stick within the same territory, and a freshly harvested field is a big draw because of all the small mammals and insects that get chopped up and scattered by the combine. The smell of all that food can be irresistible to a cub that hasn't yet learnt all the dangers.

Foxing at this time of year inevitably means keeping some very unsocial hours. In the winter, when it's dark by 5 or 6pm, you can get your foxing done while the rest of the world is watching TV or down the pub, and there's less need to stay up through the night. Some keepers switch their routine at this time of year, taking their sleep during the middle of the day like a night-shift worker.

One good tip is to keep your body topped up with food and liquids so you don't run out of steam halfway through the night. We don't generally go for hours on end without eating or drinking during the day, or we'd expect to feel very tired, yet people will stay up through the night without taking a break for a meal. It's no surprise they start to feel whacked.

You can take a flask and sandwiches with you, so plan a pit stop partway through the session, just like you'd take a big lunch-break during a full day of shooting. Small meals scattered through the night are best, however. If you have a big blowout you may want to sleep afterwards, just as in the day. Little and often keeps you going.

Remember that at this time of year there's a considerable window of daylight, after sunrise and before the human world really gets going, when foxes will still be out. It's another chance to catch up with them on the stubbles and elsewhere, and with the light in your favour.

So, sit in your high seat of an evening – out all night – then go back and wait at first light for the one that gave you the slip! ■

Above:
Many foxes will fall during the harvest, but it's worth spending extra time to get the problem foxes and not just the easy ones

so you can see your target clearly, and you should know the size of your fields as well. If not, a laser rangefinder will give you the range, as it will read off the dark fox body contrasting against the stubble. Provided you know your gun's trajectory, have a good solid rest and allow for any wind, then long range needn't be a problem – provided you put in the practice beforehand!

Be careful if you see only see one eye, or the eyes are flickering, when reflecting the light of the lamp back at you in some tall stubbles. That should alert you to the fact that there may be an obstruction. Stubbles cut high such as rape, maize or linseed, can be very tough, and may be enough to blow up or deflect your bullet and cause a miss. At harvest time in particular you need to be very careful with the lighter calibres such as .17 HMR or .204 Ruger, or even ultra fast light ballistic-tipped bullets in .223 and .243. I prefer a heavier 69-grain bullet in my .223, because I can rely on it to work in most conditions. It may tumble, but it will not blow up and fail to reach the target.

SCENT SENSE

I recall an occasion when I was clearing up a litter of fox cubs around a nine-acre field on the farm. It was a good spot, and it attracted the youngsters because one side has an acre clump of scrub willow, called appropriately enough 'the bog', and it always lays wet, with a couple of small areas of open water. Once cubs are weaned they need a ready supply of water in the warm months of June to August. Being lazy, they tend to set up camp by a reliable source. You will often find that a litter that has moved in on you is constrained in its choice of hunting ground by the need to drink regularly.

For several evenings, I drove up to the field in the pick-up, and parked near a corner that gave me a good view along two sides of the crop of wheat. I could see any fox that came out onto either of the 10-metre-wide grass headlands. They are not conservation headlands, so they can be kept mown to allow wildlife easy passage and give me a good chance to catch any local foxes in the open.

On one night, it was 10 past 10 and pretty dark when I saw a darker patch 160 metres down the headland on the edge of the crop. I raised the binoculars; yes, it was a fox. I raised the rifle into position on the padded wing mirror. When the fox stopped to smell something, I was ready and dropped it quickly. It was a testament to good optics – I couldn't have shot that fox without good binoculars and a top-end scope. How many foxes have succumbed because an interesting smell stopped them at some point?

The next evening I returned to the same position, but the wind had changed. It was blowing my scent directly towards the spot where I'd shot the fox the night before. Would that ruin my chances?

Hunters understand the importance of scent. We know that animals rely on their sense of smell more than their senses of sight and hearing. The smart hunter is always thinking about how the wind will carry his scent – it's usually the first thought before the initial decision of how to proceed.

He'll usually start a night's lamping at the downwind end of the estate, so he's always working into the wind. But with a high seat it may work the other way round.

Scent is a complex subject, and we can easily get it wrong because we don't fully understand how it works. To learn just how complicated it can be, ask a huntsman. He'll tell you that there are good and bad scenting days. Sometimes the air scent of a fox hangs near the ground, and hounds can follow the line quickly. Another day, he may be able to smell the fox from his raised position on his horse, while hounds can't find a line at all. On other days all they can find is a ground scent, so things will go slower.

All these factors work equally the other way round, when it's a fox catching a whiff of human. Sometimes the fox will detect you from far away, and other times he will appear unaware even as he cuts downwind of you. Perhaps the air currents are carrying

ROBERT'S TOP TIP

Learn to understand how foxes use scent to scout their surroundings your scent over his head, or further to one side than you thought. On the other hand he may be aware you are there but choosing to ignore you. It can be interesting to take a child's bubble bottle out with you and watch how the wind carries the soap bubbles – you'll soon see that wind and scent don't travel in straight lines.

Ground scent behaves differently to air scent. It tends to stay in one place. It's a mixture of crushed vegetation, disturbed earth, and whatever smelly stuff you might have picked up on your boots. Foxes, like dogs, can read this mixture of scents like a book. They can tell the difference between fresh human scent and something a human has touched a while ago. A fox will happily take a dead rabbit that you have handled earlier in the day, while it wouldn't come nearer than 400 metres if you were standing there with it in your hand. Town foxes have a different comfort zone, of course, and are much less bothered by human scent. Some even come closer to beg for food.

The fox's curiosity is often his downfall, and that goes for scent too. The scent of a chicken farm or pheasant pen can draw them in from miles away. But it doesn't have to be food. A while ago I was waiting by a hedge at night, watching through night vision, and saw a fox cut my scent 200 yards downwind. He sniffed the air, looked about, and trotted towards me, quartering across my scent, curious about what he could smell.

He kept stopping, sniffing and coming closer to me until eventually he seemed satisfied, turned and trotted off. Luckily for him I didn't have a gun with me. I paced it out and discovered he had come within 16 yards. Must change my deodorant, I thought.

Back to my nine-acre field. Many fox shooters will set up facing an open field so the wind is blowing towards them across the field. Their thinking is that a fox approaching across the field won't scent them. But that's totally wrong. A fox may come from any angle, but the least likely direction is the convenient one for you – straight across.

Foxes are a lot smarter than they used to be, and it's rare for one to come piling in directly towards a call. It will want to check it out first by getting downwind. If the wind is blowing across the field, the fox will sneak up through the undergrowth behind. You may not know it's there until it's right under your high seat or peering into your pocket to see if you have brought a sandwich. I think you realise this last scenario is very unlikely – it will, of course, have legged it to somewhere much safer without you even being aware of its presence.

But suppose you've set up, back to cover, with the wind blowing from you out across the field. The only way for the fox to get downwind is to go out into the field for a sniff. He'll have to trot across the open ground around you before he can catch your wind – giving you a perfect chance of a shot before he gets there.

In the event, that evening it was a roebuck that cut my scent only 60 metres out. He walked out through the wheat crop on my right, in full view of my vehicle but quite unalarmed until he caught the scent of the truck and me. He barked and ran to the hedge on the left, then doubled back across the wheat field and barked his way right across to the other side by the hedge 150 metres away, calling all the time. What a racket!

You might expect that would be it for the evening, but it's always worth waiting to see what happens. This is especially true with cubs – they may be curious to see what all the fuss is about. Sure enough, a little face popped out of 'the bog' right beside where I'd shot the cub the night before.

He stepped out and sniffed the air, 160 metres away and seemingly straight downwind. An older, more experienced fox may have vanished again in a flash, but this cub was curious and I was ready. My rifle was to hand. He stood a moment too long – and never knew what hit him. The wind may have appeared all wrong on paper, but it was all right in practice. ■

A WEIGHTY PROBLEM

It can be hard to tell one fox from another at distance, but I felt confident I would recognise one my neighbouring keeper described to me a few years ago. "Dog fox. Fat as a mole," he said. This one had been seen during a pheasant drive on the next shoot to mine as he slipped away through the open gap between the line of beaters and the guns. He was last seen heading towards my ground.

I had a sneaking suspicion he would stay there, probably having a go at my partridges. They are vulnerable because they jug down in the fields at night instead of going up to roost in the trees like pheasants. On shoots where there are a lot of rats owing to an abundance of food – especially in maize cover – partridges stay out in the middle of the field, away from the hedges. On my farm the rats are controlled heavily so you're more likely to find partridges near the edge, which means a fox is more likely to find them and trap them as some flee into the cover.

Going round at night, you can always tell if the partridges have been disturbed. If a covey is huddled together in the field, all hunkered down facing outwards, then all is well. But you know something has disturbed them when you see one here, one there and another wandering across the road looking bewildered. An owl or badger might have moved them, but much more likely a fox will be the culprit.

We'd had some foul, wet weather that had restricted fox shooting. With the ground saturated, you can't cross the fields in an ATV, never mind a truck. That means sticking to the roads and tracks, or heading out on foot – and with the weather so unpredictable you're bound to get caught in a downpour sooner or later. That's when you're glad you spent a few extra pounds on Butler Creek flip-up covers to protect the scope lenses.

Knowing this barrel-shaped fox was likely to be on my patch, I decided to take a drive around in the truck. I would have to stay on the farm roads, but that gave me a chance of spotting it and at least I would stay dry.

The first time round I saw nothing, then the heavens opened and I returned home for a coffee and a bite to eat before heading out again a couple of hours later. At least the rain had ceased. This time I was in luck – there was the fox, or a fox anyway, out in the middle of a field. I couldn't get a safe shot, however, as it was in line with someone's house. It moved off directly away from me, and I thought it might stop within range of the track near this farm.

Driving round to the other side, I realised I would be no more than 60 or 70 yards from the very bedroom window that had prevented me shooting earlier. It was 2am by now and the lights were off, so I was confident the occupants would be asleep. I pulled up on the other side of the farm barn that would help shield the report left over from the use of a Jet-Z moderator. They would probably never even hear the shot.

The fox was still there, sitting on the ditch line at the far side of the field, a range I knew

ROBERT'S TOP TIP

Your shot can be good, but a fox can still run a good distance before dropping dead

82

to be about 200 yards. Sure enough he looked rotund, although without putting the HID lamp full on him I couldn't be sure. The ground is flat here, but knowing the land, I was confident the backstop was good, especially taking into account the drop from the bullet's trajectory. If I did miss, it had 40 acres of muddy wheat to land in and a good clear mile behind that.

I lined up on the white chest; the bullet would be an inch low out there. The wind was coming in over the left shoulder, but not enough, I thought, to move the bullet too far. Tight hold – don't hang about. I squeezed the trigger and a fraction later heard a good solid thump as the bullet hit. In case the gunshot had disturbed the neighbours, I switched off the lamp immediately and waited 10 minutes before walking out.

All was quiet, so I set off to find the fox with my Global Rifle head torch. At 220 paces I reached the ditch – no fox. I looked round to the left in the direction it had been heading. Fortunately there was no cover out there and I could see a body in the distance. It had run exactly 107 paces before dropping dead. If it had been near a hedge or wood, I might have doubted the evidence of my own ears and wondered if I had missed it altogether.

On closer examination I found that my bullet had struck the fox's chest at a slight angle and exited just to one side of the backbone. An inch left and it would have dropped on the spot, but the slight quartering breeze had pushed my bullet that vital fraction sideways. The fox was as good as dead when my bullet struck, but it was a useful reminder of how far a 'dead' fox can run.

The fox fitted my neighbour's description perfectly. It was not especially big but plump and round, "fat as a mole" indeed, and with its fine winter coat adding to the bulk. It's a shame to waste these pelts. You can understand people objecting to the idea of breeding foxes just for their skins, but if the fox is going to be shot anyway it seems such a waste.

This one was a reasonable weight for a dog fox, probably 17-18lbs. Its teeth weren't in good order – there was one canine missing and the rest were yellowed and worn down to three quarters of their original length. It had been around a while, but was clearly able to feed itself well. Perhaps it had been hanging around the town three miles away and this was the first time it had been shot at – and the last. ■

Below:
The unpredictable weather can render a truck or ATV redundant

GOLD MEDAL FOXING

Like many shooters, I was thrilled when Peter Wilson, 'Pigeon Pete' to his friends, won the Double Trap gold at the Olympics in 2012. It was a tremendous personal achievement, and it helps the sport of shooting generally if a British athlete can achieve success on the world stage. We couldn't ask for a better ambassador for shooting: Peter comes across as a genial, likeable, sensible and dedicated young man, the opposite of the image the antis would like to portray.

I'm sure many shooters also became engrossed in watching the other sports, from swimming and rowing to athletics and cycling. Perhaps, like me, you saw lessons in many of these sports that we can apply to our everyday lives, fox shooting included.

One comment that really struck a chord with me was not about shooting at all, but cycling. There was much debate about the technology behind Britain's success in the cycling events – did we have a secret weapon? Perhaps the Brits' bicycles had special wheels that gave them an advantage, or high-tech suits to reduce wind resistance. The media was desperate to find out, but when they got their interview the truth was even more revealing.

There was no secret weapon – just a determination to work at every tiny thing that could deliver even the smallest improvement. Refining the helmet shape in a wind tunnel might give you a fraction of a second's advantage; adjusting the seat height to give the legs the best possible leverage is another fraction of a second. Then there's perfecting the athletes' diets to maximise stamina and power – and even a campaign of thorough hand-washing in the training camp to reduce the risk of a stomach upset.

Taken individually, each of those things might seem too tiny to worry about, but added together they could make a difference of as much as a second. That's a lot of effort for just one second, but a second can be the difference between winning and losing, and that makes all the effort worthwhile.

Now apply that way of thinking to your fox shooting. You could put in a lot of time practising your shooting at different ranges, and from a variety of positions and rests; you could spend more on your scope to give slightly better performance in low light; you could experiment with different brands of ammo, or even load your own, to achieve the best possible accuracy.

All of this time, effort and expense might mean you can shoot slightly smaller groups, or get an accurate shot away a fraction of a second faster. It won't do much for your social life, and will probably cause more than a little friction with your partner too.

Is it worth it? That depends on your point of view, because sooner or later it will mean shooting a fox that would otherwise have got away. Only you know whether that makes it worthwhile. If you were aiming for an Olympic gold medal, the choice might be easier, but it takes a special kind of person to apply that level of dedication to fox shooting.

That's one lesson we can take from the Olympics, but there are others. Here's one for the kit junkies, the sort of people who are constantly tweaking their gun and ammo in a search for the ultimate in accuracy. If you watched the rifle shooting events at the Olympics, you'll have seen that many of the rifles were virtually identical, and most competitors were using the same ammo too. If you could test each of the guns on the line, you wouldn't find a bad one among them – every one is capable of putting round after round through the same hole in the target. Yet some competitors shot 10 after 10 to build a perfect score, while others dropped a point here and a point there, and failed to make it to the final.

It's obvious really, but we forget too easily that the kit is just part of the equation. Once you've got a gun that fits and ammo that

ROBERT'S TOP TIP

Dedication to fox shooting will make you a better fox shooter, it's as simple as that

Left:
Pete Wilson's gold
medal at London
2012 should be a
source of great pride
for British shooters,
but also a reminder
to dedicate time to
practising

can shoot accurately, you need to put in the practice with that combination so that shooting with it becomes second nature. If you're constantly chopping and changing in search of perfection, you never get the chance to develop the level of understanding so you know exactly how your bullet flies. I have been shooting with the same brand and bullet in .223 since 1986. Just the other night I saw six foxes and dealt with them at 108,157,174, 236, 254 and 263 yards.

Now for the gun. One of the Olympic rifle shooters at London 2012 was competing with a Soviet-era rifle and ammunition, while everyone around him was using modern, high-tech kit.

Asked why he doggedly stuck to his antiquated gear, he replied, "I have a new rifle back at home but when you are getting ready for the Olympic Games it is too late to change anything." What he was saying was that he had used the old gun so often it fitted like a glove and could be used without conscious thought. His name was Sergei Martynov, and he won the 50-metre rifle prone event.

Not long after the Olympics, a friend who shoots a .22LR visited me. He had read an article in one of the shooting magazines that said you shouldn't take longer-distance shots with a rimfire. "That's true for most people," he said, "but I'm going to carry on regardless."

He bought his .22 rifle years ago for £150, settled on a brand of ammo that worked well in it, and has shot nothing else ever since. He has some natural ability too, and the combination means that he can hit just about anything up to 150 yards – I know it's true because I have watched him do it.

In his case, the definition of a long shot is stretched far beyond what would be long for most people because of his skill and familiarity with the gun and ammunition – and, another attribute to long use, an uncanny ability to judge range accurately.

In the modern world, people often expect to be able to splash out a load of cash and get instant results, but as any Olympic athlete will tell you, buying the best gear is just the start.

There is no substitute for practice, application and dedication.

I remember one competitor in the days of practical pistol shooting who, after winning a world championship in South Africa, swapped guns with one of the other shooters for a bit of informal fun. He noticed that the other chap was shooting tighter groups than he could with his own gun. Not being the sort to let it pass, he went back to basics and practised shooting slowly to improve his groups, then gradually built his speed back up again. "After 15,000 rounds I was shooting as fast as before – but tighter groups," he said. Although he had won, he was thinking of next year's competition.

Not many fox shooters are that dedicated – in fact, you'd be a little bit bonkers if you were – but it's an insight into what it means to take your shooting to the Olympic level. Come to that, you may even decide to take up one of the Olympic shooting disciplines: Pete has done it, so can you. ■

FOX RIGHT OFF

HOWARD HEYWOOD

HOWARD'S TOP TIP

Never forget the basics, no matter how difficult a fox may seem

If I had a pound for every time I've been questioned about dealing with difficult foxes I would be a very rich man indeed. The trouble is that there's no straightforward answer, as every situation is different; many are similar but no two are ever the same.

Shooters who boast they have the foxing job sussed are as often as not outwitted due to their blinkered attitude towards their own ability. Don't get me wrong, I'm not painting a picture of doom and gloom here that foxing with lamp and rifle is inherently difficult or above the average shooter's ability. Not at all, the point is that we all make mistakes. But to improve our ability we must realise them and try not to give a repeat performance. Every foxer, myself definitely included, remembers the red-letter days – or should that be nights? Failures are very easily forgotten, but the reasons for the failure should not be.

There are some myths in particular that need to be immediately dispelled by the budding fox shooter and possibly even some of the more experienced ones. It is a common belief that one cannot over-call. This is folly. No two foxes are the same and not all will come in – no matter how good you are at manually calling or how hi-tech your electronic digital gizmo is. It's not just dependent on the particular fox but also on his mood or how full his belly is at the time. I suppose what I'm trying to say is, please don't go out with the preconceived idea

that it will be just another night spotting eyes, calling up the sighted fox to a sensible range and rolling him over with a good shot before moving on to the next one. If only it were actually that simple.

The fox is a born survivor: it's top of the food chain in its own environment and we are really the intruders into the fox's world. A world where there are no convenient supermarkets, central heating or audiovisual entertainment. An environment many of us decide not to venture into when the weather turns nasty. I am like many other shooters – and probably many non-shooters too – in that I enjoy those long summer evenings when I can take a break after work to have my evening meal, put my feet up for a couple of hours and still be up on the fell before the sun slips behind the horizon to let the moon take over for the nightshift. Those evenings are precious and seem to be getting fewer as each year turns.

Despite my warning about over-calling, in summer you are just as likely to call a few foxes out of their lying up spots in suitable cover before nightfall as you are slogging over field after field in search of a sighting during darkness. I've done full nights without sleep, far too many to count, and worked the next day in pursuit of a particularly troublesome fox. The irony is that, on so many occasions when you aren't trying that hard you almost trip over the damn fox and after taking a successful shot it seems so easy it is almost untrue. In fact, tales of the times I've just had a casual walkabout with the rimfire and happened across a normally-elusive fox would fill these pages on their own.

Fortunately though, I've usually been quick enough to react to the fox while within range with a well-placed headshot and stolen a welcome result. The key point here is not to become complacent, expect the unexpected and be ready to exploit an advantageous position to the full.

What do you suppose a fox actually sees when it looks at the glare of a lamp shining back at it? If it isn't lamp shy I don't for one instant presume that it immediately thinks danger. I believe it is a mixed sense of curiosity, confusion and a fair dose of caution to what to Charlie must be a big ball of daylight. Of course most experienced foxers will have on occasion had foxes steaming in, almost suicidal, but this is definitely not always the case. Far from it; the times when Charlie hangs just out of range, circling, appearing to the side and trying to catch your wind are much more commonplace.

A mistake many will make when dealing with difficult foxes is the tendency to think of them as rogue animals with a mythical ability to avoid danger. They accredit more difficulty to the situation than really exists. This has certain shooters trying elaborate ruses to outwit old 'Super Charlie', but in their haste to dream up the ingenious they quite often forget the basics and educate the fox more with their lack of success. This will create a frustrating perpetual cycle. Yes, a fox has acute senses and an uncanny ability for self-preservation, but he does not walk on water or need a silver bullet. All animals survive by being adaptable and having the ability to learn quickly from experience. Take four fox cubs waiting by the verge side to cross a road. The first cub attempts a crossing and is reassembled into a flatter profile by a passing car. Then there were three fox cubs – but all are now very much educated about the dangers of the tarmac. Equally, a fox that had been half-mesmerised

by a high powered lamp while being drawn in by a tempting squeak that promised an easy meal but actually culminated in a terrifying crack and a close shave with a bullet, has plenty of new notes to make for his further education in survival course.

Don't forget the basics throughout the year, such as searching for fresh earths or likely holes the vixen may be using. Those old regular runs that foxes have used in the past are all worth checking out, but don't venture too close at cubbing time or the vixen will move her charges before you return. Also, when the weather leaves the ground muddy keep an eye out for fresh tracks and other

clues to Charlie's routes and routine. Look for vantage points over obvious travel paths and above all remain focused. As you search the area where the fox is causing problems, it is so easy to become complacent. Time put in is time well spent, and knowing Charlie's ways will give you the edge over the educated fox, enabling you to eventually bring him to book.

Sometimes when lamping you will come across foxes that are actually put off by the call for no apparent reason. I have seen this many times, even when using a proven call, and am convinced that it was the call that put the fox off. If you find yourself in this situation and the fox is behaving cautiously circling out of range, just pocket the call, turn off the lamp and sit tight. When your eyes return to what natural night vision humans have you may or may not make out movement in the area you last saw the fox, but never ever presume it is a fox. Often as not Charlie, without further visual or audible disturbance, will carry on the way it was heading. If this was across your sightline or in your general direction you've nothing to lose by waiting those extra five or 10 minutes before flicking the lamp on again to see if he is now in a safe position to shoot. But be ready, Charlie will not hang around this time.

Another lamping mistake commonly made by the inexperienced is to switch off the lamp when the fox is totally committed and, although out of range, is coming in strong. All of a sudden the lamp goes off, the fox sees your silhouette and is gone. This has often happened to me when lamping with a new companion and his inexperience has led to us losing a dead ringer. Needless to say I do run through the dos and don'ts with my lamp man, but instructions are often forgotten in the excitement. Joking about mistakes and laughing it off does far more good than chastising a beginner. Just because they don't have the experience you have does not make them a bad person. It will prove much more fruitful if you are constructive when correcting a newcomer's errors – who knows, a new shooting acquaintance may well be formed. He could even turn out to be the guy you can call on when you are dealing with difficult foxes and going solo is not an option, or your regular light man is unavailable. That is when your patience will be rewarded. ∎

DINNERTIME DISTURBANCE

Some days it seems I've hardly sat down for a brew after work when the phone rings with a farmer or landowner on the other end frantically relating how he's just seen a fox take a lamb or chicken and can I go immediately to nab it.

If only it were that simple. You are now faced with a dilemma in these situations. You may have other shooting commitments or a night out socially planned, but, on the other hand, you have to keep the people who allow you on their land happy and prove you serve a purpose. Nine times out of 10 you do have to drop everything and rush over there – and

the experience gained over the years has you 99.9 per cent certain there will be nothing around when you get there. The fox will be well away, back in the den or wandering off somewhere else to cause problems.

You can't really explain this to the majority of people who have just seen a fox up to no good. So make the best of the situation and use your visit to try to gain some insight into the problem, either by waiting for the fox or going to the spots you've found that could hold clues as to its route and intentions. Some clues are obvious, others not so obvious.

Golf courses are the most difficult places to weigh up tactics and successfully target foxes.

Any animal that visits could be opportunist, transient or nosing around because it's part of its territory.

Smallholdings and farms with free range hens and other such birds are the most basic as you know the fox is coming to dine on the fowl, but again, if called to such a place, assess the area. Some birds will be penned in, some will be so free range they're allowed to walk on the farmhouse garden and spill on to the private road or track leading to the farm. It's these birds a fox will grab. No netting for it to dig under or gaps to squeeze through, just a quick dash in, then cut and run once it has got one. This kind of fox is often seen during the warmer months because at that time more people are pottering around the garden or looking out of the window at the countryside surrounding them.

The fox-shooting textbooks often say that if you see a fox at a certain time more than once, you can be pretty sure it has got a routine. The books add that if you are there half an hour either side of this time you'll be in with a chance of catching it out. Foxes don't read books and I think it's about time this supposed truism was revealed as the misconception it often is.

Sure, a fox with a small territory will regularly visit areas where it has previously found food, but no situation is the same. On some land, the fox will turn up around the same time two or three days running but then the pattern can change dramatically. It can come anytime, day or night.

One reason for change is that a fox has come across something tasty on its way there, so doesn't need to go to its favourite diner at the same time as its usual booking. In the warmer months I have found foxes to be the least predictable. The reason for this is there's so much more daylight for it when people aren't around at sunrise, and there's much more food in the 'natural larder' so it doesn't need to come close to farms for easy pickings. More often, they haunt the farm area when

times are hard – keep those basics in mind as I relate the next stage of this tale.

I had a call from a farmer. I went to look. Nothing. I had another call. Another visit. Still nothing. This went on for a while. As the losing of birds continued I then began getting calls at work. The fox had been seen at midday and again ducks or chickens were taken. When this happens the all-round fox man knows it's time to set snares or bait live catch cage traps. These devices are the patient hunters that work 24/7. The only time you're needed is to

Above and below:
Tracks and gaps underneath fences are tell-tale signs of fox ingress

check them daily, reset any knocked snares and put fresh bait in the trap.

As this was an area the chickens roam and badgers are regularly seen I couldn't use snares, so I set out two live catch traps. One was in the wood near a well-used fox track I'd found and the other right at the back of the farm itself against a boundary wall. Within the second day I had one in a trap; two days later I had another in the trap placed at the edge of its woodland route. As you can see, there's no pattern to this supposed timed visiting, and it's not just one fox doing the dirty work.

If the taking of stock continues, the traps will become less successful. If this happens then move them around, and vary the bait. If they want chicken, then if you have a dead hen use it. Put it in a cage trap and you might catch one out, but you still need to go and wait with the rifle day and night.

Strangely, I'd never glimpsed anything at night on this farm, either by lamp or night vision, so the penultimate part of the job had to be done very early morning or in the evening.

By now I'd spent a lot of time sorting these foxes, not only watching and waiting in ambush but also advising on repairing netting and fencing and checking traps. All time-consuming but necessary jobs.

Anyway, getting back to the shooting part of this job, the area was still being targeted by local foxes and their timing coincided with my meal times. There was nothing else for it but to go up to the farm straight after work, first of all stopping off at home to pick my rifle up and then going back up to patiently sit up and wait for the foxes. Due to my previous searching for signs of fox activity I knew where the animal could come from.

For once this was a little more cushy for me as I parked the Jeep up near some farm machinery with a view of the steep rising field the fox has to cross to get to the farmyard and hens.

The first, second and third evenings drew nothing. Then on the fourth, as if it'd read all the books, the fox came ambling out of the wood at the top of the hill, stopping every so often to sniff around, then it trotted alongside the wood to my far right, I presume to sneak down the hedge line.

However, it would at some point still have to cross the field as it headed for some chicken supper and this was my opportunity for getting the shot. Though I've made the waiting up sound easy, I had only a few windows of shooting opportunity to stop the fox or take it moving as, in front of me, there where three large trees. Their trunks did obscure some of the field but they also helped me be partly hidden from view from my intended target.

A good pair of binos are a must, so my Meopta 7x50s were getting a lot of use on this job as I scanned the top of the field and the edge of the wood. From my shooting position to where the fox could first appear was over 250 yards. I mention this as for once, though shooting near the farm, I decided to use my latest acquisition – a synthetic stock Tikka M595 with a 1-8 twist custom barrel in 6mm BR calibre. It was safe to use as I was shooting away from the farm into a solid backstop on this steeply rising field. The rest of the rig comprises a Schmidt & Bender 8x56 scope with a Wildcat Predator 8 sound moderator up front.

You might think this a bit OTT but, believe me, I wanted stopping power and range as the fox could get wise and stay quite a way out or keep moving so it might be a long range shot or 'one on the hoof,' so to speak.

As it was, the fox began crossing to my left between the first two trees to my right and, due to my careful scanning, I was already behind the scope rested on the large window-mount shooting bag from Dog-gone-good shooting bags for the shot.

A quick squeak on the back of my hand and the fox stopped to look up. Without hesitation I put an 87-grain Hornady V-Max Ballistic Tip bullet using a recommended home load using Varget Powder straight into the boiler room, and boy what a mess that 6mm round made of Charlie at a little over 140 yards.

I knew that I'd be able to eat my tea in peace – for a short while at least. ∎

FOXING IN THE SNOW

There's an old saying I have that sums up shooting pests: "You've got to be out and about to get 'em." I always harp on about it, but too many foxers and deerstalkers won't venture out unless conditions are perfect. Trouble is, if you've got a few pesky foxes nabbing precious poultry and generally causing headaches, then you've got to be out to catch them out.

Horrendous winter conditions should see many good fox controllers out doing their duty. Prolonged snow coverage and low temperatures will see an increased hunting activity in foxes. A trait of fox behaviour is to sometimes bury an excess of food, but any buried food ends up in very hard ground after a deep freeze. I recall at the start of one year that the local foxes were desperate. Also, vagrant foxes finding it hard on the higher hill ground were coming down to invade others' territory. The fox situation, like the road system, was becoming congested. I don't think there was a day that went by when I didn't get called to one farm or another to sort out marauding foxes. The vulpine menaces were much bolder, coming closer to farm outbuildings and into the farmyards in search of an easy meal. Some farmers had noticed foxes rummaging through gardens or uncollected rubbish bins looking for discarded festive fare, which shows just how quickly foxes adapt to

the changing weather conditions. There are few better species survivors in the UK than the fox.

The fox was much easier to target than usual at the start of the year, in the wintery conditions that caused chaos throughout the country. Charlie was abroad at all hours and the snow showed his runs and regular routes of travel.

Even in good weather, no predator wants to waste precious energy reserves trotting across hill and over dale; they'll generally go straight to the larder (an area where they know there's likely to be food) and be back in the earth before *Eastenders* has finished.

The first of the two most memorable fox outings during this snowy period was on a farm I've not been called to for a while. The other was on a farm where I'm a regular visitor. Even if it's new ground, a fox man should remember the basics. Although the farmer may tell you where and at what time he's seen the foxes about, you should always have a good look around during daylight hours. It surprises me how few take the trouble to do this. I know a lot might say they haven't the time, but to be successful you've got to make time. Although I had walked this ground many times before, it had been almost 12 months since the farmer had last needed me. When he did, the situation was desperate. Foxes, apparently, were everywhere.

I quickly visited the farm and had a good look around from key vantage points with my Meopta binos. If you haven't been on your permission for a long time, give the farmer a knock after you've phoned to say you'll be down, and just have a few friendly words face to face. It'll stand you in good stead for future relations – that call has shown you are there and taking an active interest in his fox problem. Some shooters think they'll be seen so don't bother, but believe me, just a few minutes' friendly banter goes a long way. After the pleasantries I got straight out on to the ground to familiarise myself with the place in daylight. Don't worry about taking the gun or being seen by foxes, just make sure no new buildings have gone up or fields turned into paddocks and suchlike. Even though you

may think you have a sound knowledge of the ground, it's very easy to forget a particular area that might be cause for concern when out at night if you've a lot of land to cover.

As the place is quite expansive, I was glad of a good quality pair of binoculars. I didn't see too many fox tracks on this piece of land so I had an idea Charlie would be using a very old, disused railway line that crosses through the ground, and I headed over there to look for evidence.

Many of us relate to the simplicity of animal behaviour if judging it against how we think as humans. Whenever possible, we'll take the fastest route from one shop to another; in the fox's case it's one meal to another. They also know they've got the chance of picking something up on the way, perhaps a rabbit or ground bird, which are also finding it hard in these harsh conditions. Along the rough part of the disused rail lines there are also occasional culverts, other drain holes and the like. These are often used by foxes as occasional dens. On my initial recce I found tracks, and ground that was exposed where foxes had been grubbing around. The fox is a true opportunist predator and doesn't differentiate between poultry, earthworms, or grubs. I had seen evidence that foxes were working the railway – I could now form a plan.

I returned later that evening. Please note I didn't say 'night', as foxes will be out as soon as daylight begins to fade, often at dusk. But as the days are sometimes dull it's very hard to differentiate the witching hour – one day there's cloud cover, the next clear sky. In these cases I won't initially use the lamp to scan the ground, merely have a good look around and call from strategic areas. Remember, though, that in these conditions you, like the fox, will stick out like a flea on a white blanket.

Let your eyes become accustomed to your natural night vision and you'll be surprised what you see. On a good, clear night you can see a fair distance on relatively flat land that rises to the hills, and believe me, when there's snow on the ground you will see even further and with

Below:
Howard familiarises himself with the farm in daylight

Above:
Snow makes it easy to
pick up foxes' tracks

after a good spy around I scanned the distant areas with the Thor handheld light and red filter. Immediately picking up a pair of eyes, I turned the lamp off and squeaked a rabbit distress call on my fingers. My position was a good one; I was well down behind a wooden fence that broke up my outline. One more call on the hand and Charlie came slightly closer, though it was obviously a very wise one as it ducked and dived, eventually disappearing back over the hill and out of sight. Even so, due to the conditions I reckoned it hadn't gone far, so I played it a tune from my favorite electronic caller – the Digital Callmaster – and it showed itself instantly. Knowing he was a wary critter I didn't switch on the lamp or call again, as he was obviously committed to his expected easy meal. He came into a range of about 120 yards but I was already rested on the wooden fencing, and the natural light made him clearly visible in the Simmons Super Nightview scope. My .223 calibre Tikka 525 dropped him where he stood. Those 55-grain Ballistic Tip V-Max bullets really do stop foxes in their tracks.

The second fox was much easier in comparison, as it was shot in a place I know well. I had visited the land frequently as I was sorting a rabbit problem there with the .22LR rimfire. The 'fluffy hopping gnawers' were wreaking havoc on the saplings that had been planted. This time though, the call was to sort out the foxes that had taken an unhealthy interest in the landowner's ornamental ducks. It's a lovely spot in the summer, but in a landscape reminiscent of Siberia, it was difficult to make out the lake. Thankfully, I knew the terrain, and where the bankside is, as it'd be so easy to go over the edge and end up in the water. When the weather was at its worst, the foxes were just nipping out from their den (I had an idea of its location) to trot across the lake and nab a duck or a goose. The landowner had said he'd gone out to spread some feed and noticed a lot of feathers and missing water birds.

This was a morning job. I simply waited within range of the lake and the 'duck cabins', as I

more clarity. Obviously you do need the lamp to pick up eyes and to make positive identification, but in the first instance it can sometimes work against you. As I said before, foxes are far less cautious the more desperate they are to feed. This isn't reason to become complacent – always ensure you have a backdrop behind you to avoid being silhouetted, or have something in front that breaks up your outline. Keep a check on the wind direction at all times, as the fox will be relying heavily on its sense of smell, along with hearing and sight, to detect danger. In these situations you'll find that once the fox has found a food source it will go to it purposefully, rather than roaming around as at other times of the year. Knowing where foxes are likely to head and the routes taken to and from that location are the keys to success.

I returned in the early evening and got into a good position with a commanding view. It was a clear night – not great for lamping – but

call them. Sitting tight near a large fencepost, I was hidden and had a good view of all possible approaches. I knew there was no need to call as Charlie was coming here regularly for the ducks and geese. In fact, calling in this situation may well have turned them away as they were intent on waterfowl. Quiet ambush was the plan and I settled in to wait. Sure enough, within half an hour on the first morning a vixen came out of the far wood, heading straight to the lake. With a good sky overhead, the fox stood out against the snowy backstop of the hill it was trotting down. I was on target immediately and took a steady rest on the shooting sticks. She suddenly stopped for a moment and, standing clear in my crosshairs, my trusty .223 Tikka stopped her dead.

Adverse weather conditions don't have to be uncomfortable if you are well prepared. The reality is that the harshness of winter can actually make catching up with Charlie a whole lot easier. On this occasion I saw the foxes, but they certainly didn't see me. ■

Above:
The fox paid the price for sticking out against the snow white backdrop

BE PREPARED

When foxing, especially in bad weather with the associated deadly ground conditions, it is extremely important to ensure you are properly kitted up. I recall visiting a local farm notorious for its wet ground, so much so that it could almost be a marsh. I'd visited a few times before and had glimpses of fox, but hadn't had the chance of a sure shot.

With my son, Michael, armed with a Thor lamp and filled with confidence, I set out for some long walks over the farm's windy quagmire for another foxing foray. We were wrapped up in fingerless mittens, some Rocky Mountain jackets and trousers, and neoprene wellies as the breeze was biting. But the most important piece of kit was my shooting sticks; not just useful for steadying my aim, they are also perfect for testing the depth of mud and to help stay upright.

We left the motor behind and squelched off in pursuit of Charlie. After finally getting across the first field, through a short wood and up a hill to a good vantage point, we settled ourselves and made ready. I know some hunters would rather call first and then switch on the lamp, but in my experience wary old foxes are often alerted by artificial distress calls. These are the foxes that can often be caught out by careful use of the lamp from a good position.

I quickly spotted something out in the field in front. Louder and louder I whispered, "Lamp

HOWARD'S TOP TIP

Once settled on a load or factory brand of ammo, stick with it

on, lamp on," but my lad was still getting his leads untangled. Eventually he lit up the area and we were met with two blinking red eyes staring straight back. It quickly disappeared from view behind some hedging. My lad knew it was a case of lamp off, wait a while and then try the call. This grabbed the fox's curiosity and when the lamp went back on the fox had trotted in to within 100 yards, stopping instantly in the lamps glare.

I took the shot and it was over and done with. It really can be that easy sometimes, but every situation is different. That fox was twitchy in the lamp but came readily to the call; sometimes it is the other way round – a missed fox becomes a wary fox. As does a fox that comes to the call from downwind, catches your scent and slinks off, often unseen but nevertheless more educated in survival.

I used a .223, an efficient, flat-shooting foxing round, though some people continue to question it. That fox had a clean, virtually cauterised entry hole, with a horrendous exit – death had been instant. Know your rifle, scope and ammunition combination, practise its capabilities at different ranges and success will soon follow. Once you've settled on a particular load or factory brand of ammo, stick with it.

My next foxing outing was also successful, though a little bit more difficult in a strange, light-hearted way. It was a farm, not on my usual patch, that had two marauding foxes that regularly took the farmer's poultry. The ground was a friend's permission and I asked him what the score was; he was honest enough to say he had lit one of the foxes up and had missed. The odds would be stacked against us, I knew, but I wanted to help out the farmer, who always puts a lot of effort into his Christmas birds.

As we left the vehicle the farmer commented on my gloves. He wasn't wearing any and would be holding the lamp. It amazes me how many shooters don't consider how cold it drops at night; he didn't think he would need them and probably didn't realise it was going to be a long session. Sure enough, as soon

as we started to cross some boggy ground he was cursing and squelching, trying to retain his balance and rub warmth back into his fingers. Yet another time my shooting sticks have come in handy. The easiest way to cross boggy ground is to place your feet on the higher clumps of grass that offer a firmer footing; the sticks become invaluable to test how waterlogged and deep the bog really is. The sticks often become a third leg for helping you walk uphill, taking some strain off both torso and knees.

When we finally reached a high point where we could do a sweep with the lamp, my companion's first words were, "my hands are cold." A little forethought goes a long way

Above:
The .223 did the job perfectly on this fox

when considering one's own comforts. In the first sweep we picked up a pair of eyes. I didn't really want to go any closer on this ground, but this fox wasn't going to come in – after trying a new electronic caller he was obviously not impressed. Luckily we were at the side of a low fence line set on firmer ground and due to a favourable wind we could walk closer for a shot. The lamp man thought this to be a good idea as he was familiar with the ground. We soon came to a large area that had gravel dumped the softer ground, to make a path for the livestock, and I made ready for the next sweep. I'd already set the sticks at the height I'm used to and was ready with my rifle rested for action in not time. Then I instructed the lamp man to sweep the field.

Again a set of eyes, approximately 140 yards out, shone brightly. Before my lamp man could get any colder the rapid, flat 55-grain Molycoated V-Max had hit its target and put the fox down for good.

Sometimes you just feel that nothing you do will be dumb luck, so I directed my companion to wait a short while, call a few times and sweep the field once again. In these situations a digital caller can make life a lot easier. I called again and another fox trotted into sight. When the light hit it, it turned to trot away. Luckily another call caught its attention. It hesitated to look back for any potential freebie. Unfortunately the only freebie was my V-Max bullet.

I walked over and brought the brace back to the farmer for a few photographs. My new friend and lamp man was happy with the result. Both marauders had been taken care of and he'd learned a few lessons – even though it'd been the hard way. ■

WELCOME STUBBLES

I recall one year when I still had some holidays owed to me, so I thought I would make a dash to Scotland for a possible last buck of the season and to have a go at the fox population that had long been untouchable because of the standing cereal crops. After checking all my equipment and hastily packing my bag for the seven-hour journey, the only thing I had to do was get an early night. Double-checking your equipment saves the frustration and embarrassment of getting to your destination and finding you have the wrong combination of rifle, ammo and moderator.

When I make such journeys I like to arrive not long after midday to give me time to unpack and check zero on my 6mm BR rifle.

All went to plan – I arrived mid-afternoon and made a small adjustment to the scope. It needed one click left, putting the point of aim spot on at one inch high at 100 yards, dead on at 200 yards and three inches below at 300 yards – all well within the kill zone.

The shooting area consists of a very large moor with a good acreage of woodland, some of which has just been thinned out. This thinning has had an impact on the deer and other wildlife. Roebucks seemed to have gone to ground as they do after the rut, only feeding during the hours of darkness. I only saw six bucks all week, and although most didn't stay out too long, I did manage to get one in the bag.

HOWARD'S **TOP TIP**

Being cautious and patient with the lamp may provide shooting opportunities

Above:
Another brush gathered in the stubble

The end of the roebuck season is also one of the best times of year to get to grips with the fox population. The farmers are busy cutting their crops, allowing us to get onto the fields lamping from the Land Rover. This is a real luxury for me, as back home 95 per cent of my foxing is on foot – another reason why I am so glad of the lithium ion battery pack from Deben. Weighing only 800 grams, it will never throw you off balance like the more conventional battery packs can do.

After a drive round in the afternoon to see which fields had been cut, we made plans for later that night. With the farmers working through the night to get their crops in, we would spend a little longer in each stubble field instead of rushing off to the next. When you have so much ground to cover, it is tempting to do a circuit of the field, lamp blazing away, and go straight on to the next if you don't see anything. I like the slower approach, so this suited me better. Geared up and ready to go, we set off on the 15-minute drive to our destination.

In the first stubble field we drove into, I picked up a pair of eyes some 400 yards away – but as soon as we went through the gate they disappeared. Rather than driving straight towards the fox's last location, we drove across at an angle. This would reduce the distance between us and our possible quarry and was less likely to spook the fox. When we got to a good range for

identification and shooting, I readied the rifle. My friend flicked on the lamp and picked up the fox in the beam at about 150 yards. I drew a bead on his chest in the scope, and that was the first fox of the night in the bag.

What I didn't see was a second pair of eyes on the edge of the beam. Luckily my number two spotted it and gave me a nudge. This one was startled, no doubt owing to the recent demise of his brethren. I switched off the lamp for a few minutes to give him time to calm down, and moved further downfield.

We were in no rush as we rolled down towards Charlie's location. Flicking the light on and keeping just on the edge of the beam with rifle at the ready, we got as close as we dared and turned the Land Rover sideways. With the beam lowered, the fox kept what little confidence it had – until half a second of hesitation allowed me to add him to the bag when the beam was placed in his face. I felt that if we had put the beam full-on to the uneasy fox any earlier, he would have been away down the field in an instant.

We accounted for another two foxes that night, making it four in total, and we didn't have to call once. The moral of this story is to be a little more patient when you pick up a fox in the beam. Instead of going directly into calling mode, watch its reaction to the lamp. If your fox moves off, ack yourself. Did it go like lightning, not even stopping and looking back? Or did it move off and calm down again further down the field? No two foxes are the same, and all this should help you make an informed decision.

If, in your opinion, the fox has been badly lamped before, then an early morning ambush might be the most appropriate way of getting a result. Or maybe it was you making a noise of some kind that the fox didn't like, putting it on extra alert. Understanding all this information and then analysing it on the spot comes with experience. Get it wrong and you could make it much harder the next time you tussle with Charlie. The more you go out, the more experienced you will become and the more brushes you will gather. ∎

IN THE PIG PEN

I know most associate pig farms with rats, but at times they can be magnets for foxes coming to take piglets, the weakly older 'snorkers' and of course to grub around in the 'muck' heaps and around the slurry tips. Then again, as most realise, the fox is an opportunist, and where it sees the chance of an easy meal it'll take full advantage.

I have many shooting acquaintances around the country and the majority like myself are keen fox shooters or deerstalkers. They have their 'beats' and regular areas to shoot as do I, but I never turn down any offer of some 'new' shooting that comes my way to join up with one of my friends in the shooting fraternity.

I recall an occasion when a friend of mine who shoots a few farms in Lincolnshire phoned to relate to me the story of a pig farm being continually harassed by the local fox population. No sooner had he thought he'd got on top of the problem than more

chaos ensued. However, what he told me even intrigued me although I had heard of it happening but on a much smaller scale – that being foxes snatching piglets. In my part of the country we don't have intensive pig farming on the scale they do in his county – well, who hasn't heard of the Lincolnshire sausage? But what he told me next was interesting. The foxes were entering the rearing units and dodging the sow (obviously) managing to grab a hapless piglet, then make good their escape. Now I couldn't at first understand how a fox was getting into such buildings but then again I've not previously seen a pig farm on the scale of this or how the rearing units where set out. However a worker driving up to the farm for the early shift actually saw a fox leap out of a ventilating window with a piglet in its mouth. The rearing units obviously have to be heated to keep the young warm but this also means these windows are left open around the clock so air can circulate to keep the sows

HOWARD'S TOP TIP

Scouting the land allows you to discover fox hot-spots

Right:
The large scale pig farm where Howard saw foxes running off with piglets

and young not forgetting the workers when on shift in there as comfortable as possible. Even so, I know that security on these buildings is tight so I was still baffled at how they were managing to pilfer so many and so regularly – so was my friend. He'd been doing a good job of lamping the foxes in the surrounding fields, but, knowing my fondness of solving problems and more relevantly shooting with night vision, as the foxes were becoming lamp shy, asked if I'd like to have a trip over to see what I could do – and to see if I could find how the foxes were slipping past him to get at the precious porkers.

As I planned to shoot early evening then most of the night I chose to take my Tikka M595 custom barrelled 6mm BR calibre with Wildcat Predator 8 Sound Moderator and Schmidt & Bender 8x56 scope in case I got the chance during daylight and when darkness fell I'd use my dedicated foxing NV rig – my Tikka .223 calibre M525 with Reflex T8 Silencer complete with the astounding Thales Maxi-Kite Gen 3 unit on board.

I met up with my friend at his home and after a few brews and another chat about the situation we went over early evening so I could have a look around. Now I thought I'd seen some big farms in my time but this place was massive. On the drive up the private track, I could see many 'prime porkers' out in the fields free to roam and feeding happily while the workers inside the rearing pens toiled long and hard so you and me can enjoy a hearty full English… He introduced me to the owner and with his kind permission was allowed to have a look around the outside of the rearing units and the surrounding area. Initially on seeing the buildings, the venting windows are obvious but even though a fox can jump a good height they did seem a little on the high side but not impossible for a determined fox to leap up onto and drop through. However, a fox still wants to take the easier route so I looked further. Around the back of one of the

units, which not so coincidentally as I was soon to discover was the unit the foxes had taken most piglets out of was a stack of black drain pipe on an earth bank. It was now obvious how they were getting in. They'd simply walked up the bank, got on the pipes and from there it was approximately two feet to the nearside open vent at the rear of the unit. So with that sorted my friend decided to show me the muck and slurry pit where he's taken many foxes – but loses as many as they slip past the mounds of pig muck stored here to be used later on the surrounding fields as fertiliser for the crops that are grown.

Like I said, this was a huge scale operation. Just in case we spotted anything, I slipped my 6mm BR Tikka from its case and headed over. Sure enough as soon as we arrived a fox was on the far side looking directly at us and skirting around continuously slipping out of view. It'd got behind a mound of this lovely aromatic mixture, but knowing its curiosity would have it show either side eventually I rested the 6mm BR Tikka cushioned under my leading hand on the gate to the fenced off area and readied for a shot. My friend acted as spotter on watching one side of the mound while I scanned the other through the Schmidt & Bender 8x56 optics. When it did appear, it was half way up the mound, possibly deciding to get a look at us but thankfully it stopped broadside on. Without hesitation, I squeezed the trigger and the 87-grain Hornady V-Max Ballistic

Tip bullet slammed home resulting in first blood down among the slurry. I say that because as we went around to collect it when we got there we realised there was no way we could retrieve the fox as even though we had wellies on (always a wise move when shooting areas such as this), my mate said he'd get it later when he'd come back with a grappling hook to snag it off. All around the slurry pit were fox tracks – this really was a hot spot!

That peek-a-boo situation in itself shows how clever a fox can be, this one might have been able to pick a careful route that gave it cover but it couldn't walk on water – or slurry – forever! So after that 'quick fire' unexpected success I decided not to overly disturb the area and waited until dark to get stuck into the serious foxing. With the dark came intermittent showers, which made the foxing all the more difficult. My friend accompanied me as he wanted to see how I use the lamp and NV tactic that I've now employed for saving time and not missing any foxes hiding in tallish cover. I thought this was going to be a long night, but I must admit the action that followed as the sun had set even surprised me.

As the area they dump the slurry is a 'known hotspot' for the foxes, come nightfall we went directly over there first. I positioned myself next to a large fencepost and switched on the compact and very effective Digital Callmaster MkII for a minute or so, then on with the Cluson lamp. I immediately picked up a pair of eyes so just as quickly switched the lamp off, set it carefully and quietly on the grass and set the rifle on the post and scanned in the direction I'd seen the eyes. Even in pitch black I could still through the superb NV Maxi-Kite Night vision sight to clearly spot the fox. It was now sitting down about 120 yards out just looking around, so without hesitation I placed the aim point of the Chevron reticle on its chest and 'drilled it.' It was obviously a big cub so I expected it wouldn't be the only one so began calling again using the electronic call. As soon as I'd put my eye back into the NV scope's eyecup I saw one steaming in around the slurry. This time I waited until it got in front of another very thick muck pile which gave a solid backstop and just as it hesitated as if it had changed its mind because it didn't like what it had run on or had got skittish, I sent another .223 calibre 55-grain moly-coated Ballistic Tip Hornady bullet straight into its heart/ lungs – again like the other it just dropped like a stone.

We decided we'd collect these as we'd already walked this area in daylight so knew the two I'd just shot were retrievable. I knew the probability of a night hat trick here was very slim, but I tried the call a few more times and used the lamp again to see if I could pick up any more eyes but there was nothing doing. I scanned all around from this position but nothing showed so I decided to walk down the private track that runs broadside to the farm to an area of grass fields that lead into a set of tall stubble fields. Using the tactic which to me is virtually an automatic action when shooting like this, I switched on the call, then after nearly a minute flicked on the lamp. Most of the time we were walking slowly scanning with the lamp and intermittently using the call, but mostly I'd use the call when I stopped somewhere that looked promising and gave good backstops. I've now come to use a lamp in my NV rig

because it helps me pick up eyes quickly especially when you've got a fox just keeping back in cover. No matter how good the NV scope you are using, you can still easily miss spotting a fox in these situations. As we walked the track, we'd just reached another set of cut stubble when something just caught my eye in the lamp. At first it was so small hardly a glint I thought it was a rabbit until it stood up and then I could clearly make out its form – it was a fox. Going straight into autopilot, the lamp was carefully placed on the ground; I set the sticks and sighted the target through the Maxi-Kite.

I could clearly see it was another big cub but a fair old distance out. I didn't have time to reach back into my pocket for the electronic call, so as I was already trained on target I squeaked sucking on the back of my hand.

At first it didn't seem to want to know, then it went from left to right towards a hedge. I thought it'd disappear but unlucky for it but lucky for me it just began trotting slowly towards us, looking around warily. It was now approximately 160 yards out and there was a gap in the hedge that at any time it could have shot through and got away but the calling must have just kept its attention as it stood looking in our direction long enough for me to carefully placed the scope aim point and again the muted crack from the all-weather .223 Tikka that proudly holds the ginormous NV optic resulted in another very dead fox.

We walked over to retrieve it and then decided to try another area, but the wind had got up and was changing direction erratically so it was becoming increasingly difficult to judge an approach to an area. We decided to head over in the direction of a wood where my companion that night has previously regularly drawn foxes.

We stopped near a drainage dyke where I again switched on the electronic call. Same routine as before on with the lamp and immediately I spotted a pair of eyes as we'd obviously drawn one out of the cover but it must have been over 250-yds away. Switching off the lamp I must admit I thought this wasn't going to come within sensible range and after a few calls and using the lamp it was a wary one as it kept coming forward then trotting back, coming closer, then backing away. This routine went on for at least 15-minutes until curiosity or hunger got the better of it and it committed itself to coming in. I switched the lamp off, and had the .223 Tikka up on the sticks and was on it in a flash. Thankfully it hadn't come in too close so it was pretty much on my zero. At night, though using night vision equipment, range is the hardest thing to judge, but presenting itself side-on I placed the Chevron aim point on its chest and with a squeeze of the trigger the last fox of the night bit the dust, or I should say corner of the maize field it had come across from. ∎

ON THE LAMB

A good sheep farmer knows two very important things: when to get the ewes to the safety of the lambing sheds and what constitutes good predator control. In relation to foxes, that's having a man or men he can trust to respect his land and get the job done quickly and discreetly.

I've learned a great deal about fox behaviour on sheep farms – its ways, routes, and the places it favours to hide or bask in the sun. It's hardly surprising, then, that I'm known as the foxman of these parts. I earned my reputation by a lot of hard work, chasing Charlie on bitter cold nights over frosty, windswept landscapes; that is, until Charlie can't resist the lure of the rich pickings in the lambing sheds and on the lower fields that lead to them.

In terms of foxing, spring is my busiest time of year. The lambs are easy to take, the foxes are always in abundance and they're more likely bolder than ever before. The foxes seem to lurk in every valley; they can be found hiding in any dip, hollow, clumps of reed grass and often run unseen alongside every other drystone wall.

As you've probably gathered, I'm surrounded by sheep farms. The majority of farms in my area use my services and on some, usually the farms with most land, I have to strip down my kit to the basic essentials as I often need to cover large plots of land on foot. I'll linger longer than usual at vantage points, overlooking areas where I know foxes come off the moor to head for the weakly adult sheep and even more vulnerable lambs.

I had come back from a trip to Scotland to a constantly ringing phone. It's good to have the land to shoot over and equally beneficial that the farmer trusts me to do the job, but it does get tiring. However, there is a price to pay for this kind of sport and if that means going without sleep, dragging myself out after a hard day's manual labour, then so be it. If you're not

Above:
Terrain like this can be even more tiring if you're laden down with heavy, unnecessary kit

prepared to do so then I suggest you take up knitting, or perhaps photography, as I've been advised to do.

Each spring brings the same challenges, yet none presents itself in the same way. Although I know the land I shoot like the back of my hand I still need to be cautious on certain areas. I say this as a reminder to fellow foxers who, in their eagerness to get out and into position, forget to beware of dips, sudden drops, large stones and, of course, the dreaded electric fencing. Even after the length of time I've spent on familiar land I'm surprised how quickly the farmer can erect fencing – almost overnight. If you don't see the wire and posts while scanning with the lamp, you can become so engrossed in chasing fox eyes you'll trip on a rock or walk straight into an electric fence. I've had enough jolts over the years to know I don't intentionally go out to get another, so watch for them day and night no matter how absorbed you've become in the pursuit of your chosen quarry.

Although most foxers are grateful to the farmer for allowing them to shoot on his land, ask yourself: 'is that bottle at Christmas enough?' As

you are already on his land, there are far more practical ways to show your appreciation. It takes very little time to check fences as you walk alongside them. If you see a sheep in trouble and you're unable to help it yourself, tell the farmer straight away. Sheep are daft animals. They'll frequently run into fences and if they don't bounce off unharmed you'll be surprised how many get caught up on barbed wire. I was walking a fence line in the early evening once, looking and calling for Charlie when I noticed a sheep in trouble. It had got its leg tangled in the top wire of some corner fencing and was tugging and pulling to the point where it was not going to free itself unaided. As I approached it I could see the poor thing was beginning to tire, occasionally slumping down and hanging from one back leg. Now sheep won't kill you (joke!). They'll occasionally come over and spoil your shooting or a frisky pent-up tup might nudge you away from his 'girls', but on the whole sheep are docile, timid creatures.

It was as I untangled this sheep that I noticed a fox lying down not 60 yards away, half hiding behind the reed grass. Foxes, crows and buzzards are opportunistic creatures. They'll hang about close by, waiting until the sheep has tired to the point that it will just lie down and give up. In the case of the fox, sometimes alone but more often in groups, it will then come in for the kill. Crows are even crueller, pecking out its eyes and throat while the sheep is still alive. Inexperienced shooters might think that bizarre, but some of the tales I could tell of foxes around any livestock are even more incredible.

A number of fellow shooters have expressed an interest in learning how to go it alone on moorland farms; being able to walk up on foxes in what can be at times inhospitable terrain. Even though I love my night vision, I now most often use the lamp off the rifle when lamping alone, because continually lifting the rifle to scan an area isn't the most conducive way to search the ground with a light. You can also lift the lamp higher to reach seemingly hidden areas. Moorland foxing is very different to what many foxmen are used to. There are so many dips, hollows, cut-throughs and walls that it would be impossible to shine the light around an area without having to lift the gun or point it at some strange unsafe angles. The very first scan of the lamp can yield crucial information. If you see sheep bunched together in one area and others bunched together lower down the field, this suggests a fox is around.

A question I'm often asked when I've been out foxing with a newcomer is why do I initially call so quietly and infrequently? A fox's hearing is possibly its most acute sense, so even though louder calls are sometimes needed, consider one could be close by. Also, rabbits and rodents don't squeal for minutes on end when attacked or grabbed by something. The fox's second most powerful sense is smell, and as for sight, I'm now convinced that the fox isn't overly lamp-shy, if lamp-shy at all. If you've kept your approach quiet, low and down wind when you switch on the lamp from its position that's all the fox will see – a bright light shining in its direction. Why do you think so many hold in the light trying to work out what it is? They see lights on tractors, workers going about their business and sensor-operated security lights, so it isn't always necessarily the lamp that has them spooked. It's more likely a noise you make getting into a shooting position that says two things that mean the same to a wild fox – 'human' and 'danger'. ■

Left:
Moorland foxing brings new challenges, even for an experienced foxer

DARK POINTS

From the outset I want to point out NV (night vision) scopes are not the be all and end all to modern day fox shooting. They certainly aren't a magic source of instant success; NV is another important tool in the gun cabinet to help you control any lamp-shy foxes on your patch. NV also allows you to operate with the utmost stealth in areas you don't want to be bathing with artificial light.

The best way I've 'invented' (after trying many other methods of setting zero on various glow in the dark targets) is as follows. Get a reasonable size heavy-duty cardboard box (decent width, height and depth) – something your local greengrocer or newsagents would throw out – and prepare it as follows. First, leave one end open then blank out all possible nooks and crannies of the front section and sides with heavy duty black duct tape. This is so no light can show through the front of the box except at the hole you are now going to make. To do this, pierce the front middle of the box with a relatively thick

biro to produce a hole of approximately ¼ inch in diameter. Now cover this with a piece or two of normal masking tape.

The reason for this and leaving the back open will become apparent once in the field. This is going to be the target and you will need to take an old headtorch or small utility light as well as the black duct tape and masking tape with you. Once you've found a piece of land on your shoot with a decent and solid earth backdrop put the box on the ground facing the direction you are going to shoot from. Once in place, switch on the light and put it into the box and fully close the back up by folding the sides in. Looking from the front in the pitch black all you'll see is the light glowing through the hole you've obscured by the masking tape. The reason for the masking tape is so the light isn't overly harsh, otherwise this could damage the sensitive image intensifier on the NV equipment by being constantly directed at the artificial light. If setting up the scope for the first time, you can, before doing all of this,

HOWARD'S TOP TIP

Use NV gear as an ambushing tool

112

set a rough zero in daylight keeping the front scope lens cover in place. The scope cover always has a pin prick size hole to allow a tiny amount of light in to aid set up in daylight. At the ranges fox shooters should be setting zero this isn't that reliable, as I don't feel it gives you a good enough sight picture. A tip is to use a laser boresighter with the moderator removed and lining up the cross hairs or chevron aimpoint (depending on NV unit) to the laser dot at the required distance. Then use the light in the box target to fine tune your zero at night.

What is important is not to switch on the IR (infrared) capability of the scope as this will over power the light shining through the hole in the box. If you've set everything as precisely as possible during daylight, then you shouldn't take long to fine tune your zero at night using the 'light box' trick. Usually I'll fire a string of six to eight before I'm ready to try a three-string group. Don't forget the duct tape as during zeroing it is also useful for blanking off bullet holes in the target

box. You should be striving to at least make a one-inch grouping for foxing and any decent quality NV scope is certainly capable of this. However, that's my self-imposed standard; others I know will be satisfied with a larger grouping, but if you're not achieving sub two-inch groups at 100 yards using any popular calibre fox round then I hardly need say – practise more until you can.

Well that's my tried and tested trick that I've discovered works best for zeroing night vision. I've been asked many times what the best method and target to use is, so there you go. Others do use reflective tape, and use IR either as an external or add on or use the unit's own integral IR to get a reflection back off the tape. Yes it does work, but believe me not half as precise as my way – try it and you'll soon be on target and grouping as you should, believe me.

Around this time I was using a Maxi-Kite NV Scope, which was fantastic for foxing. However, not everybody can afford the high £6K price tag, so I was testing the Pulsar Sentinel G2+ 3X50

Below (left to right): Howard's method for zeroing his NV units

with the optional extra 'doubler lens' and add-on high power Laserluchs IR torch. I paired it with a Tikka 525 in .222, a lovely rifle for both day and night use and one which has served me well on long range crows and of course foxes around the back of farms where I do not need much more range than 175-200-yds.

Though I look at any prospective scope specifications as an idea to its possible capabilities, it is only in the field you will get the true picture of what any day scope or NV is capable of. With

the IR on full I found I was easily spotting fox size targets out to and over 200 yards. For clear identification in good ambient light conditions I'd recommend you keep your shots within the 120-yard-mark for a sure precisely placed clean killing shot.

Also remember with NV comes total stealth and if you mind your fieldcraft and use the call correctly, a fox will more likely come steaming in unperturbed as you're not alerting Charlie with a lamp.

I also use and recommend NV be used as an ambushing tool. Waiting up near a run or other area foxes are regularly visiting for food you'll soon spot them undetected, often without having to resort to the use of the call. A good example of this was prior to lambing one year at a local farm that had foxes coming closer to the farmstead than usual. The reason for this was the farmer had the ewes penned close to home to keep a better eye on his charges. I'm convinced a fox can sense when ewes are ready to lamb and if Charlie manages to miss the young they'll take the afterbirths.

I had positioned myself behind a drystone wall and keeping low I watched the area leading to the temporary sheep pen using my Yukon Ranger Pro 5X42 digital monocular. Eventually Charlie turned up trotting straight for the sheep. This fox stopped a way out which gave me time to carefully put the monocular down and get myself settled behind the Tikka and NV scope combo. The reason the foxes are coming closer isn't just because of the imminent lamb arrivals but owing to the few rabbits available they're also targeting mice and rats around the outbuildings. This fox wasn't presenting me with a good clear shot at his kill zone so I made a short squeak on the back of my hand. It immediately put its head up to look towards my position leaning on the wall in ambush. I took the shot at around 85yds and the .222 calibre 50-grain Remington Express bullet did its duty, hitting it smack in the upper chest and killing Charlie instantly.

Another one chalked up to my trusty NV and rifle combo. ∎

PATIENCE IS A VIRTUE

As an experienced fox controller, I've probably got every piece of kit that a foxer could ever want. During my time fox shooting, I've amassed so much equipment to help me in my chosen trade I often wonder how I ever managed to shoot foxes in the past. I've got numerous electronic calls, various calibres of rifle, different lamping systems, high seats, hides, 4x4s and ATVs at my disposal, and now even the most high-tech night vision equipment, but there are still occasions when I think: is there something I haven't tried?

The farmer who allows you to shoot on his land does so because he trusts you, and to a certain degree relies on your help to keep his livelihood safe. When it comes to the waiting game there is no easy option. In the past, if the fox was coming near the farm we'd ask them to leave a light on for a few nights so the fox gets used to it, and then start the vigil. Dead poultry or a shot rabbit on the fringes of the light will add incentive. This has worked for me many times, though just as often it hasn't.

The fox is an opportunist and will feed where appropriate – it doesn't necessarily content itself with stealing ornamental waterbirds, chickens and lambs. Sometimes you must go to extraordinary lengths to nab a difficult fox.

I'm sure other foxers will have experienced a fox coming into their patch from an area they don't have permission to shoot. They've seen Charlie next door but don't want to upset the owners of the DMZ by even shining a light across it. To do so would, at the very least, invite exaggerated accusations about one's conduct.

Quite often you will find that these safe zones are also animal havens, with no vermin control at all. As such, they are a regular nightmare for both farmer and keeper. This

HOWARD'S TOP TIP
Foxes tend to gravitate towards freshly cut fields as there is usually a free meal on offer

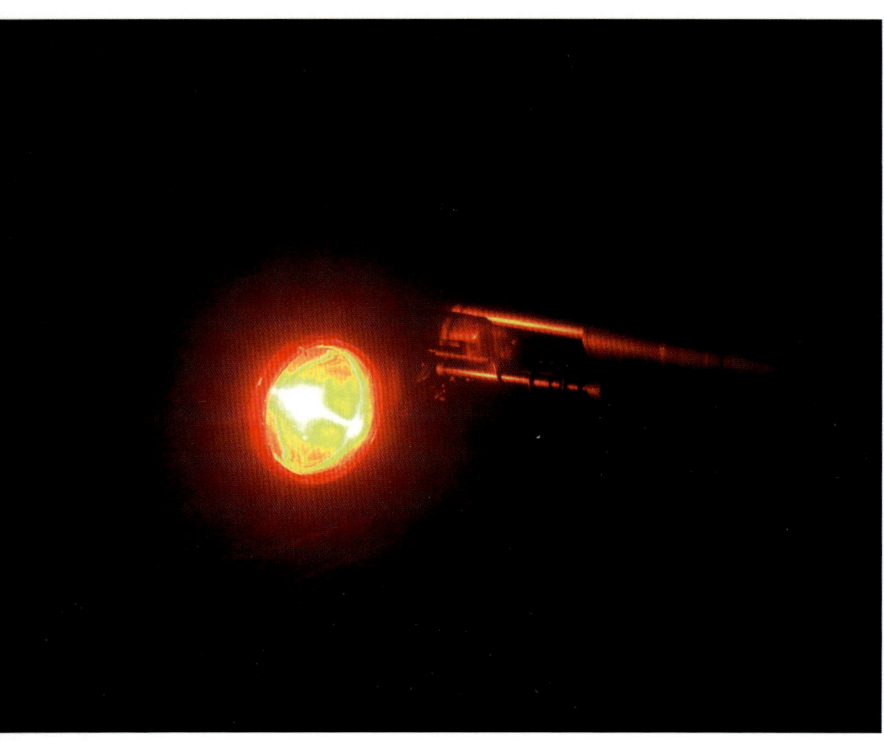

Above:
Use the lamp sparingly to allow your vision to adjust to the dark more quickly

permission', at certain times of year the odds are back on my side. I say times of year, because when the grass isn't too high or has just been cut, the foxes are out in the open and aren't used to being targeted there.

Prior to arranging the permission to shoot on the adjoining land, the foxes had become increasingly troublesome yet still elusive. Knowing that foxes revert to opportunism, I knew it was highly likely that there would be foxes in the freshly-cut field grubbing around for mice, frogs or slugs. If not, a mouse call could hopefully draw them into the field, where they would likely feel secure despite being in the open.

This field had previously been a sanctuary, and the rows of turned grass would also give cover to crouch or lie behind. Sure enough, on the second visit after the tractors had left, I got to the top of the hill and waited a while, watching over the expansive freshly cut fields and letting my eyes get accustomed to the view. My silhouette wasn't showing an outline due to the trees directly behind me. I shone the light across the field to see a couple of roe. I immediately switched off the lamp to let my eyes get used to the darkness once more. Incidentally, an old military tip about using night flares applies equally to lamping: keep one eye closed when scanning and your limited night vision returns much quicker. I watched the roe disappear, the larger doe springing and prancing as if showing off until they were lost in the gloom.

This was a perfect situation to try the mouse call. Many mice get caught in blades and the fox soon recognises the mower as a dinner bell announcing diced mouse on the menu. Plus many displaced survivors take refuge in the laid grass.

I switched on the Digital Callmaster and saw something dash out across the field. Readying myself for a shot, I switched on the lamp to see the fox crouching down and looking in my direction, not because it could see me

was the situation that had arisen on some land I was called to, where the owner was plagued by visiting foxes. It was an awful scenario. I had only two or three places that I could walk to and wait for a safe shot adjacent to the boundary. But behind this land is an expansive area of ground, and in the middle of this is a chicken farm. It's an intensive rearing facility and no fox or two-legged thief could get in there without a degree in espionage.

I knew the foxes used the surrounding area for approaching and leaving the woods that ran up to the boundary, as that's where they were dug in. I was having trouble targeting them. This was a result of a lack of safe shooting positions and also because the whole area is generally difficult.

After pulling a few strings (politeness and a bottle of whisky go a long way), I managed to gain access to some adjacent landed grasses used for grazing. Thanks to my 'new

but because this was the source of the sound, and now also a light. Being ready meant I'd got myself rested for the shot off a fencepost. Keeping the light on, I carefully took aim, and Charlie's lights went out permanently. It may sound a very simple result, but many shooters in similar situations make classic mistakes due to angle of fire, and therefore shot placement.

I was higher than the fox and so could still see it as it lay down, believing itself safe. When foxes are close to the 140-150 yard mark, they are only offering you a small target for a clean kill. Especially this fox. Although it was looking at me, most of its body, including the major kill area (chest/heart/lungs), was obscured as it was crouched low. A head shot could have easily missed as it wasn't that close, but if you lower your aim you can put the bullet into the vital chest area, due to the angle of fire. When I retrieved the fox, that's exactly what had happened.

Suffice to say that this fox was probably the one I'd been having trouble with, and it was a job well done. Now that I'd secured the legal right to shoot over the new area, the fox's safe zone was no longer a sanctuary. She didn't know that, and unfortunately for her she'd been well and truly caught out.

At times you need to go to great lengths, and these don't always include walking for hour after hour searching continuously. Although that can sometimes be the case, it wasn't an option or solution here. It was politeness and patience that won through. ■

Below:
Asking for access on previously unshootable land can lead to good results

TEN TOP TIPS

Over the years, people have asked me countless questions on foxing. What's the best kit for foxing, or the best calibre, or rifle scope combination, right down to what's the best footwear. I suppose it is to be expected – the range of kit readily available to the discerning foxer is immense. A good rule of thumb is to take note of what experienced fox controllers are already using.

Quality equipment does not come cheap, but it will often make the difference between success and failure. Nowhere is this truer than with optics. A top-end scope will prove to be the single most important piece of kit in your arsenal. Most factory rifles have straight-out-of-the-box accuracy nowadays, and your choice is best made by fit. Buy a rifle that mounts well in a fast, flat-shooting calibre. Look after it and it will serve you well for many a year. If you don't home-load, buy quality ammunition. Try different brands and you will be amazed at how much tighter your groups are with a brand that suits your rifle.

Another commonly asked question that always amazes me is: "What's the best time to go out looking for a fox?" There is no easy answer – all I can say is that to find a fox you must put the time in. Believe me, there is never enough time available, but you won't get your fox sat in front of the box or downing a jar in the pub. There really isn't a best time to go out – it very much depends on where you are and what the situation is. If, for instance, you are on open moorland, the foxes may be moving about early. The moorland on my patch is very bleak, especially late in the year when food is much harder to find. In this situation, I find that one of the best places to ambush foxes is just off the moor, on the lower ground, where there are richer pickings to be had.

Think like a fox. Pick your spot and wait, and if at first you don't succeed, try again. Time in the field is always well spent, even if you draw a blank. You may see where Charlie is coming in from and be able to alter your position accordingly on your next outing. However, in many scenarios I wouldn't take the chance of calling the fox. If he knows exactly what's on the menu, it may have an opposite effect to the one intended and spook him. Remember, the fox is a calculating creature and isn't likely to give up an easy chicken dinner to come to a dubious rabbit or hare in distress. In this situation, calling should only be a last-ditch attempt if your quarry is moving away – by giving it a quick, sharp squeak you may get it to stop long enough for you to get a shot away. You must be ready, though, as Charlie will only stop for a second. But do not rush or (worse still) chance a shot – if you miss him you may never get another chance, as you have educated that particular fox and made him that much harder to put down. If you do miss, give yourself a good kick – you will now have to outsmart it in some way. This is where time in the field comes in handy yet again. Learning the habits of a difficult fox is certainly the secret to success. We have all missed foxes and made all the excuses, some of which are very inventive – but the most important thing is to learn from your mistakes. Only a fool makes the same error twice.

Of course, knowing the ground is more than just an advantage in getting to grips with Charlie. It is also absolutely essential from a safety point of view. The shooter must be familiar with where the backstops and livestock are, which is knowledge you must have before even thinking of firing a shot. On new ground it is essential to familiarise oneself with the terrain before doing anything else.

Checking your zero is another oft-overlooked practice that, if left unattended to, can cause many cock-ups. A couple of shots at the target on a regular basis boosts confidence as well as alerting the shooter to any deviation from the point of aim. When checking your zero, it is also helpful to change shooting positions so you are familiar and comfortable with shooting from the different positions that may be presented to you in the field. This may sound obvious, but you would not believe the amount of times I have seen a shooter shuffle about and miss an opportunity because he is trying to shoot from an unfamiliar position. I regularly vary the position of my practice shots – off the sticks, kneeling, prone, or even leaning against a tree or post to improvise a steady aim.

HOWARD'S TOP TIP

Time in the field is always well spent, even if you draw a blank

Left:
There's no shortcut to becoming a better foxer, though determination and the best gear you can afford will help

"Practice makes perfect" may be an overused phrase but it is forged in truth.

The quality of today's shooting clothing is fantastic. When I started shooting, most of my gear was ex-military stuff I had bought from the army and navy store. Today there is a vast variety of commercial outdoor clothing, and nearly all of it is comfortable, breathable and waterproof. Remember not to lose sight of the basics: if it keeps you concealed, warm and dry, and does not sound like a crisp bag, that's all you will ever need. Virtually all the sporting garments on today's market are well thought out and designed, with all the necessities (hand warmers, pockets, hidden hoods and so on). Taking into account the technology involved in waterproof but breathable garments, they are exceptional value for money in my opinion.

You cannot buy experience, but if you listen to others you will soon learn to decipher the knowledge from the dross. Always remember, a listener learns a lot more than a teller. Buy the best kit that you can afford, put the time in, be sensible and above all be safe – these are the prerequisites for successful foxing.

Finally, remember that politeness costs absolutely nothing, and doesn't just help you gain and keep shooting ground – it can also go a long way to defusing a potentially difficult confrontation with members of the public. If someone is anti-shooting, you are unlikely ever to change their mind. However, if you politely explain that you are providing a valuable service and point out the benefits of your actions to both the economy and the surrounding wildlife, you will placate all but the real diehards.

Humankind has upset the balance of nature; it is down to us, the countrymen of the present, to address that balance. The fox is a worthy quarry – he is, after all, just trying to make a living. Unfortunately, he has to be kept in check, and as long as we as enthusiasts cull him in an ethical and efficient manner, our sport will continue long into the future. ∎

QUIETLY CONFIDENT

MARK
NICHOLSON

Over the last 10 years, my main tool to keep fox population down in my area has been a Heym SR30 straight bolt in .25-06, loaded with Hornady 75-grain V-Max pushed out at around 3,600fps by VarGet powder. I knew if the fox presented itself at 300 yards it would go down. However, hot loads have taken their toll on the barrel, and its accuracy isn't what it was, so I invested in an Antonio Zoli rifle in .243 Win.

I immediately had it screw-cut for the T8 moderator, and with Leupold base and rings mounted a Zeiss Duralyt 3-12x50 illuminated scope. Once I was happy everything was screwed up tight and aligned, I took it to the range. The first two shots from 50 yards showed the windage 5cm left and the elevation slightly low. After turning the windage dial 5cm right, I moved back to the 100-yard mark where I attained a sub-one-inch group. This was from a rifle straight out of the box, so letting the barrel cool and tweaking the zero, I repeated the process. Happy with a three-shot group of less than an inch and one inch high of the target, I unscrewed the bipod and shot off the sandbag to confirm no difference in zero. This is always worth checking as some rifles do change.

Eager to try the set-up in the field, I headed to the farm that night and deployed the vehicle overlooking a muck hill frequented by foxes. I placed the rifle on the bonnet, supported by the bipod; I had the lamp close at hand and soon chambered a round before flicking on the safety.

Beyond the muck hill was a grass banking littered with rabbits about 100 yards away. My plan was to call a fox, and if nothing showed I would take the test to the rabbits.

Switching on the illuminated dot on the Zeiss, I checked that the variable magnification was on 8x. While looking through the scope, I pressed the minus button to decrease the brightness and size of the illuminated dot until the glare had gone completely, leaving a minute dot that could accurately be placed on a rabbit's chest. Even in the red filter, the clarity was exceptional.

At the end of the field is a marsh from which I often call foxes. Trying a manual distressed rabbit call on the back of my hand brought a fox in after 20 minutes. Keeping the main beam on the fox and continuing the squeaking, I took hold of the rifle and lined it up, tracking it through the Zeiss. I stopped calling, as the fox slowed to a stop at 80 yards or so. With the illuminated red dot fixed on its chest, I squeezed the trigger of the Zoli and dropped the fox with a sound bullet strike.

Reloading, I put the lamp back on the fallen fox, and to my disbelief, it was moving off slowly but looking rather worse for wear. I rushed the follow-up shot, missing completely, and it disappeared behind the muck heap. Reloading, I changed position, hoping the fox would reappear in the expected quarter. I readied the lamp, and seconds later the fox showed, still struggling – but I missed again.

The vulpine was now getting close to escaping into a thick hedge. With round number four in

the breech, I tracked the maimed fox and took my chance as it stopped momentarily before entering the thorns. This time I connected and he was fortunately dispatched. On closer inspection, the first strike had been high across its shoulder, causing a flesh wound only.

The following day, I checked that all the screws were tight on the rifle, took it back to the range and shot a sub-1.5in group just above the point of aim at 100 yards. Putting the previous night's performance down to pilot error, I took the rifle out on a serious foxing foray that very night.

This weekly excursion around arable farms would allow me to give the new set-up a fair test shooting from a solid rest. My regular driver Pete and lamp man H turned up about nine o'clock and we headed off. Turning off the road, I climbed into my purpose-made shooting box and powered up the Lightforce 240 Blitz lamp covered with a red filter. After stocking up the .243, we made off, scanning the open fields.

Initially events were unremarkable until we tried a couple of pastures running alongside some woodland. Sweeping the red beam across the grasses, we spotted a fox laid down only 100 yards away. With my lamp man pressing the in-line button to signal Pete to stop, I readied the rifle and got into position to shoot as H kept the lamp on the fox. However, it thought it better to make haste rather than wait for a 75-grain Accutip. I tracked it through the Zeiss, and as it reached the far fence it did as expected and stopped broadside to us. The report of the .243 was answered by a thwack of the bullet dispatching the fox at 200 yards.

After collecting our quarry, we proceeded onto another farm, lamping both sides of the track. As Pete carefully drove on at around 10mph, we spotted a brace of foxes in a field to our left some 500 yards away. The track direction would close the distance, so turning off the lamp, we drove on until we were well within range and pulled up. I chambered a round and got ready before the lamp went on.

Spotting one of the two foxes right away, I drew a quick bead and confidently took him out before homing in on the second, reloading in an instant. It gave a sideways glance as it searched for its mate before disappearing over a ditch at the top of the field. Leaving the shot fox for now, we carried on to the end of the track, but to no avail – the fox had gone.

Collecting the fox on the way back, we now had two on board. We lamped the ground back towards the farm for a second time. As the end of the final sweep drew near, H spotted some eyes in a wild bird mix conservation crop opposite the farmstead running along the edge of a wood 180 yards away.

Stopping, I had a closer look through the scope, confirming it was a fox. I chambered a bullet, focused back on the fox and waited for a clear shot. I could see it mousing about in the crop and showing no concern towards the lamp. As I was debating whether to give it a call, the vulpine began to move back towards the wood and paused, giving me a wonderful opportunity to take him out, which I gladly took.

Our last call was a smallholding at the bottom of the village. As we turned through a gate, H caught the flash of vermin eyes in his initial sweep of the lamp. Pete stopped straight away, but this fox seemed to know the score, disappearing into a dip in the field. As H tried to keep the lamp on the fox, which was now lost to sight, I covered the dead ground with the rifle.

The fox came back into view, but he was mostly covered by the contour of the land. I carefully followed the fox through the Zeiss. Knowing that it was 300 yards from the gate to the field corner, I knew I would have good range on it if it did stop. Keeping silent, we watched and waited, willing the fox to stop for that last look back. Our wish was eventually granted as he turned just short of the fence. I immediately steadied the illuminated dot high on his shoulder before squeezing away the round. He reacted to the shot by jumping forward even before the sound of the bullet strike reached my ears, and completely disappeared from sight.

Opting to walk across rather than drive, I grabbed the HID Lightforce and began a diligent search for the shot fox. I soon found him at the side of the fence, hit slightly low in the chest but dead nonetheless, taken well at 290 yards. Confidence had been redeemed in under two hours without a call being made, and a successful alliance with a new foxing tool had been formed. ∎

Below:
A good night's work for Mark and his team

CHICKEN PROTECTION

Although the rifle is one of the most effective tools with regards to controlling foxes, sometimes you'll have to deploy other methods to catch up with them. I recently had a flustered visit from the manager of a local chicken farm who was experiencing some vulpine trouble.

Apparently he had been going about his regular rounds and found evidence of where a fox had dug into one of the sheds. These sheds hold several hundred birds. After investigating further, his worst fears were soon confirmed: the culprit had committed mass murder.

I followed the manager back to the farm for a scout around to see if there were any signs of which direction the fox was going. The hole dug into the shed had been blocked, but I told the manager to leave a couple of dead chickens outside, both as bait and to deter the fox from excavating back in. Trails of feathers led away from the poultry housing, across a field, under a hedge and away over the boundary. Clearly the fox had taken at least one victim away to feast upon later.

The farm manager agreed to leave some of the dead birds out as requested before the end of the day. I soon picked my spot for the evening vigil some 150 yards from the shed, but with a full view of where I expected the fox was travelling in from. I guessed it was a dog fox feeding a nursing vixen. Unfortunately, beyond the farm boundary was serious hunting country, so a search for the earth was a no-go for fear of upsetting the huntsman. It was therefore down to catching Charlie in the act, but owing to work commitments, I could not get out with the lamp until 9pm.

The hour hand soon sped forward, and armed with the .243 and my Lightforce lamp, I was soon in position and scanning around the shed and the neighbouring fields from the truck. After checking the immediate area and confirming all was clear, I parked up in my chosen spot overlooking the field and towards the shed where the fox had last done

its damage. A couple of hours quickly passed without seeing a glimpse of any marauder. Eventually I began to nod off as the time approached 1.30am, so I decided to call it a night and accepted a blank outing.

A report from the farm manager the following morning revealed the fox had been back, but thankfully only to take some of the carcases left over from its previous antics. That night I was on a similar time schedule, and another blank was the result. Deciding on a change of tactics, I set the alarm early the following morning and made it to the farm a good hour before dawn. Parking the truck well away from the chicken sheds, I opted to sneak round on foot with the lamp and battery pack hooked up along with the Tikka .223 supported by the shooting sticks. I lamped the whole area over the next hour or

MARK'S TOP TIP

Snaring is an effective way of taking a fox that has previously escaped the rifle

so, but once again the elusive fox was not to be seen.

Almost in desperation, I picked a good vantage point and waited for the fast approaching dawn. The darkness receded and it soon became light enough to see without the lamp. I then started calling using the palm of my hand on my mouth to imitate a rabbit in distress. This went on intermittently for well over an hour to no avail. Another blank.

Making my way back to the chicken shed, I met the farm manager, who informed me the fox had again been back and took a couple more of the dead. This puzzled me – I could only guess that Charlie was coming in the very early evening. Unfortunately I wasn't able to get back out until the weekend. This did not fill the manager with confidence. I assured him that I would arrange for a foxing companion of mine to have a look out after dark that very night, and I also promised to set a few snares before the weekend if the culprit stayed at large.

On my way home, I called in on Steve who would take over duties in my absence. We discussed the situation and he agreed to have a look out that evening. I am sure he saw his chance to get one up on me, so I had no worries about his diligence regarding the task.

After work, I called at Steve's house and was met at the door by his huge grin. He had seen the fox and called it in. It all sounds good so far – but that's when things went pear-shaped. He suffered two misfires and then a complete miss. The result of all this was a further educated fox.

On closer inspection, the cause was proved to be a cracked firing pin. Our only consolation was that the fox had made its way in over a footbridge across a large ditch, betraying its entry route and offering me a superb snaring scenario. That being so, I set off the next morning at first light, armed with a dozen snares in the wiring bag as well as the rifle. I deployed six snares in total, two at either end of the footbridge and four on other likely spots. I then informed the landowner where the snares were set, to avoid the embarrassment associated with any unlucky individual suspended upside-down from the bridge by a snared ankle.

The beauty of snares is that they work 24 hours a day. Set correctly in the right places, they can be very effective. So with a couple of days off work and with the back-up of several snares, I was totally committed to bringing the culprit to justice. With the Lightforce Xenon HID lamp and battery pack fully charged, I was in position by the following dusk. I opted for a conveniently placed round bale as my ambush point.

I assessed my current position. With the aid of the lamp I could see the chicken shed to my right. Across the grass field running down from the hedge to my front was the entry bridge just less than 150 yards away. I scanned the field at 10-minute intervals for an hour or more with the filtered lamp beam before I spotted a fox behind the chicken shed.

Below:
The snares caught two further foxes to the one Mark called in

Credit: Nick Latus

Keeping the main beam of the lamp below the fox, I watched it as it went about its business, totally oblivious to the lamp. However, at 300 yards away, I would have preferred it to be closer for a sure kill.

I watched as the fox quartered across the field from the shed. As it came closer, I guessed that this was a different fox to the one Steve had encountered the previous evening – either that or it was bulletproof. As it came in to around 200 yards, I took hold of the rifle and spied the fox through the 8x56 Schmidt & Bender scope. Easing off the safety, I anxiously awaited my chance.

At 130 yards, the dozy fox suddenly stopped and stared straight into the lamp, almost as if it had come to its senses. However, its undoing was already complete as I touched off the trigger and sent a 55-grain V-Max into its vitals. Although I was happy at the result, I wasn't convinced that this was the villain who had eluded me all week. Thankful for small mercies, however, I retrieved the dog fox and retired from the field.

The following evening I checked the snares and approaching the footbridge, I could see that the brashing on either side of the snare had been demolished. As I got closer, the culprit turned out to be a small, barren vixen that was still very much alive under the bridge. She was quickly dispatched. I found another fox in the next snare, and a well-aimed tap completed the trio.

To make sure the fox that had dug into the shed was one of the three I'd taken, I kept the snares running for another week, checking them daily. With these efforts proving fruitless, it seemed that the threat to the chickens had finally subsided.

The rifle is often the best answer for fox control, but it is well worth remembering that it isn't the only option. It had taken me nearly a week to outwit the marauder, but that's what makes fox control so addictive and rewarding. ∎

OBSERVATION AND INTEL

A few years ago, in my part of East Yorkshire, foxes started to pair early, from mid-October through to mid-January. On one occasion the following spring, I was out on a foxing foray covering a small farm pheasant shoot, and successfully shot three small foxes out of a narrow belt of trees. They proved to be two dogs and one vixen. Generally speaking, at that time of year cubs are about to be born, but this vixen showed no signs of having cubs or being in cub, despite being in obvious good health (before being shot of course).

But for the foxes who do birth cubs, feeding a litter of hungry mouths is a full-time occupation, and the parents' continuous comings and goings can be their undoing. This regular activity often betrays their presence and points towards the earth's location. When the cubs are active, signs of occupation are obvious – fur, feather and assorted old carcases strung about the earth makes it easy to confirm where they are living. However, do not approach too close – any disturbance of the area normally results in the vixen moving the litter post-haste.

Conversely, when the cubs are first born, often in a benign-looking rabbit warren just big enough for the vixen to squeeze into, there will be no trace of fox activity. Sometimes the vixen will choose a badger's sett, where excavation of soil, changing of bedding, and badger latrines confirm the excavations as brock real-estate. The vixen may give herself away by leaving signs of passage in the soft, newly dug earth at the set entrance. It is not uncommon for foxes to use the same sett as badgers – fortunately they don't know our laws protecting badgers and their setts, or we would find Charlie squatting in every sett I'm sure.

During early summer, the arable crops are high enough to conceal a fox, especially at night, rendering the lamp less effective. Therefore at this time, I tend to change tactics to early morning and evening. With hungry cubs wanting to be fed, the dog and vixen are active both sides of dawn. One or two well-positioned high seats can be a good asset at this time of year. If you are able to view over a large area with the binoculars and rifle in hand, it is surprising how many opportunistic fox shots you can tally up. However, the real advantage is observing the comings and goings of a fox through a certain gateway or tramline, possibly with a rabbit in its mouth, indicating the general direction of the maternity den.

Another thing to look for is a fox sat upright on guard duty. This is often the vixen positioning herself within a couple of hundred yards of the earth on the lookout for any threat towards her cubs. Ideally you need to take out the vixen and then the dog fox before dispatching the cubs as humanely as possible, but if only it was that easy. In reality it is often very different.

By April, most cubs will be at an age where they can survive on some form of meat alone, but still will not be able to fend for themselves, and would certainly starve to death without parental assistance. Therefore, if I have accounted for the adult pair, I tend to feed the cubs with rabbits at the sett entrance, enabling me to sum the size and number of the cubs. Positioning a high seat within 50 yards of the earth wherever possible, I can sit out well before dark with the .22 rimfire and lamp to wait for the cubs to come out above ground.

On a nice evening, cubs will venture out well before dark, allowing a silenced .22 rimfire with subsonic ammunition to take care of them with very little disturbance. The job can often be done before dark. If not, having the lamp as back-up will allow you to carry on into the night until you are satisfied all the cubs have been dispatched.

There are situations where it is not possible to place a high seat, but using a vehicle or simply getting into a good position where you can see the entrance to the den will suffice. As long as you keep your movements and noise to a minimum, the cubs will venture out.

I remember an occasion when I was repositioning a high seat in some woodland when I noticed a clump of pheasant feathers. Investigating further, I found two more places where a fox had mauled even more pheasants. They were all hens, so it was clear that the culprit was nailing the pheasants on their nests. Pheasants are known for not being the brightest of birds – when it comes to their self-preservation, they are practically suicidal.

Although I had been keeping an eye on the earths in the area, I'd seen no sign of cubbing. This pointed to the fox travelling a greater distance from the cubs as some nursing foxes do, setting their sights further afield and deliberately not hunting the area around the earth.

Over the following couple of days, I sat out with the rifle in various positions around the wood during the morning and the evening – but to no avail. The third evening, I headed away from the woodland and took position on some silage bales, using them as an opportunist high seat. A railway five fields away had embankments on either side covered in four feet of tall brambles, and an obvious haven for foxes. I got into position a good three hours before dusk.

With the woodland behind me, I used the top bale of the stack as a blind and a solid rest to shoot the rifle. Once I'd clambered up the bales, I loaded the .243 with Remington 75-grain Accutip bullets and laid the rifle close at hand. It was one of those late spring evenings with a cloudless sky and a light westerly breeze into my face. I diligently searched the hedges and fields through the binoculars towards the railway. Over the next couple of hours I was entertained by the nature around me, including a mature

roebuck seeing off a lesser rival – but no sign of a fox.

As the sun began to set, a cock pheasant slinked past the bales towards a small copse of trees some 200 yards away. As the light faded, a mist closed in, limiting my view to 300 yards. Nevertheless I could hear the pheasant chirp, as they do before fluttering up to their chosen roost for the night. But as I listened on, something was not right, as the rooster began his alarm call: 'Kok...kok...kok...kok...'

Visibility was dramatically decreasing. I tried to focus the binoculars in the pheasant's direction, and slowly scanned around the copse. Momentarily, I saw some movement down the hedge running towards me, before losing whatever it was. Slowly lowering the binoculars, I grasped the rifle to see if I could make out what was through the illuminated Zeiss Duralyt optic. I spied a greyish-red patch, belonging to a fox. As it turned in my direction to come down a tractor's wheeling on the edge of the field, its white chest dispelled any lingering doubt. I kept him in the scope and followed him down with the illuminated dot as more of him was revealed. Target confirmed, I waited for him to stop for the shot.

At around 70 yards he halted, looking in my direction. I centred the dot on his chest while pushing off the Zoli's safety, and squeezed away the trigger. The fox slumped to the ground, instantly dispatched. If he had been 10 minutes later or the optics had been of lesser quality, I would have probably have been none the wiser to his presence.

As suspected, he proved to be a dog fox. It was a welcome result, and I now had a good idea where the cubs and vixen were residing. A bird in the hand is always worth two in the bush, but never lose sight of the bigger picture, and always try to locate and deal with the cubs. Good relations with neighbours are often essential to achieve this – an annual bottle of malt is a good way to maintain necessary relationships with neighbouring landowners. ∎

THINK BEFORE YOU SQUINT

A question often asked is: 'Which scope is best?' The general answer given is: 'Spend as much as you can afford.' A good quality scope can cost more than the rifle itself depending on make and model. But when choosing a scope, take into consideration what you intend to use the scope for.

I prefer simplicity in a scope. A few years ago I made the mistake of buying a benchrest scope, which had more knobs and dials on it than cockpit on a jumbo jet. After mounting it on a foxing rifle I took it down to the range and zeroed the rifle easily. The fine reticle and 20-plus maximum magnification made cloverleaf bullet holes at 300 yards a reality. Parallax adjustment was nothing short of impressive. But having to adjust the focus dial at 100 yards, 200 yards, 300 yards and so on would prove to be a nightmare in the field.

I didn't recognise a problem until I was out lamping. I just could not get to grips with focusing during night-time manoeuvres. During daylight hours it wasn't a problem but when that fox ran out to 250 yards in the lamp before stopping for a look back, the last thing I wanted to be doing was adjusting the focus on the scope.

This is just my personal opinion – a gamekeeper friend of mine swears by Nightforce benchrest scopes, and uses them to the efficiency of the design by ranging his target with the latest Swarovski EL rangefinding binoculars. By knowing the ballistics of his bullet intimately he is able to dial in his scope, and consistently takes quarry to 500 yards.

I realise these ranges are beyond most folk – me included – and even frowned upon. Long-range varminting is much more accepted in the USA than it is here. That said, if a professional has intimate knowledge of his ground, has clear sight and the necessary equipment to do the job both safely and ethically, I really don't have a problem with it. Remember, there is a big difference between sport shooting and professional pest control.

At the other end of the spectrum are the lesser-known scopes that look good on paper – say, 6-24x50 AOE illuminated with range

MARK'S TOP TIP
Don't be tempted to buy bottom-end scopes for serious night shooting

focus at the objective lens end – and all for less than half of your planned budget. Don't be tempted to buy bottom-end scopes for serious night shooting. The field of view is far less than in quality optics, and a poorer sight picture of your target when you are looking down the beam of the lamp will be your undoing. Another problem with most of the illuminated versions is that the centre cross of the reticle illuminates, rather than using a dot, and often the dimmer setting is inadequate, creating glare back, which can obscure your target completely in low light conditions.

I'm not saying that what won't work for one won't work for another. But practically speaking, if you intend to buy a scope for dusk, dawn or lamping, a quality non-illuminated fixed or variable power scope with 50mm or 56mm objective lens and a clear reticle would be a better buy than an all-singing, all-dancing illuminated scope of lesser quality that looks like a lit up Christmas tree when in use.

There can be too much going on with some scopes, especially when lamping foxes. The last thing you need to be doing is focusing the scope on the fox or having trouble finding it in a narrow field of vision. This is time you should be using for positive identification of quarry, setting up a steady shot, and a clean kill. Poorer scopes will mean missing opportunities, or worse still, educating a fox after rushing the process and missing.

Next up the scale is the quality illuminated variable powers with a standard cross reticle and an illuminated dot at the point of aim. On most, the size or brightness can be reduced or increased depending on the situation. My personal choice is the Zeiss Duralyt 3-12x50 illuminated, retailing for less than £900. For a mid-range scope, it has proved its worth on numerous occasions.

This was never more evident than on a recent evening on fox patrol. I set out to sit in a box seat I had situated along side a belt of trees towards the corner of a rape field. Having made a mental note of deer movement and deer paths or runs, I positioned the box at a focal point where deer approached from four different directions. It is also a good vantage point for shooting foxes travelling in from beyond my boundary.

My Duralyt is mounted on the Zoli .243 and zeroed one inch high at 100 yards. Fuelled with Sako 90-grain soft points, this efficient foxing tool is finished off with a T8 moderator.

It was a typical early summer evening with a warm south-west breeze blowing. The forecast was a chance of thunderstorms later in the evening. I didn't give this a second thought as I soaked up the surroundings watching wildlife go about its business – not until the sun was beginning to set and the clouds began to thicken. Up to this point I had not seen a deer, it was getting darker by the minute and looking as if the evening was going to be cut short by the light. Plus I had forgotten my binoculars, which wasn't helping matters.

I heard the rumble of thunder in the distance and was just considering packing up when I spotted a deer walking through the yellow carpet of rape towards the belt of trees to my left. Just the top of its neck and head were showing above the rape crop. I raised the rifle to determine if it was a buck or doe. The Duralyt scope was essential with the ever-decreasing light.

I focused in on the deer, quickly realising it was a buck. I activated the illumination and decreased the magnification down to 6x, but as the buck stepped out of the rape into the shadows of the trees I lost sight of the deer with my naked eye.

It was only when I re-mounted the rifle and looked back through the Zeiss scope that I could see the buck heading towards me. He turned broadside at about 60 yards, at which point I placed the red dot on his vitals and squeezed off the shot to guarantee him a place in the larder. With a lesser scope I have no doubt I would have had to let him pass by to live another day as the optic would have proved inadequate in those light conditions.

Out lamping on another occasion, I came across the reflection of the eyes of a fox on a muck hill well over 250 yards away. Through the Duralyt scope, the fox tended to blend into the background under the red filter off the lamp. It wasn't until I increased the magnification of the scope to 12x power that I could clearly see the outline of the fox. On higher power, its outline was much clearer defined, and using the illuminated dot on a low setting, I was able to take a safe, confident and successful shot. ∎

Below:
Mark knows his scope... and it gets him results

131

DESPICABLE PRACTICE

Most of us who have anything to do with foxes will have heard stories or even witnessed fox behaviour that doesn't always ring true. For instance, some 20 years ago a local farm manager used to drive around the fields in his Subaru Estate, with his son stood up out of the sunroof shooting rabbits and the odd fox with the shotgun. That is, if they happened to be out in the middle of a field where they could give chase before they reached the safety of the hedge.

I'd speak to him on a regular basis and he was always keen to let me know how many rabbits they had shot, and of course it was a red letter day if they had shot a fox. I often wondered how many were getting a lesson in avoiding both vehicle and lamp beam. But he looked after his own ground and was happy, so it wasn't for me to say.

One particular harvest, the pair shot over 20 foxes in a period of four weeks. This may not have seemed unusual except that they were all within a couple of fields of each other and three quarters of them never moved while the farmer drove up to within shotgun range.

It was apparent they were not familiar with their surroundings, and soon he had come round to the idea that they had almost certainly been dumped.

Of course, the societies and organisations believed to be involved in this stupidity deny such acts. I can remember in my later school years, rough shooting close to home. We would see covey after covey of grey partridge, and a couple of us could shoot up to 10 brace in a morning. I know modern farming has not helped the grey partridge, but releasing vermin like the fox into any area is bound to have a massive impact on certain wildlife, particularly the partridge. Last September I walked my dogs on the same farm stubbles, and flushed but one covey of eight greys.

Four years ago I had been out for a drive with the lamp for a few rabbits on a local farm. As I returned down the lane towards the farmhouse, a fox came onto the track from the direction of the house – only 100 yards away. The fox turned and headed directly towards me. The vehicle was running and the side lights were on, but the fox was oblivious to the mortal danger he was in. I ended up shooting him with the .22 at 15 yards.

Apparently the dumped vulpines are more educated nowadays. The latest info I have heard concerns practices before release. They are allegedly placed in a dog cage in total darkness, and a beam is then passed over them while someone clatters and bangs the cage to condition the captives to associate light with danger. If this is indeed being carried on, it is a shocking state of affairs and must be ruthlessly stamped out.

I remember once being out foxing around a couple of farms towards the coast and close to my home. Apart from a couple of standing bean fields, the harvest was over.

During the previous few weeks I had shot a dozen or so cubs and foxes from this farm, but on my last visit I hadn't seen a fox over the whole 100 acres. But I just assumed I was on top of the fox population, especially as the cubs were breaking away from the family unit and dispersing.

I arrived at the first field around 10 o'clock. Picking up the Tikka .223 and the new Lightforce Xenon HID lamp, I locked the 4x4, grabbed the stalking sticks and quietly moved into the wind. I had opted for the red filter as I had used a green one on the last two visits. Perhaps a change might bring me a bit of luck.

The farmer had no objection with me driving around the headlands as long as I stayed off the drilled rape, but sometimes Shanks's pony is best. I lamped the whole bottom half of the farm in this way without seeing a fox. The Xenon HID Lamp was impressive – perfectly balanced, light but toughly built with extreme light penetration.

The only stubble field actually left on the farm was a rape stubble. Being on foot is definitely best on a cut rape field, as the chopped stalks make a lot of noise under the vehicle. As I entered this field I picked up a fox in the lamp. I was at the far side of the stubble to me at around 200 yards, and it seemed to be in no hurry. Placing the rifle in the v of the stalking sticks, I chambered a V-Max round. As I picked up the fox in the scope, it decided to move along the hedge and out of the beam.

Lifting the rifle once more, I corrected the sticks and swung the lamp beam back onto the fox, placing the crosshairs on the fox's chest in one swift movement. The same thing happened again – the fox moved out of the beam, went 20 yards up the hedge and

stopped. So once more I had to alter both my position and the Xenon HID lamp.

Although going solo is an excellent way of lamping foxes, there are obvious limitations – like on this occasion, when you get on fox that won't stand still long enough for a shot. The process happened once more, and by now the fox was edging out towards 250 yards. I was getting more and more frustrated, and I'm sorry to say I rushed the shot and did not connect.

Disgusted, I decided to lamp the rest of the farm before changing venues. It was quieter than expected until I went over an old railway

Above:
The 'distressed rabbit' on the Mini Colibri drew the fox in

line, dropped down the embankment and spotted a pair of eyes in the far hedge. As there was a safe backstop, I took a look through the Schmidt & Bender. It was definitely a fox, but it was obscured by the hedge bottom.

Taking the Mini Colibri from my pocket, I tried to use the electronic call to lure him out of the hedge. 'Distressed rabbit' was already programmed in to the call, and I soon set it going on low volume. After a minute or so, I turned off the volume and had another look with the lamp. The fox was en route towards me, so leaving the lamp on him, I increased the call volume and made ready with the rifle.

He was picking his way through the long rape stubble, when another appeared: both were easily visible in the lamp. I quickly shot the closest and instantly reloaded, picking up the second fox, who was stood looking at his deceased companion. I settled the Schmidt crosshair onto his chest and took him cleanly. The caller soon brought in another fox to the left of the first pair, and that made it a trio for three shots in less than three minutes.

Believe it or not, two more came strolling down the field at around 80 yards out, and I shot that pair within five yards of each other. I kept the caller going on for a further 10 minutes, but it was to no avail. I collected my spoils, marvelling at this surprising result from such a small area in so short a time. The farmer always informs me of any fox movement he had seen, and he had only seen activity post-harvest. Judging from the size of the foxes, he would definitely not have missed seeing them.

Once back at base, I had a good look at the vulpines, and I could not get over the size of them. They were certainly that year's cubs, but I would say they were bigger and heavier than most foxes I'd shot that year. The five foxes had displayed no fear whatsoever. Even when the unmoderated .223 dropped the fourth fox, his companion just stood a few yards from him, totally unperturbed. Furthermore, all five were dog foxes, shot in a 15-acre field and all within five minutes of each other.

It just didn't ring true to me. They seemed to have been fed well and had little exercise. You may argue that they came to the call, but I believe it's an instinct that the fox has, similar to the young ferret whose instinct is to home in on a rabbit even if he has never seen one before. But these foxes, I am sure, were expecting a bowl of cat food and a pat on the head. They got a lead pill instead. I am convinced that this despicable practice of releasing foxes is going on, and it should be stamped out, as there is nothing that can justify it. ■

Below:
Five foxes in five minutes, but Mark believes these fearless foxes were released onto the land

DUSK TILL DAWN

Owing to the wet weather one August, the harvest had been delayed. This had put my fox control operations seriously behind. I control foxes over a mixture of arable, pasture and woodland. Around 80 per cent is arable, and any cubs that get away from the earth are tricky to mop up until the harvest is completed.

In general, modern cereal farming means big fields. What were once four or five separate fields are now combined into one larger field, often exceeding 100 acres. This means lamping is more viable from a vehicle rather than on foot on these larger holdings. Successful lamping is a team effort, requiring an experienced and accomplished rifleman and an equally experienced lamper and driver.

Thankfully, a certain number of cereal fields had been cut at last. Keen to get going, I arranged to meet my cousin and lamping partner, Paul, at the estate's timber yard the first night there were enough stubbles for us to have a crack at the foxes. There was good cloud cover with a light south-westerly breeze. On arrival, I fitted the suction bar to the roof of the Ranger over the driver's window for me to use as the spotter. Paul would work the handheld Lightforce lamp from the cab once I had located a fox, leaving me to do the necessary with rifle and call if required.

Eye shine is what many rely on when lamping foxes, but often I have watched someone sweeping a field with the beam pass a fox by, simply because they are looking for the glint of an eye and nothing else. Eye shine is what gives most foxes away, and most will fall to the rifle. However, a hunting fox with his head down working across a stubble field or running low down a tramline will often take no notice of the beam. Spotting the movement or outline of a fox uninterested in your illuminations can account for many difficult foxes.

Mounting up at the yard, we soon set off down the estate track and turned into the

first barley stubble, which ran alongside a field of standing beans. At the far end stood a wood. Flicking on the lamp, I made the first sweep of the field with the red filtered lamp. A good-sized cub was sat no more than 120 yards out. I cut the light and took hold of the rifle, chambering a round before Paul stopped the engine.

A fox will tolerate the sound of a vehicle much more than it will the 'clink clink' of a rifle bolt being worked, so Paul always gives me a couple of seconds before silence ensues.

Taking a good rest on the mirror, Paul illuminated the cub, which was still sat bolt upright. I settled the crosshair on its chest and squeezed off the round to see the fox drop instantly. Another set of eyes appeared 200 yards beyond the shot cub – no doubt its attention was attracted by the moderated 'tunk'. Killing the beam, we kept quiet for a few minutes before I began to squeak using my mouth on the palm of my hand. A few

MARK'S TOP TIP
It's better to decline to shoot than to educate a fox with a shot beyond your abilities

Above:
Mark calls and lamps
separately until the fox
is within range

him up and shoot if safe. Again, when to shoot is all down to experience, but it is better to decline than to educate a fox with a shot beyond your abilities.

After a further 15 minutes of calling nothing showed, so we gathered the two shot cubs and pressed on to a series of rape and pea stubbles. A fox soon showed in the middle of one of the few ploughings about 250 yards out. It looked back a couple of times but made off before we even stopped the truck. We left him for the moment, and carried on towards a grass valley with woodland on one side and 100 acres of maize on the other. Paul had seen a couple of cubs two days before by the maize.

I drove into the valley before stopping, getting out of the truck and setting up the bipod on the vehicle bonnet as quickly and quietly as possible. The first sweep along the valley side showed three cubs in the lamp along the hedge below the maize.

I switched the lamp off and started calling just loud enough for them to respond. Paul put his lamp on and held it low as the cubs made haste down the hill. Two of them were racing in and the third was a bit of a plodder. As the two sprinters got within 50 yards, Paul lit up the furthest cub around 100 yards away. He stopped broadside on as the main beam dazzled him, and I settled the crosshairs on his chest.

Squeezing off the trigger, I heard the unmistakable thwack of success, and instantly reloaded. Paul tracked one of the other two cubs with the lamp, and I gave out a loud hare squeak to stop him just enough to add him to the bag.

I racked another bullet up as Paul picked up the third cub heading back up the valley. I gave out a screechy bark and settled behind the rifle. At just over 200 yards I steadied the Schmidt crosshairs on his shoulder and squeezed the trigger. I saw the cub roll over before I heard the welcome bullet strike. Satisfied all three cubs were dead, we

minutes later I flicked the lamp back on, and the fox was seen making his way towards us.

Leaving the lamp on, with the beam circle just in front of this cub, I kept calling and raised the rifle. Paul picked him up in his beam, and I tracked the cub in my Schmidt & Bender 8x56 optic. As the fox filled the scope, I stopped calling and gave out a bark, bringing the cub to an abrupt halt.

He was then instantly halted for good when the V-Max entered his chest and destroyed his vitals.

Once more I let things settle down before calling again, in between sweeps of the field with the lamp. I tend to call and lamp separately until the fox is within range. Only then will I keep the beam on – in front of his general direction, not on him – and I always keep calling. The closer he gets, the softer, quieter and less frequently I call. The trick is to call just enough to keep the fox interested. If the fox becomes hesitant, it is fine to line

scanned the valley for signs of more litter members but nothing showed.

After gathering the cubs, we drove further into the valley, scanning all the way. I soon got a glint of eyes from a nettle patch only 50 yards or so up the hill to my right. Leaving the lamp on the nettles, I reached for the rifle and slid home a round with the truck still running.

Moments later we spotted the eyes of an unmistakable fox, which was now stood at the near side of the nettles showing us some interest. At no more than 40 yards away, he too paid the penalty.

Cub number six was safely in the truck before midnight. We carefully scanned the area before turning round and heading out over the stubbles on the wooded side of the valley, and cleaned up another six cubs and a very old vixen.

I then headed in to the main part of the shoot in the central park of the estate. After scanning a suitable field above a disused quarry, I clicked the Mini Colibri to the rabbit setting and increased the volume to about the same as a regular back-of-the-hand call. I let the call play for three or four minutes before turning the volume button down another notch and having a scan with the lamp.

Nothing showed, but I was impressed with crispness of the sound. I increased the volume, then turned it off for five minutes. Turning the call back on, but at reduced volume, I began searching with the lamp on the far side of the quarry.

A rough grass field ran up the hill away from the pit, and beyond the beam of the filtered lamp. However, the red beam was able to detect the glint of another fox's eyes. In the distance I watched for a few seconds before turning off the lamp and turning the caller volume down and then back up before reducing it once more.

Every so often, I find that a louder squeak when calling a fox at distance will focus him

more, and this is very easily done with the Mini Colibri.

The fox came down the hill towards the call. I estimated the fox at around 300 yards away, and he was still closing. I got behind the rifle and spied him through the scope. He looked like a biggish dog fox, and I decided to take a shot before he reached the quarry. At around 250 yards he stopped and turned broadside, and with a good-sized target to shoot at I settled the scope on his engine room and touched off the trigger.

He disappeared instantly, but, owing to a slight muzzle flip, I did not see him go down. We marked the spot where the fox was stood, and drove around for a look. Happily, it didn't take us too long to find him dead on the spot.

After shooting two more in the park and one in the last field, dawn was almost upon us and we decided to call it a night with a dozen cubs, a vixen and a dog fox. ■

Below:

A bumper bag with 14 fewer foxes on Mark's shooting permission

137

VULPINE ARMOUR

MARK'S TOP TIP

Don't get caught short: make sure you're equipped to switch quarry if a night of unexpected foxing is on the cards

During the harvest, I usually get one chance of bagging more than 10 cubs and adult foxes in a night's lamping. But I recall one year that produced three such double-figure bags, two of which were on consecutive six-hour sessions with the lamp and rifle.

However times like that seem a far in the distance when the new generation is in the making. Conditions might not be ideal for lamping at that time of year, but when your local farmer rings to say he has foraged his maize and I need to get out and take a few rabbits, it's all systems go. I attached the Light Force suction bar to the roof of the truck, along with the 170 Strike Lamp and the T Bar handle, before placing the CZ .22 along with the trusty Tikka .223 for any foxes I may come across.

The first field I entered with the truck was one of the few with wheat stubbles left for the winter, with a mind to sowing spring barley. As soon as I drove through the gateway into the field, I readied the magazines on the rifles before having a quick flick around for a fox first. Beyond the ditch, 500 yards away, I picked out two sets of eyes in the lamp moving across the field. They were oblivious to the beam of the lamp, and I was 99 per cent sure they were foxes. One followed the other – presumably the dog following the vixen. Bringing the truck to a halt, I called for a short time, but the pair showed no interest whatsoever and disappeared over the brow of the field. With very few rabbits around, and the freshly cut maize stubble stretching across to a plantation on my right, a spot of foxing seemed a better option.

Changing direction towards the maize, I carefully began lamping both sides of a boundary ditch that separated the stubble from a drilled field of winter rape. Across the ditch, a good number of hares were happily munching away on the new plants. Beyond the hares on the far side of the field, I picked up a fox well out of range. Killing the lamp beam, I chambered a round into the .223 before quietly getting out of the truck. I have a small benchrest bag for use over the truck's bonnet in these situations, and I quickly deployed it to support the rifle.

Flicking on the roof-mounted lamp, I checked the fox was still in the same area. It had moved slightly to the right, but was certainly still out there. The lamp was extinguished once more, and after setting the Mini Colibri caller to the 'distressed hare' setting I let her rip and increased the volume. After a short spell, I turned the caller down to zero and had another swift look with the lamp. The fox had moved further to the right down the hedge, and strangely was showing very little interest in the call. I again switched off the lamp and repeated the process with the caller, increasing the volume even further.

Taking another look, I was halfway through a 360-degree sweep with the beam, but the targeted fox had gone. However, I illuminated another fox that had responded to the call and come in behind me. It was stood no more than 60 yards out. It had caught me in no man's land with the rifle laid over the bonnet of the truck, and pointing in the opposite direction. Quickly taking hold of the rifle, I turned towards the fox, but Charlie had realised that all was not what it seemed, and immediately turned toward the safety of the plantation.

My first thought was a free hand shot, but the fox was alert now so I opted to get behind the driver's door and use the open window sill as a rest. The lamp was still on, but the fox was now disappearing out of the main beam.

After correcting the lamp, I placed the beam directly back onto the fox at about 120 yards. I gave out a fox bark to stop it, and mounting the Tikka, I picked up Charlie through the Schmidt & Bender. The fox bark impression did the trick and Charlie courteously stopped broadside for the crosshairs. I touched off the trigger and the fox was slammed to the ground. An instant later the thwack of the 55-grain V-Max reached my ears as the bullet destroyed the ribcage.

After a quick scan around with the lamp to make sure no other foxes had sneaked in, I made the rifle safe and placed it back in the truck before driving on to collect the fallen fox.

Now totally in fox mode, I left any rabbits and carried on lamping the rest of the farm without any sightings until I got to the chicken shed. By this, I do not mean a hut with a dozen hens in – these are commercial free range egg-laying units, protected by miles of electric fencing to deter predators on three sides, with a river on the other. However, the electric fencing stops short of the river bank, allowing the fox entry at both ends.

As I drove down the side of the river bank, I spotted two foxes in the lamp beam on the electric fence side not far from the furthest shed. They were too far away from where I was for a shot, and from past experience I knew my best chance would be to try and get between them and the river. Keeping the lamp on them, I kept driving at steady pace along the riverside. The foxes kept appearing then disappearing in the same place time and again, but showed no concern about my presence at all.

It wasn't until I got within 150 yards that it became clear it was a vixen and a dog chasing her back behind the shed and out of sight. I proceeded until I was parallel with the end of the shed. To my knowledge, the escape was 100 yards in front of me. I drew to a halt. The rifle was at the ready, placed in on the rest out of the vehicle window, with the lamp directed on the area between the shed and the electric

Above:
The window sill of
Mark's truck makes
for an impromptu
shooting rest

fence. I didn't have to wait long before the courting couple came out from behind the shed, oblivious to the danger that awaited them.

The dog fox proceeded to chase the vixen round in circles for nearly a minute before they came to a stop, tight alongside the electric fence. They were still not phased by my presence. I made a couple of mouse squeaks from the palm of my hand, and instantly the dog fox hurtled down the beam of the lamp, failing to stop until it was within 20 yards of my muzzle. Its body filled the 8x56 scope, and I squeezed off the V-Max to finish him.

The vixen had started to come too until I took the shot. However, at the dog's demise she soon disappeared into the darkness beyond the shed. Reloading, I waited with the lamp to cover her exit. Within seconds she slowly sneaked around the corner, heading in the direction of the river. The vixen made it into a patch of thistles, completely covering her lower body. Most of her front quarter was obscured by cover, but there was a small window in the foliage exposing her engine room, and a well placed shot ensured the third and final fox of the night would join the other couple on the truck. ■

SHY BUT NOT INVINCIBLE

Once the glut of shooting foxes during the harvest has passed, it's back to tactics and outwitting them. With the breeding cycle starting all over again and the colder weather kicking in, it's worth keeping a close eye on the earths and bail stacks for activity, and not forgetting to listen out for the verbal signs when out at night as the foxes pair up. This can be a giveaway as to which area they are in. They tend to act differently at this time of year – less interested in the distress calls and more interested in each other. So the more efficient you can be with the rifle, the more chance you have.

When lamping, I use a box on the back of the pick-up made from a 2x2 frame and exterior ply. (The width and length may vary according to the size of the pickup back – that is, single or double cab.) The main measurement is 54in (height) from the floor. You need the sides to be low enough to be able to take a shot downhill or close in so you are not overstretched.

Although I do use the box for staking out areas, its main use is for lamping. I have it wired straight to the truck, with a socket inside to plug in the lamp and a switch wired to a small light in the cab to indicate to the driver when to stop based on one person lamping and a rifleman in the box.

With 360-degree lamping and shooting, no matter where the fox is, if it's safe and within range the shot can be taken anywhere very quickly. It also enables you to lamp over hedges or off farm roads and tracks without entering the field and spooking wary foxes. When I spot a fox in range from the box, I try to keep the lamp fixed on the fox while the vehicle stops and the rifleman prepares to take the shot. More often than not, it's over in less than 10 seconds.

A good tip for when you drop on that wary fox that's well within range and has been eluding you in the past few weeks is to keep the lamp on him when he sets off and get the rifleman to track him through the scope. Keep quiet as the fox will often stop for that one look back – just long enough to take the shot. Based on my theory, using a red or green filtered lamp, you can see if it is within range.

Three miles down the road on an arable farm, one particular fox was always in the same area of three 100-acre fields of winter wheat, always sticking to the brow of the fields. He was not really lamp shy, but seemed educated enough to stay at a safe distance with no backstop to make a safe shot.

Post-harvest, I take the box out with two colleagues twice a week, covering a vast acreage over four or five hours each night. The vehicle driver knows the lie of the land and the farm tracks, with enough land to lamp for seven nights on the trot without covering any area twice. I probably lamp most of this ground once a fortnight unless a fox is causing a problem. Then I adopt a more intensive approach.

I often find that with shorter days and longer nights, if I go out at the same time lamping the same route, I hit a quiet period where I hardly see anything. If this happens, a good tip is to alter your routine and go out a couple of hours earlier or later – or change your route and lamp the ground in reverse, starting out where you would normally finish. The weather can play a vital part

MARK'S **TOP TIP**

When you drop on a wary fox that's well within range, keep the lamp on him when he sets off and get the rifleman to track him through the scope

141

too. I try to avoid cool or frosty, clear nights, as for some reason I tend to see very little.

An occasion that stands out for me was when I was out with two regular lamping companions, doing the rounds lamping from the box. I was on the lamp: A Lightforce 240 Blitz with the red filter on. My rifleman was using his C2 Limited ebony edition with a candy twist barrel in .223 calibre, using 50-grain Remington Accutip bullets and fitted with a T8 sound moderator. At the wheel was our regular driver who is my brother-in-law and the local farmer's son.

We set off just outside the village down a farm track. It was a mild evening, overcast with a slight drizzle in the air. Ideal conditions with a decent breeze, you would think. I scoured the open winter field with the red beam for half a mile, probably covering 500 acres, only seeing hares and rabbits.

We were heading towards the 100-acre wheat fields where a fox had been eluding me for the past month. The farm track went along the bottom of the fields and then turned along the

right side of the last field. I lamped the fields as we drove steadily along the track, and sure enough, on the last field the fox was stood some 300 yards away. He was at the highest point on the field with only the dark sky as a backdrop.

I pushed the button wired to the truck cab to indicate to the driver to stop. Keeping the lamp on the fox, Paul, the rifleman, had a quick look through the scope and confirmed the fox was lying down. Anxious not to spook the fox, I indicated to the driver to continue as I had a cunning plan.

Once we had passed the fox up the right side of the field, we went on for a quarter of a mile and stopped upwind of the fox. I explained to Paul and Pete, the driver, that I would get out there and they would drive back around to the bottom side of the field and position themselves in the box 150 yards to the side of a grass balk that ran up the field towards the fox. Over the years, I have seen a lot of foxes using this technique and if my plan worked, the fox would come down it.

I grabbed the lamp and battery pack before they had made it back around. I waited for 10 minutes or so for them to get into position and for Pete to get into the box to lamp for Paul. The pair knew exactly which direction I would be coming down. I would certainly not try this with an excitable rifleman – only one that would think first and shoot second.

I set off to the other side of the field above where the fox was laid up. I was trying to push the fox into a safe area to shoot, bearing in mind it was sat in a 100-acre field and I could only approach it from one direction so I would be nowhere near the line of fire. Once I was in the same field as the fox, I had a flick around with the lamp. He was nowhere in sight, which was a good thing. If the fox was still in the same place, I would not pick him up in the light for another couple of hundred yards.

I pressed on towards the red glow, which I could see over the brow of the field coming from the truck's position with the lamp. It was beginning to look as if the fox had put the slip on us once more. Then, at no more than 70 yards, I saw the fox. It had been lying down, and it was not until the fox stood up that I could see him. I kept the lamp on him, and he disappeared towards the direction of the bottom track where the truck was stationed.

I turned off the lamp and stayed still, watching the red glow in front. It seemed that the fox had outdone me again. A minute or so passed before I heard the report of the .223. Had the plan come together? Or had we made the fox much harder to lamp?

As I approached the truck, Pete was on his way back from the field below the truck with a dog fox in hand – a great result. Paul explained that it came down the side of the grass bank but had not stopped until it had crossed the track and gone into the field below, where it turned and looked straight towards my direction. He took it out at around 170 yards.

The whole excursion may have taken 40 minutes, but it was well worth it. ■

FOXING FOREPLAY

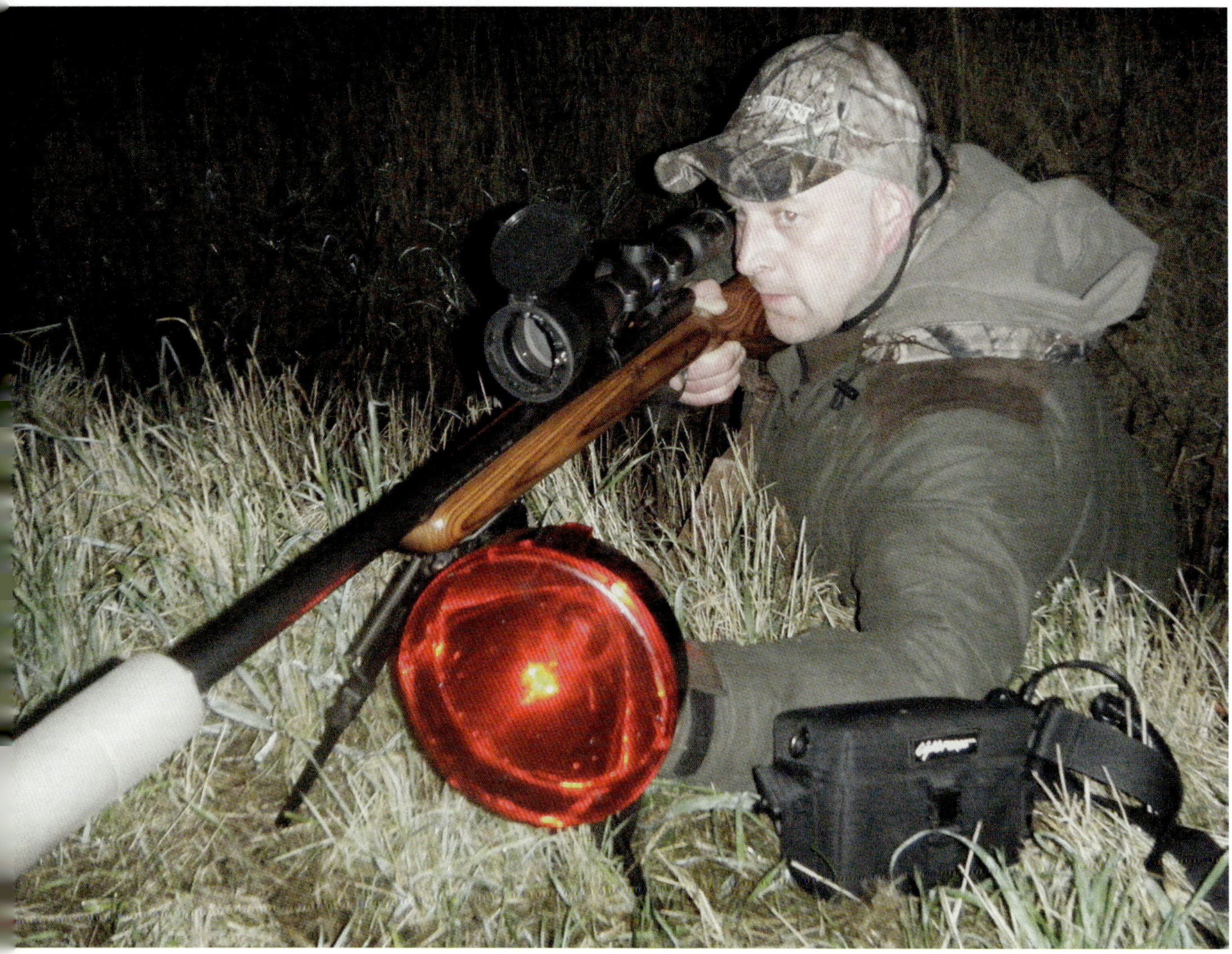

MARK'S TOP TIP

When baiting, secure the bait down so a fox can't sneak off with it when you've cast the lamp's beam further on

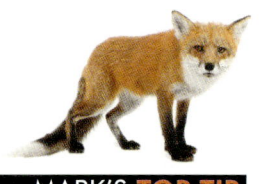

When the fox mating season is active it can be eventful to say the least. I've seen everything from paired-up dogs and vixens running into the calls like six-month-old cubs, to the other extreme where foxes show no interest at all in the regular calls.

When this happens, in addition to the regular rabbit or hare distress call I also use the fox bark call every one or two minutes. This way of calling certainly attracts the foxes much more at this time of year. Don't expect them to come steaming in, though – they often sit or stay hovering 150-200 yards away.

I find certain areas show more fox activity than others during the pairing up spell. I often use the baiting method to get the foxes into a safer position to shoot. With signs of fox activity at the bait, I then set myself up in an ambush position.

It was during the mating season that I sat up on an overcast night with a south-westerly breeze blowing directly to my position. I was equipped with the Mini Colibri electronic caller and a Lightforce 170 Xenon HID lamp and 12V 9AH battery pack – a very impressive bit of kit, enabling far-out viewing with its high-density spot beam even with a colour filter in place.

Earlier in the week I had set up the bait using a hare and pegged it down securely. The workmen on the nearby chicken units finished around 5.30pm and would often see a fox about as they were locking up. With this knowledge, I left home in enough time to allow me to be in position just before 5pm, and ready for the fox's arrival. I parked the truck behind one of the chicken units before loading the magazine of the Remi .308 and checking that the chamber was empty. With the battery pack over one shoulder, the holdall over the other and lamp and rifle in hand, I made my way to the ditch that overlooked the bait.

Scanning the area with the lamp as I walked in to my position revealed that the vicinity was clear of any foxes at present. After quickly checking the bait was still there – without going too close – I soon settled into the dry ditch. Remaining comfortable is paramount in any ambush job, and all the necessary equipment should be immediately at hand. I adjusted the bipod legs so as soon as I took hold of the rifle I would be steady on the baited area. Placing the battery and caller alongside the rifle, I chambered a round and applied the safety.

After allowing the immediate area to settle down after my arrival, I took hold of the Lightforce lamp and scanned the field in front of me for a few seconds until the xenon bulb had warmed up to full brightness. This enabled me to look further afield into the next acreage. All was quiet apart from the odd rabbit and hare munching on the grass.

My method of lamping over bait is to flick the lamp on towards the baited area every five minutes or so, keeping the main beam of the lamp low for five to ten seconds – just long enough to see if the fox is in the baited area. This is the main reason I secure the bait: it allows me to sit without lamping constantly. If not, a fox could sneak in and be away with it without being detected. Keeping the lamping to a minimum avoids deterring any foxes, whereas sweeping the lamp across the area will often put the fox on the alert and arouse suspicion. After three or four flicks to the baited area, I would have a complete scan around every 15-20 minutes to make sure an opportunity away from the bait is not missed.

Although the light does not get to full brightness for at least 20 seconds, it is still more than powerful enough to spot anything out to 200 yards. I was using the filter as this was a low-key, sensitive operation. After an hour or so, I was sweeping the beam beyond the bait and along the hedge when I noticed a couple of rabbits sat up on their hind legs, obviously not comfortable with something. The cause of their concern soon became apparent when I spotted the glint of eyes in the hedge beyond them.

Below:
The pegged down hare made attractive bait for this *Vulpes vulpes*

145

on and could clearly see the fox in the edge of the beam, trotting unconcerned alongside the bank of a small beck.

I quickly shouldered the Remy with my right hand and steadied the lamp along side the bipod with the other. Keeping the lamp fixed on the fox, with the rifle already in position pointing towards the hare bait, I easily picked up the fox in the Zeiss scope. The fox must have dined here previously as it approached the bait directly and began taking a few tugs at the flesh before turning broadside. As it enjoyed its last supper, I eased the cross onto its chest and took up the trigger. The report and recoil of the .308 moved me off the target, and I could not confirm the outcome until I refocused on the mauled bait and saw the fox lying motionless beside it.

Leaving the fox where it lay, I poured a coffee and sat back for quarter of an hour before starting the lamping sequence once again. An hour passed without a sighting, and I decided to set the Mini Colibri caller going on the distressed hare setting on a low volume, intermittently changing to the fox bark.

As the call echoed out into the cold, still night, I scanned past the bridge that spanned the beck, and instantly lit up a fox. It crossed the bridge and headed down the bank at a brisk pace, catching me by surprise. The caller was still going on its lowest volume as the fox trotted past the bait and its deceased relative with not as much as a glance towards them. By the time I had settled behind the rifle and focused on the fox, it was within 50 yards and filling the scope up with every step.

I shouted to make him stop. With his white bib filling the scope, I centred the cross and squeezed away the 150-grain ballistic tip. That brought an end to the night's proceedings.

Unloading the rifle, I picked up the closely encountered dog fox that had come in like an August cub and collected the vixen by the bait. It had been another great result, and it was high time for me to go and get thawed out. ∎

After watching for a few seconds, I switched off the lamp, hoping it would come out into the open. Once the fox got to the end of the hedge it was working, it should be in range. A couple of minutes later, I turned the lamp back

VULPINE BID

The *Sporting Rifle* Save the Rhino auction has raised a lot of money for a fantastic cause, and one year I put up a lot for a reader to come out foxing with me. I had arranged with the winner Howard Stott to come foxing the weekend after the Midland Game Fair, hopefully hitting that spell after harvest when foxes turn up everywhere. This is the time when what they have known as home has been cut or harvested, making them move about looking for sanctuary elsewhere.

Howard arrived mid-afternoon on the Friday and showed me his rifle set up. He had brought two rifles, both Tikka T3 Stainless Varmints – one in .223 and the other in .22-250, with identical ASE sound moderators. The .22-250 was topped with a Cobra night vision scope paired with Cobra night binoculars, whereas the .223 had a Nightforce 8-32x56 for Howard's day shooting or with the lamp.

We met my cousin Paul at dusk; he had volunteered to drive while Howard and I were in the fox box fixed to the truck back. Within five minutes of setting out I had the lamp on a fully grown cub no more than 150 yards out on a stubble field. Paul came to a halt as Howard pressed his back into the corner of the box for a solid rest. I gave the fox a couple of squeaks and the cub responded well, too well in fact, not stopping until it got within 10 yards of the truck and disappearing into an adjacent hedge. Keeping quiet, I lamped back and forth for at least two minutes. Eventually I spotted the cub moving back out into the field. Stopping him with a quick squeak, Howard was soon on him, taking the cub at around 40 yards. Number one was in the bag.

The next stubble field revealed nothing, but being optimistic, we parked up and started calling. After five minutes a cub came into the field from some woodland at the far end of the field. It wasn't as keen as the previous victim but I managed to coax it in to around 100 yards. Howard followed it through the Nightforce scope as I kept the cub in the outside of the main beam of the lamp. Killing the call, I then dazzled the

fox with the full beam. It paused long enough for Howard to rack up fox number two.

Howard's confidence was now growing but the next fox we came across was less accommodating. He moved off away from the lamp as soon as the truck stopped. I kept the lamp on it while Howard positioned himself to take a shot while he still could. A couple of hare squeaks from me were just enough to stop and turn Charlie at 150 yards out. The .223 cracked and although the fox ran 20 yards before dropping, the bullet strike sounded good. On inspection the bullet had hit just behind the ribcage, missing all the vital organs, but did enough to kill the fox in seconds nevertheless.

Over the next three stubble fields two more cubs came to the squeak and fell to Howard's rifle. It was still well before midnight and it seemed everything was sticking to the script. Moving on I picked up another fox, which would not respond to the call. It just kept on hunting about 400 yards away oblivious to our presence.

Above:
Howard Stott, a *Sporting Rifle* Save the Rhino auction winner, enjoys his foxing trip with Mark

MARK'S **TOP TIP**
Put a miss out of your mind. Everyone does it at some point

I signalled to Paul to drive on towards the fox in 'diesel stalking' mode. Paul knew the ground well, and without instruction brought the truck to a halt. I flicked the lamp on and made a sweep of the area, the fox was now around 200 yards away still going about his business. Howard readied the rifle as I mimicked the call of a distressed hare, stopping the fox, but Howard unfortunately missed the target. The lucky fox headed for the next county, and my guest was understandably annoyed with himself for missing – but we've all done it.

During the next hour we changed to a different location. This proved to be a good move, adding another five foxes to the bag. By 2.30am we had changed again to an area with wiser foxes that tended to keep their distance. Fortunately I managed to call a couple of juveniles in, which Howard dispatched with no trouble. As the clock crept up to 4am we called it a night.

I was looking forward to the next evening's outing as much as Howard, keen as I was to test the Cobra in the field. The plan was for me to drive and spot with the lamp while Howard would be in the passenger seat of the truck with his Tikka .22-250 fitted with his Cobra Centaur 165 night vision scope and Laserluchs illuminator. Once I had spotted the fox, Howard would dismount the truck to take the shot over the bonnet if possible while I switched from lamp to the Cobra Tornado 165 NV Binoculars – also fitted with a Laserluchs illuminator.

The first farm we went to saw us lamping two fields at once as we drove up the mile-long private road. It wasn't until we had nearly reached the farmstead that I spotted a fox, 100 yards in front of the house and about the same from our position. Turning the lamp off, Howard got out of the truck as I cut the engine and set up on the bonnet. Unfortunately I was totally blind to what was going on as the NV binoculars were out of reach, and I did not want to move about too much in case Howard was trying to steady himself for a shot. Talk about the blind leading the blind.

Fortunately the fox was as unaware as I was when I heard the crack of the .22-250 followed by a pleasing 'thwack'.

Moving on the next farm, I made sure the Cobra NV binoculars were closer to hand. I soon caught a glimpse of a fox as it disappeared through the hedge. It was a way off so we stopped and set up outside the truck. Howard placed his bench bag on the bonnet as I set the Mini Colibri caller going. Using the Cobra NV binos, I searched the field and was amazed at the quality of vision even without the added Laserluchs illuminator.

Spotting a fox some 300 yards away, I indicated it to Howard. Working the NV units as a team, Howard soon picked up Charlie in the scope guided by the illuminator emanating from the NV binoculars. This fox unfortunately disappeared through the hedge and was gone.

A mist began to swirl in so we moved to a good vantage on higher ground. Howard set

Left:
Fifteen foxes fell to
Howard's rifles during
the two-day foray

up over the bonnet while I set the caller going and switched the Cobra binos on. We had only been calling a couple of minutes when on the second sweep of the field I spotted a fox coming alongside a maize crop 300 yards below. I watched it with the beam of the Laserluchs illuminator on the fox, and I could see Howard's illuminator beam sweep across the field as he quickly locked on to the closing fox.

I turned the volume down on the Mini Colibri, coaxing the cub in to 100 yards. The fox paused, oblivious to what was going on stopped giving Howard the chance of a shot. Howard placed the cross of the Cobra at the top of his shoulders and squeezed away the bullet. The fox crumpled as the Sako B-Tip found its mark.

We headed for a farm out towards the Yorkshire Wolds to try to get away from the mist, which was now forming a blanket across most fields on the lowland areas. As we turned off the public road I flashed the lamp across the field on our left spotting a fox straight away. Applying the brakes, I brought the truck to a halt. Howard disembarked and came round to my side of the truck and set up his rifle on his bench bag before I switched off the engine. Picking up the NV binos and looking out of the passenger window, I could see the fox bolt upright facing in our direction. Howard took his time and clinically dropped it at 219 yards.

We finished with a total bag of 15 foxes for the two nights. Despite the mist hindering Saturday's outing, the foxes had called well and Howard had shot straight. I had been impressed by both the Cobra gear and Howard's shooting. Furthermore it felt good to know that the money Howard had bid for this hunt had gone to the hard-pressed anti-poaching units in Africa, who risk their lives daily to save that most iconic of big game species, the rhino. ∎

GARY GREEN

Gary Green has a number of foxing permissions within striking distance of his home in Essex. They range from the huge free-range poultry farm to a couple of smallholdings with just a handful of birds each. The numbers may be different, but the smallholders care every bit as much about their birds – indeed, the loss of a single bird is far more significant when you own 12 rather than 12,000.

One of those smallholdings is a constant problem for Gary. It seems that every time he turns his back, another fox moves in. It threatened to turn into more of a problem on one occasion when the farmer called up at the end of his tether. Since Gary's previous visit a fox – or perhaps foxes – had been breaking in and taking his chickens.

The farmer had lost a handful of birds, at which point he called enough and shut the birds in their coop. They hadn't been allowed out since. It was a temporary solution, but not one he could use indefinitely. The birds needed to get outside and scratch about, like chickens are supposed to.

Gary applied his fox-detective skills, honed over many years of controlling foxes in all sorts of situations. He quickly found a gap in the hedge where he thought the foxes must be coming through. There was plenty of fox scat in and around the hedge, which supported his theory. It looked like a family with cubs was to blame.

Next step was to sort out a firing point that would give him a clear view and a safe shot. With the lie of the land not in his favour, Gary moved one of his high seats into position using a big, mature oak tree as support. Its branches would give him a bit of cover, supplemented by a piece of camouflage net draped from the shooting rail to hide his lower body and legs.

He used his favoured method of rigging up a small floodlight to cast a light out across the

area where he expected the fox to appear. The light is very dim, but just enough to see a fox moving in by the glint of its eyes. As the fox approaches the bait point, at 100 yards or so, the light is enough for a proper identification and an accurate shot through his Swarovski Z6i scope, without the need for any extra lamps or night vision gear. This spot was some way from mains power, so Gary had to chain together a few extension leads to reach the farm buildings and plug it in.

The light is a security lamp from a DIY store and comes with a built-in day/night sensor. That saves electricity during the day, but turns on the light before darkness falls. The foxes soon learn that the light is always there, and get used to ignoring it as they come and go.

On the first night Gary got into position and a fox showed itself within 10 minutes. This could be the quickest fox control job he's ever undertaken! What Gary assumes to be the vixen appears at the top corner of the field. He can see her clearly through the scope but the shot isn't safe. Even though the high seat, lamp and bait have been in place for a few days now, this fox seems very cautious of the additions to the scene, and melts back into the wood. Gary waits, knowing there's every chance she will reappear before too long.

Sure enough, she does, this time a bit further along where the safety margins are good. Gary is ready and eases the RPA .223 into position. The illuminated aiming dot

of the Z6i is already switched on and Gary quickly lines up and fires. The reassuring thump of impact is missing but Gary can see what's happened. The bullet has broken up on a piece of grass just in front of the fox. She jumps and spins, but falls dead just a couple of yards away from where she was hit.

Gary reloads quietly and waits. There's no point creating any more disturbance, as there could be other foxes in the area. Another 40 minutes pass before the dog fox appears, very close to where the vixen lies still. He seems less cautious though, and moves towards the bait. Gary lets him come – no point in making this any harder than necessary.

He tracks the dog through the scope as it trots in towards the bait. When it reaches the halfway mark he gives a small squeak. The fox stands broadside, offering a perfect shot, and as the bullet strikes he falls dead on the spot.

With the dog and vixen dealt with, Gary's attention turns to the cubs. By now they should be fully coloured and look like small adults. Perhaps they will come out later. Three hours pass, and as the clock strikes 2.45am Gary decides to call it a night, surprised the cubs haven't shown.

Gary knows there are no guarantees with foxing, but he's as confident as he can be that there are cubs about at the smallholding, and they will appear at some point the following night. Wanting to give his brother some sport, he puts him into the 'guaranteed' spot and takes himself off to sit in another high seat at the other side of the farm.

Three hours later they've both seen nothing. They head home empty-handed, but determined to come back the next day. Surely the cubs will show then. But they don't, and it's the same story over again – and Gary's brother can't try again because he's back to work and doing late nights.

Gary can't afford to leave the job half done though – the chickens are still locked indoors and the sound of them scratching at the door is preying on his mind. Back he goes on Monday for his fourth night in a row.

He's been in the seat for close to two hours when, at 8.40pm, a fox strolls in like it owns the place and walks boldly up to the bait point. Bang – it's down. Gary reloads and waits. An hour and 20 minutes later the next one comes; down it goes. Another hour passes, and the same thing happens. Gary

waits a while longer, but by 1.15am he is starting to see shadows of foxes that aren't there, and decides to call it a night.

That should be it, thinks Gary, but he wants to make sure. He returns the next evening expecting to see nothing – but to his surprise he shoots two more foxes in a couple of hours.

He's back again on Thursday and Friday night to be quite certain. Nothing stirs, not even an alarm call from the ever-vigilant local owls. It's looking good, and the farmer confirms that the bait hasn't been touched. Fingers crossed!

Two weeks later, the chickens are enjoying sunshine and freedom. Gary is even enjoying the odd early night himself, although for him 'early' means anything before midnight. It seems his week of perseverance has paid off, but he's confident it won't be long before a new fox moves into the area and the farmer is back on the phone again! ∎

Below:
Gary waits for the cubs to appear

152

A FOX IN BROAD DAYLIGHT

Fox shooting is generally a night-time activity, and most of Gary Green's work is done in the dark. But foxes don't keep strict hours, and you can find one up and about at any time of the day or night. That's a good job, because there are some places you simply can't go letting off a gun in the middle of the night – places like the smallholding I visited recently with Gary.

The owner here has a real problem. His chickens and geese are regularly raided by marauding foxes from the surrounding farmland. He does what he can to protect them, but there are limits, both financial and practical, and sooner or later the foxes always find a way through his defences.

He would love to give Gary free rein to tackle the foxes 24/7, but he simply can't. There are other houses nearby where folk wouldn't take kindly to being woken by gunfire in the middle of the night. Plus there are horses stabled in the yard, and the farmer's own dogs need their regular exercise. At least the land isn't criss-crossed with public footpaths, although like many places there are a few locals who consider it their birthright to wander where they damn well please without regard to those who actually live and work on the land.

It all adds up to a very restricted window for Gary, but he does his best for the farmer, visiting when he can. That explains why we find ourselves climbing into a high seat under a

GARY'S TOP TIP

With a remotely operated caller, the fox's attention is on the caller and not the shooter

153

scorching mid-afternoon sun – hardly ideal fox-calling conditions!

Gary sets great store by his Foxpro FX3 electronic caller. He ordered it direct from the US and was one of the first people in the UK to get one. He is particularly keen on the range of sounds built into the caller, his favourite being No.15, a 'cottontail distress' sound that seems to work very well on British foxes. The unit is rugged and reliable, and has the power to throw the sound well. Best of all, it is operated by a hand-held remote control. He places the caller unit at ground level – or in this case on an old upturned bathtub in the middle of the field,

about 80 yards from the high seat which is built against the wall of a brick and tile barn.

This directs the attention of any approaching fox away from Gary himself and towards the caller, which is controlled via remote. Gary can switch sounds, change the volume, or stop the call mid-flow if he judges it might put the fox off.

With the call set up, Gary climbs into the high seat and gets ready, filling the magazine of his RPA rifle with Geco .223 Express 56-grain. He chambers a round and sets the safety catch. It feels a little stiff, but moves into the 'safe' position. The safety on this rifle is a lever with a knurled knob that sits just in front of the

Below:
Despite the misfire, Gary still took the vixen out with a well placed shot

trigger. When it's on 'safe' you can't attempt to pull the trigger without your trigger finger encountering the safety, which saves the embarrassment of forgetting to release the catch. It also avoids the need to change your hold on the rifle to release the safety, keeping movement to a minimum.

He checks the picture through the scope, then looks all around, taking in the view from his commanding position. To the front, the field is rough pasture, with a few small patches of nettles and thistles. It rises gently towards the hedge about 200 yards away, beyond which is an arable field. Leading off from the top-left corner of the field is a wood, with an area of thick bramble where it joins the hedge up the left side of the field.

Before long the wildlife has forgotten the minor disturbance of Gary's arrival. Rabbits come out to graze, and a woodpigeon swoops across the field to drink from the water trough near the high seat. Gary smiles as he notices goldfinches feeding on the downy-headed thistles beneath his feet, but quickly remembers why he's here and reaches for the remote control.

He starts at low volume, in case there's a fox close by. In similar situations, he has had foxes appear almost underneath the high seat, and he doesn't want to alarm a nearby fox with a full blast of distressed cottontail.

After a few minutes at low volume Gary is convinced there is no fox nearby. If there had been one in the hedges, or lurking in the bramble thickets, it would have shown itself by now. Time to crank up the volume and reach out to the wood and beyond.

The call sounds unnaturally loud in the stillness of this baking summer's day, but perhaps it is working. From the wood comes the alarm call of a single cock pheasant: "K'kok!" The call is repeated regularly. "If it's every three seconds, it usually means there's a predator about," says Gary, and counts. "Yup, three seconds precisely. We could be in business."

He keeps up the calling, his eyes scanning rapidly around the perimeter of the field but always returning to that top left corner by the wood. "Here we go," he whispers. A rabbit has rushed into the open, then stopped bolt upright, looking back into the bramble.

Seconds later our fox appears, stepping nonchalantly on to the edge of the field, then lying down, stretching and yawning. It sits up, gives the rabbit a sideways glance, then has a good hard scratch behind its ear. It's doing its best to look uninterested, but it's clearly curious about the sound of the call and sets off across the top edge of the field at a trot.

Gary is using all his skill on the call to try to draw the fox in, but it's not having it. It scampers past the call without stopping. Gary doesn't want it to keep going and reach the cover of the hedge on the other side. "Oi!" he shouts, pushing off the safety catch.

The fox stops and looks about, searching frantically for the source of the sound. Gary lines up the crosshairs of the Swarovski scope, squeezes the trigger, and... nothing! The trigger is locked solid.

Time to think fast. Quickly he works the bolt and aims again. The fox still stands, staring. Bang, and it's done. The fox drops on the spot, a clean kill.

What happened with the misfire? Gary isn't sure. "I'm sure it was my fault, not the rifle," he says. "I probably hadn't chambered the round properly." Still, he's happy the job is done, and the farmer will be relieved too. The fox turns out to be a mature vixen, not one of this year's cubs as Gary had first assumed. He measures out the shot at 171 yards, and notes the solid hit with satisfaction. "She never felt a thing," he muses.

The farmer's problems don't start and end with a single vixen. Over time, though, his efforts pay off in the area. Not only are livestock losses down generally, but the lapwings are nesting again on the hill above the farm. "That's a real result," says Gary. "It shows we're doing some good for the wildlife round here." ■

DOG EAT DOG

Gary Green's reputation as 'the fox man' goes before him, so he often gets calls from farmers and smallholders about a troublesome fox. The latest request, however, took him by surprise. It came through his contacts at the turkey farm, but this time it wasn't about protecting poultry. This was a boarding kennels – and the marauding Charlie had killed two Chihuahuas.

Fortunately – if that's the right word – they belonged to the owner rather than one of the paying customers who leave their pet pooches at the kennels when they go on holiday. But that was little consolation to the distraught owner who had lost two much-loved pets.

The bold fox had managed to climb into an enclosed area of garden despite a high fence and a pair of Alsatians that shared the area with the little dogs. This was one determined customer. It would be a sensitive job, too, so Gary took the time to visit the owners and answer their questions as well as finding out more about the lie of the land.

He was able to reassure them about safety and noise before inspecting the area and working out a plan. It's a tight spot, and the only place suitable for a shot was an exercise area of neatly trimmed lawn measuring no more than 20 yards wide by 40 yards long. The area is surrounded by thick conifers that would allow a fox to approach unseen, and beyond that is a mixture of farmland and rough ground that to Gary looks decidedly foxy. He picks his shooting position, which will be a portable high seat leant against an ivy-covered tree near the main reception area. It's not ideal, but it's the best of the limited options and will give him a clear view of his target area. The elevated position will ensure he is shooting steeply down into the ground and that, combined with the fragile 56-grain ballistic tipped .223 Geco ammo, removes any risk of a ricochet.

Gary picks up his portable high seat on the way back from another job. He's brought his tools as well, because he will have a bit of clearing to do before he can place it in position. The base of the tree is surrounded by thick brush, and he needs to remove some thin branches and ivy higher up to ensure a clear path for the bullet.

Next he needs to lay a scent trail to draw his quarry in. He reaches into the back of the Land Rover and pulls out a green plastic bucket. It smells pretty bad even before he snaps off the airtight lid; the stench rising from the contents would knock you backwards. Even Gary seems unsure exactly what's in this concoction, but it certainly includes muntjac gralloch that's been festering for a fortnight.

Without knowing which direction the fox might approach from, Gary wants to cover all the angles. He lays trails in a cross pattern, drawing a loose interpretation of a Union flag across the grass and into the edge of the trees. That should catch the attention of any fox for miles around and lead it into the centre of Gary's crosshairs.

As the sun drops towards the horizon, Gary climbs into his perch. He doesn't have long to wait – it's still light when a fox shows up 25 minutes later. Unfortunately so does the first customer, who has come to fetch her cats. "I'm sitting there waiting to shoot the fox, which is in a nice shootable position, and they're standing a few metres away having a good old chat," he says. The fox is used to people being around, but eventually it's had enough and slips back into the conifers before the customer has left.

Half an hour later, all is quiet and the light is failing. Even with the exceptional light-gathering abilities of the Swarovski scope on his RPA rifle, Gary can no longer see into the shadows, so he switches on the light he rigged earlier. It's a small LED headtorch with a focusing beam and dimmer control. He taped it to the front rail of the high seat to shine out across the grass. With the brightness set low, it gives just enough light in the scope to shoot by.

GARY'S TOP TIP

Always react quickly to pleas of help if you want to keep your permission

156

Left:
Gary cleared
obstructions out of the
way before settling into
his portable high seat

As the lamp comes on, there's the fox again. Gary makes ready, getting the rifle into position and checking the safety catch – then there's a noise from below. It's one of the kennel's staff, asking if he'd like a cup of tea. She felt sorry for him because it's getting cold!

The fox has gone but there's no point being cross – she doesn't understand and it was a nice thought. Gary resigns himself to more waiting and turns the light up a little. Half an hour later the fox is back, and once again Gary prepares for the shot. It's just stepping out onto the grass when – yes, you guessed – it's closing time and the staff pile out of the door chattering among themselves. The fox slips back into the conifers for a third time.

At least now it's all quiet, but of course the fox is nowhere to be seen. The minutes tick by and the temperature is falling towards zero. Gary is glad he wore his thickly padded Deerhunter Rusky suit.

By 9pm he's had enough. He was up at 5.30 this morning, had a busy day, and now he's been in the high seat for more than four hours. Time to call it a day. He packs up the head torch, pulls the magazine from his rifle and removes the round from the chamber. One last check round the high seat and he's ready to climb down. He can't resist a final look round with his handheld lamp – and would you believe it, there's the fox!

Knowing this fox is used to a bit of disturbance, Gary doesn't muck about. He quickly slaps the magazine back into the gun and chambers a round. Into position, he double checks the backstop and bang, the job is done and the fox is lying dead on the grass. It wasn't a difficult shot. At 30 yards the biggest problem was allowing for the parallax error between the scope and the barrel. That's easily forgotten in the heat of the moment, but Gary got it right.

To Gary's surprise, the fox turns out to be a vixen. She looks as if she may still be in heat – very late, but they do vary. If that's the case there will almost certainly be a dog around, perhaps the "huge" one the kennel staff had described.

"It's better this way round," says Gary. "If I'd shot the dog first, I'd never have got the vixen. Now I can use her body to help lure him in – and I'll be interested to see if he's as big as they say." ∎

POULTRY EFFORT

Fox shooting is a sport and a way of life for Gary Green, but it's also a big responsibility. One of his customers is a free-range poultry farm that supplies many of London's most famous restaurants. It's where Gary built his luxurious fox box – basically a garden shed with a wide opening to shoot from, on top of a shipping container.

There's a steady stream of foxes moving onto the farm; the sight, smell and sound of thousands of free-range hens is an irresistible draw. Gary visits regularly, and shoots well over 100 foxes at this one spot each year. That usually keeps the farmer's losses down to a bare minimum, just the odd chicken now and again.

One year, though, it threatened to go pear-shaped. When spring finally arrived, the grass really took off and quickly grew to nearly 18 inches high in front of Gary's hide, with taller tufts and weeds here and there.

Gary restricts himself to light, fast bullets in his .223 rifle at this spot. It's too close to roads and houses to risk a ricochet, and he knows that the ballistic-tipped bullets are guaranteed to break up at the slightest impact. The bullet will blow itself to tiny pieces even on a blade of grass.

It's extra safe, but it does mean you can't risk shooting at a fox through even the thinnest cover. The bullet could easily hit a stalk before

GARY'S TOP TIP

Don't skimp on comfort when putting in long hours

159

Above:
One of the mauled
chickens makes for
effective fox bait

it reaches the fox, causing a complete miss or, worse still, wounding the fox without killing it.

So when the grass grew up, Gary had to stop shooting. He explained his problem to the farmer and asked him to get it cut – otherwise the foxes would soon move in on his chickens. "Yes, of course," said the farmer, but other jobs took priority and the grass continued to grow.

And then one day Gary gets the call he's been dreading: "Some £@%*! fox has killed 43 of my chickens!" Oh dear. And the grass? "I'm cutting it now!" Gary cancels his plans and prepares to head down to the farm that very evening. When you depend on a farmer's goodwill for your shooting, you have to be ready to work for it, especially when it really matters to him – and 43 chickens mean a lot to any farmer.

Arriving at 6pm, Gary picks a white chicken from the sorry pile. The birds all show signs of a fox attack, with bruising and puncture marks to the legs, back and occasionally even

the head – but nothing has been eaten. Gary shakes his head – all those chickens killed for no purpose.

The white chicken is destined to help catch its killer, so perhaps that one won't have died in vain. Gary walks to a gap under the fence, plucks out a few white feathers and starts laying a trail to the spot right in front of his hide where he wants the fox to end up. He sets down the white chicken and fetches the big green tub from his Land Rover.

"Yes, it's a bit ripe isn't it," he laughs, pouring the oozing remains of long-dead rabbits and deer onto the ground. "That should bring the foxes in from miles away!"

Next he sets up a remote controlled electronic Foxpro caller – Gary is using every trick in his book to get this particular fox. He can't afford a repeat of last night's massacre, and neither can the farmer.

With the scene set, Gary climbs the ladder to his fox box. It's a cosy place to wait up as long as it takes. It's even connected to the farm mains electricity, with an electric kettle and two fan heaters. Gary feels no shame at being comfortable. "You do long hours at this job," he says. "There's no point being uncomfortable or making yourself ill – and I've done that before, sitting up high seats till all hours."

As Gary sips on his steaming mug of tea, he is tuning in to the surroundings and fully alert. The rifle is set up and ready, with a round in the chamber. It's his RPA .223 calibre, shooting Geco ammo. It's a heavy rifle with a target-style stock and topped with a Swarovski Z6i. The scope has phenomenal light-gathering, so Gary won't need a lamp.

There's a 150-watt floodlight that shines out across the field from the top of the fox box. It provides enough light for Gary to shoot by at up to 100 yards, even on the darkest night. The light is on a timer, so it comes on at dusk every night and the foxes have grown used to it.

The blackbirds are kicking off down to the right and Gary peers round. It is probably just a

160

cat prowling round the farmyard that's set them off, but even in daylight it could be a fox.

A pair of crows have spotted the trail of white feathers. One sits on a fencepost calling loudly, while the other waddles along the trail picking at the feathers to see if there's any fat left on the quills. It loses its nerve before it reaches the dead bird, though, and the pair flap away to roost.

Darkness falls, and Gary is surprised that no foxes have appeared yet. The farm has been undisturbed, and he'd expected something to happen at twilight or soon after. A badger snuffles around the field 30 yards away, but it's after midnight before there's any sign of a fox. A tell-tale glint of eyes appears in the hedge directly across from the fox box, 150 yards away on the far side of the field.

It trots up and down the hedge, glancing across at the bait – or maybe us – all the while, but it won't leave the safety of the hedge. Eventually it disappears. Gary thinks it has headed off to rummage in the bins of the houses away to our right.

An hour later, and I've nodded off in the warmth of the fan heaters. I'm woken by Gary tapping me on the shoulder: "Look, it's back!" The fox repeats its earlier trick of trotting up and down the hedge. Out of frustration as well as hope, Gary reaches for the Foxpro remote control and gives it a good blast, then another and another.

To his surprise the fox does exactly what it's supposed to. It trots obediently towards us, rounding one of the chicken sheds and making straight for the Foxpro on the ground just 30 yards in front of us. It stops, hesitates, and bang! Gary is in no mood to mess around and he wants this fox on the floor.

We climb down from the box to take a look at this fox that was so wary to begin with, then changed its mind and trotted in as bold as brass. It's a youngish vixen. She has already had a litter this year, and they are weaned and away. Perhaps the responsibility of having a family to feed has stayed with her, and instinct

has led her to kill more than she could ever eat. The reason is unimportant. Gary isn't after retribution, he just needs to prevent it happening again. This vixen is a good result – and Gary has certainly earned one of those. ∎

SUNSET STAKE OUT

Gary Green shoots a lot of foxes, but there was one that had eluded him for more than 12 months.

This trickiest of tricky foxes lived near the chiller where Gary processes the deer he shoots. It's an idyllic spot surrounded by farmland and close to a nature reserve. With ready access to the waste from deer carcases, Gary had baited copiously in the adjacent field. He saw his tricky vixen regularly on his way to the chiller after an early morning stalk. She sat munching his bait and thumbing her nose at him. But it's as if she has a sixth sense: when Gary has his rifle to hand, she is nowhere to be seen.

Not to be beaten, Gary built a high seat overlooking the field in question. The high seat was set back in the hedge beside the driveway, behind the trunk of a horse chestnut tree, with a commanding view across the field. Gary sat up there night after night but never got a shot at his tricky vixen.

Other priorities then took over, but some months later the vixen reappeared on his radar as she had been taking an interest in the farmer's collection of ducks and geese. With the nesting season getting underway, Gary feared for the game birds and other wildlife in the area. To cap it all, she was regularly on the bait when Gary visited his chiller in the mornings. Gary hates to shoot a vixen that might have dependent cubs underground, but something would have to be done. An early morning session seemed to be in order, since the vixen's routine saw her on the field by 6.30-7am.

Gary is usually up with the lark, and on this particular morning he climbs into his high seat at 5.45am to be there in plenty of time. As he arrives, a small group of fallow deer trot away, disturbed by the vehicle.

He is certainly well equipped for the job. He has a heavy target-style .223 RPA that he bought second-hand, and shoots Geco ballistic tip ammo. The rifle has a blue synthetic stock with adjustable cheekpiece and chromed barrel. It's topped with a Swarovski Z6i, with 56mm

objective lens for superb low-light performance. Gary prefers to shoot foxes without a lamp when possible, and the scope with its illuminated reticle allows him to aim and shoot well into the dusk – and even through the night if the moon is clear.

The rifle is a bit of a beast to carry, but for shooting off a vehicle or from a high seat it's ideal. Gary can be confident of putting shot onto shot at normal foxing distances. The field here is no more than 150 yards across, and any fox that comes to the bait will be well inside the 100-yard mark.

Gary spends hours waiting for his quarry to appear but he's never bored. "It's better than watching TV," he says. It's a glorious spring morning and the wildlife is going about its business. Pigeons make their clapping, swooping flights across the field, and a muntjac picks its way through the wood on the far side of the field. It stops in a gap between the bramble bushes and Gary is tempted, but reminds himself how important it is to get this fox. He can catch up with the muntjac later.

GARY'S TOP TIP

Make the most of the time you get to just watch the wildlife

The wider world is starting to wake up. There are stirrings at the farmhouse, and before long the farmer passes beneath the high seat, glancing up and giving Gary a cheery wave. The time has passed; the vixen has evaded Gary once again.

There are other jobs to be done, but over a hearty fried breakfast of duck eggs and home-made venison sausages Gary's mind keeps returning to that clever vixen. She hasn't fed this morning, and the bustle of the farm will keep her off the field through the day. By evening her stomach will be rumbling, and she has to eat sometime. He resolves to return this evening and wait as long as it takes. It could turn into an all-nighter, but this fox is getting under his skin.

At 6pm Gary climbs back into his high seat. He has refreshed the bait, adding a tin of strong-smelling dog food for good measure. He is equipped with the RPA again, and this time has brought night vision gear as well in case things go on after dark. The RPA's Weaver rail allows him to replace the Swarovski with his

Pulsar NV550 digital night vision scope. He has tested it thoroughly, and is confident that the combination holds zero when he swaps the scopes around.

A heavy shower soon passes and the sunset is, if anything, even more spectacular than the sunrise. Cock pheasants strut in the last rays of sunlight, and crows fly across the orange sky to roost. Still, there is no sign of this tricky vixen. Gary shifts his weight carefully so as not to make a noise, and resigns himself to a long wait.

As the last light drains from the sky, Gary takes a look through the scope and decides it is time to switch to night vision. He reaches for the bag – and at that exact moment a shadow moves from the thick cover at the far left of the field.

It's definitely a fox. Gary can't be sure if it's the fox he's been after, but feeling safe now in the near-darkness it moves boldly across the field towards the bait point. Gary brings the heavy RPA rifle to bear and squints through the scope. The light-gathering power of the optics provide a clearer view than the naked eye, and with the illuminated aiming mark he feels confident taking the shot.

He gently takes up the pressure on the trigger, checks the alignment and – bang-thud! It sounds good, but the fox jumps like a scalded cat, turns and zig-zags away in the direction it came, its tail spinning like a helicopter rotor.

That wasn't part of the plan. Gary can't bear to leave it now, and climbs down from the high seat to search. He's sure that fox was hit hard. He crosses the field and busts through the brambles – and worse – but after a thorough search there is still no sign of the shot fox. "I'll have to come back in the morning with Polly the teckel," he says. "I'm sure we'll find that fox, it won't have got far. I just hope it's the vixen I've been after all this time."

The next day Gary is on the phone. "Got her," he says excitedly. "The bullet must have hit a stalk just in front of her, because it had started to break up. That's why she didn't drop on the spot."

And yes, it turned out to be that same tricky vixen that had been giving him the run-around. She had a nasty case of sarcoptic mange, which partly explained her dark colour. She seems to have had a litter, but her milk was almost dried up, so the cubs are likely to be at the stage where they will be able to look after themselves. This pleases Gary in a way, because he wouldn't want them starving underground. On the other hand, it could mean he will face the same problem next year with the daughter of his troublesome fox. ■

Below:
Gary was able to recover his shot vixen with Polly the teckel

THE WHITES OF ITS EYES

Most of Gary Green's foxes are shot between 80 and 150 yards. His favourite technique is to sit up in a high seat or fox box, waiting over a bait, or a caller, or both. When all goes to plan the fox comes in, stands at 100 yards or so and bang, job done.

He's set up his RPA rifle to shoot one inch high at 60 yards with the relatively flat-shooting Geco .223 Express 56-grain ammo, so he can aim dead-on at anything from 60 to 200 yards and still be sure of hitting the kill-zone.

Just now and again though, a cunning fox or a tricky spot calls for a change of plan – and that's what happened with a poultry-killer on a smallholding near his home in Essex. The fox had already taken several geese and chickens when his friend the smallholder called for help.

It's not a commercial farm, but if anything that makes it worse. These birds are almost family pets, and it's upsetting for the owners to find them ripped apart with heads missing and pieces strewn around. Gary drops his plans and nips round the same evening to check out the site.

It's immediately clear that this fox won't be straightforward. The site is a tangle of buildings, patches of rough ground, hedges, bramble thickets and an orchard with long grass. This fox has no need to show itself in the open; it can sneak in through the deep cover almost to within pouncing distance of the poultry.

The farmer himself is narrowing the options too. "It's not his fault, but he's restricting the time window when I can shoot," Gary explains. "He has a couple of small dogs that run about the place, and there are people stabling horses here too. I'll be shooting close to the buildings, and they don't want a gun going off when they're riding in and out. I'll need to get my thinking cap on and work out how to get around all the restrictions to nail this fox."

It takes Gary a few visits to work out the fox's routes and plan his approach. "I don't think I stand a chance of catching it on the way in," he says. "The cover is too thick. But it passes the end of a barn as it leaves the farmyard, following a grass track before disappearing into the hedge and dropping down into an old drain. If I wait on the end of the barn, I may just be able to do the job."

GARY'S TOP TIP

Tailor your equipment and approach to the environment you're shooting in

It won't be easy. Gary needs to get some height to look down on the fox's route. He will need some light on the scene, and even then the fox will be very close indeed – no more than 10 yards away. Even the slightest sound or movement will mean a wasted evening.

He has a plan, though. There's an old shed at the end of the barn, which he can climb on top of. Then he'll be in the shadow of the end of the barn, looking down on the small patch of grass where the fox passes through. Better still, there's a security light on the barn, right beside where Gary will be standing. It has an infrared sensor that switches the light on when it detects movement. The fox must be used to it coming on as it passes by.

Gary needs something to hold the fox's attention so it stops long enough for a shot, rather than scampering on past. A cooked chicken carcase pegged to the ground should do the job, with a liberal sprinkling of fish oil for good measure.

For once Gary leaves his trusty .223 in the cabinet and takes out a semi-auto shotgun instead. It's a Beretta A391 Xtrema 2, and he's loading it with three-inch magnum No.1 shot. That should be plenty to stop any fox in its tracks, certainly at this distance, and it's much better suited to this sort of close-range work. With livestock and buildings all around, Gary doesn't want any chance of a ricochet or bullet deflection.

A little while before sunset Gary climbs into position. He leans an old metal ladder against the shed and heaves himself onto the roof. It's more rickety than he expected, and he can feel it swaying beneath him. Better walk carefully around the edge rather than stepping straight across the middle of the roof – he doesn't want to crash through!

He loads up the shotgun – one in the chamber and two in the magazine – and flicks the safety catch on. There's no seat, but he can lean against the end wall of the barn. Even so, his legs will be stiff if he has to wait here all night.

As darkness falls the daytime sounds peter out, and there's just the distant rush of traffic and the familiar night sounds. Bats flit past Gary's head, and an owl calls in the wood across the field. A couple of times something sets off the security light but there's nothing there – a bat passing the sensor perhaps. Gary works out that he can activate the light just by raising his elbow in front of the sensor; that could be useful.

Suddenly there's a terrible racket from the yard: squawking, cackling and flapping. It must be the fox. The noise dies down but Gary's senses are on full alert – has he predicted the raider's escape route correctly?

In the dim light he can just make out a movement by the chicken bait, but he can't afford to make assumptions. He must see the whites of the fox's eyes and make quite sure of his quarry.

He brings the gun to his shoulder, and lifts his elbow so it cuts the sensor beam. The light blasts on. There, frozen for an instant in the beam, is the fox. It's still holding a dead goose in its mouth but the chicken and fish oil has caught its attention and it's stopped for a sniff.

A second later it's all over. The sound of the shot echoes round the buildings and the fox lies dead on the grass, the goose still in its mouth. Talk about caught red-handed! Gary climbs gingerly down from his perch, tidies up and heads home for what's an early night for him – it's not yet 1am.

Next morning there's a text on his phone from the farmer. He'd been woken by the shot, but he didn't mind – in fact, he was delighted when he saw the fox lying there. A bit of good fieldwork and careful planning has produced another good job done and another happy customer. It all adds to the word of mouth that keeps Gary in foxing permission for miles around. ■

TURKEY SHOOT

Do you enjoy a traditional turkey Christmas dinner? Thousands of families up and down the country do but how many realised they only get to have one because people like Gary Green had kept the foxes at bay?

In the countdown to one Christmas, Gary received a call from one of his regular fox control customers, a huge free-range poultry farm not far from his home in Essex. The farmer was finishing 10,000 turkeys ready for the festive season. The birds were fully grown, ready to be slaughtered and packed off to butchers and supermarkets – if the foxes didn't get them first.

This farm is a regular gig for Gary. They keep chickens throughout the year, as well as raising turkeys to meet the seasonal demand. The birds are free to roam in large grass fields during the day – that's what makes them 'free-range'.

Electric fencing protects them against predators when they're outside, and most of the time it's effective, though nothing is 100 per cent fox-proof (or turkey-proof for that matter), there's always the odd one that somehow finds its way onto the wrong side of the wire).

It's at night that the birds are most vulnerable, even though the farmer is meticulous about rounding them all up and shutting them in their sheds before nightfall. That's when the foxes come prowling, and when it's cold and their bellies are rumbling they can be very persistent in their attempts to break in.

Gary explains that the fox doesn't need to bite the birds to kill them. When a fox is scrabbling at the shed, the birds will panic and rush to the far end of the building, where they all end up in a heap on top of one another and die of suffocation. There can be hundreds dead in a

GARY'S TOP TIP

Keep noise to a minimum when shooting from a box

single shed even if the fox never managed to break in. That means a massive financial loss to the farm, not to mention families missing out on their Christmas dinner.

Gary values his foxing permissions, and never ignores a cry for help, whether it's from a massive poultry farm or a little old lady with six chickens in her back garden. So he's straight round to the farm that day to set out his bait and make a plan.

He has one of his fox boxes already set up here. It's a wooden shed that he built on top of an old shipping container the farm uses for storage. Gary had set it up a few years back and has shot literally hundreds of foxes from it. A river running up the valley channels the foxes towards the farm, and the scent of all those birds is a massive draw to inquisitive foxes.

It gets dark early at this time of year, and the twilight provides an ideal opportunity for a smart fox to sneak in and nab any birds that haven't yet been locked away for the night. So Gary gets set up in position before 4pm. He's prepared for a long wait.

The fox box is a cosy refuge from winter's chill – in years gone by Gary has made himself ill sitting out in freezing weather in the high seat, and he doesn't want to make that mistake again. The box protects him from the worst of the weather, and it has sockets connected to the farm's electricity supply. That means he can run a fan heater and a kettle, as well as the 120W floodlamp that provides enough light to shoot by.

Tucked in the box, with a comfy seat, sandwiches and a hot cup of tea, Gary can happily sit out all night, and in fact, he often does. "I'd rather be doing this than sitting at home watching *Eastenders*," he laughs.

Despite the home comforts, if a fox appears he can be on it in a flash. Beside him his .223 RPA rifle sits ready on a sliding shelf that also provides elbow support for a steady shot. As he sips his tea, his eyes are constantly flicking across the view through the observation slits.

He usually gets plenty of warning of a fox approaching. They tend to come through

Above:
A fox caught on camera making off with a turkey

the hedge 150 yards in front, or through one of the gateways at either end of the hedge. Even at that distance, the floodlight produces a distinct eye-shine – Gary can see the big, amber, headlamp-like eyes of a fox as soon as it glances in his direction. That gives him plenty of time to move the rifle gently into position and prepare for the shot.

It's important to keep noise to a minimum inside the box. As Gary says, it's a lot like a big speaker box, and amplifies even the tiniest knock or cough in the direction of the quarry.

Today the first fox comes early. At about 5.15pm Gary spots the distinctive flash of eyes by the hedge. The fox doesn't come straight in – it circles round to Gary's left. Gary is worried it will head off up the field, so he produces a few rabbit squeaks by sucking on the palm of his hand.

169

The next time we see the fox, it's trotting obediently towards the bait – its route took it downwind of the rotting roadkill and carcase trimmings, and the stench has caught its interest. The fox stops a foot from the bait, its nose outstretched to check it out. Bang – the 56-grain bullet hits its mark and the fox goes down where he stood. His tail twitches twice as Gary chambers another round and checks through the scope; but this fox isn't going anywhere.

A couple of hours later another set of eyes shows in the other gateway. Once again this fox heads up to the left, and disappears from view behind a chicken shed. Again Gary calls and after a short wait it comes in on an almost identical line. This one is moving faster, though, and Gary is worried it might discover the dead fox and run off in fright.

Gary doesn't hang about; the fox hesitates and he fires. It's an almost identical shot and the second fox lies stretched out, nose into the wind, a few yards behind the first one.

Normally Gary would wait on well into the night. Often the first fox doesn't appear until near midnight, and they can still come in at six or seven in the morning. But tonight he has chores to attend to, so he's glad of the chance to finish here early.

He climbs down and collects the fallen foxes: they are a dog and a vixen, both good, healthy specimens with thick coats and no sign of diseases such as mange. Gary is pleased – even though he spends so much time trying to kill foxes, he had the utmost respect for them and likes to see a healthy population. He gives them a pat almost lovingly as he checks their claws and teeth for clues about how they have lived: "This big old boy has long claws," he muses. "He's not spent much time on the streets – a proper country fox."

The farmer will be happy to hear of Gary's success in the morning, knowing his turkeys are that bit safer. And Gary will be back several times between now and Christmas, making sure those turkeys end up on the dinner table surrounded by trimmings rather than making a meal for a hungry fox. ∎

BACK UP THE HIGH SEAT

Gary Green had some catching up to do. On top of the usual demands of Christmas and New Year, he'd spent a few days away in Orkney shooting geese. With all that and the need to protect the turkeys at the local free-range poultry farm, he hadn't spent as much time as usual at his other permissions. He just knew that the foxes would be taking advantage, especially at the time of year when the dog foxes are on the move.

So it was no surprise when he learned that a fox was causing trouble on the farm where his chiller is located. He stopped by for a chat with the farmer, who told him that this particular fox was taking too much interest in his waterfowl collection. To add insult to injury, it was making a mess of the farmer's garden, scratching things up and defecating all over the place.

You can't blame the fox for its territorial behaviour, Gary points out. It's just doing what comes naturally. But this isn't about

crime and punishment – it's dealing with problems as necessary. To the farmer, this fox has become a problem and he expects Gary to remove it.

Gary already has a permanent high seat set up overlooking the field next to his chiller. It's built into the hedge that runs alongside the farm track. The front of the seat follows the hedgeline, and there's a tree in front that helps hide Gary when he's inside. It looks out across the centre of the field to a narrow spinney on the far side, about 140 yards away.

The entire field is within range of the seat, but Gary prefers to make extra sure so he plans to draw this fox to a bait point 70 yards out, directly in front of the seat. That will allow him to place the shot with pinpoint precision, making absolutely certain of an instant kill.

It's also close enough that he can check for grass or weed stems in front of the quarry. Gary is using fast, light bullets in his Geco .223 ammunition. They fragment on

GARY'S TOP TIP

Shooting down from a high position reduces the chance of the bullet hitting an obstruction

171

impact, giving superb knock-down power and eliminating any risk of ricochets – an important consideration in this densely populated part of Essex.

The flipside of the coin is that the bullet will start to disintegrate if it hits a stem in front of the target. That could mean a miss, or worst-case scenario, hitting the fox with fragments of the broken-up bullet. Shooting down from a high position helps reduce that risk, and Gary regularly strims the grass down in his bait area, but it's good to be able to make that last-minute visual check.

Today Gary has only a brief window before he has other business to attend to, but it seems worth a go. He can try for the fox late afternoon, and wait until daylight fails. If that doesn't work, he'll have to think again – but he reckons it's worth grabbing the brief opportunity to try to deal with this problem fox quickly. If it works, the farmer will be impressed and it will take a bit of pressure off.

The plan is to use a combination of sound, sight and scent to bring the fox out. Gary sets up his Foxpro electronic caller, set to his favourite call: 'cottontail distress'. The caller allows him to select the front and back speakers individually, and today he elects to

switch them both on – the fox could come from any direction today, and with Gary up in the high seat it won't matter if it comes from behind. "Foxes certainly seem to sense the direction of the speaker," he comments. "Wind direction is important too, of course, but often they will line themselves up and come straight in line with the speaker. You can use that to bring them along a tramline to give you an easier shot."

With the caller set up and checked, Gary turns his attention to the 'sight and scent' part. He's brought a leftover turkey carcase that's been festering in the bin for a while. It certainly hums a bit, even to a human nose, so any fox downwind should find it interesting. Plus it's going to stand out like a white beacon in the field, which will give the fox something to focus on.

"Foxes are curious creatures, and they are fascinated by a bit of white in a field," Gary explains. "They're always keen to check it out. I sometimes use a bit of white fur or feathers in conjunction with the caller. It's even better if you can give them a little movement, perhaps tying them to a springy stick so they jig about in the wind."

This turkey carcase is quite a lump so it won't be jigging in the wind, but he has brought a hide pole so he can set it up above the height of the grass. It's important to remember that the fox's point of view is much closer to the ground than ours. Placing the carcase on the stick at about 18-inches high will ensure the fox can see that intriguing white object from the edge of the field. Combined with the scent and sound, that should pique Charlie's curiosity and keep his focus on the bait point rather than any tiny sound or movement in the high seat.

Gary takes one last look round to check everything is right, then heads back to the track and climbs into the high seat. After a minute or two to let things settle down, he begins calling – quietly at first in case there's a fox nearby. The remote control allows him

to stop and start the call at will, as well as changing the volume. That's important when a fox appears, because he will want to use it subtly depending on how the fox reacts.

"It's down to experience really," he says. "I can tell by the way a fox acts whether it's a bold one that will come rushing in, or one that's shy and cautious. Some don't need any more encouragement, but with others I'll need to call a couple of times to persuade them out into the open."

As the sun sinks in the sky, the magpies and jays beyond the spinney start to kick up a racket, and Gary goes on alert. The rasping alarm calls probably mean a fox is on the prowl. Blackbirds raise alarm calls too, and it's looking promising. Gary calls again, but nothing appears.

Gradually the light fails and still the fox hasn't shown up. Gary is confident it will come eventually, but he deliberately didn't bring his night vision because other jobs are pressing and he didn't want to be tempted to hang on. He calls it a day, collects the caller and leaves the carcase in place. "Next time I'll try an early morning stint, I think," he says. "If that doesn't work I'll come in the evening and bring the night vision – then I can stay out as long as it takes." One thing's for sure: Gary won't give up until he's got this fox. It can only be a matter of time.

Other demands take their toll on his time, and Gary can't get back to the spot for a couple of days. But he wants to keep the bait topped up. He spots a roadkill muntjac at the side of the road – just the job. He throws it in the back of his Land Rover and drops by the field on his way home.

"Would you believe it?" says Gary. "I pull up at 3.30 in the afternoon, in broad daylight – and there's the fox in the middle of the field looking at me as if to say 'Where's my dinner?'"

The fox trots away to the hedge as Gary pulls up, but it isn't going far. Gary sets out the muntjac bait and retreats to the vehicle.

The fox is still skulking in the undergrowth at the far side of the field, and Gary's sure it won't wait long. He slips into the hedge by the track, and creeps along to the high seat using a well-worn deer run inside the hedge.

Climbing into the high seat from the back, he gets into position and makes ready. Within seconds the fox is boldly trotting across to check out the new bait. As he stops for a sniff, the crosshairs are already on his chest. Bang, job done.

"That must be one of the easiest foxes I've ever shot," Gary laughs. "There will be more; there always are. But at least I've got one to show for my efforts and that will reassure the farmer that I'm on the case." ∎

REACHING NEW HEIGHTS

ANDY
MALCOLM

ANDY'S **TOP TIP**
Cover all eventualities
when packing your
gear for foxing trips

When foxing season arrives, it brings with it the realisation that I'll be walking the beat again. I remember an occasion when my five colleagues and I met up early and set off without delay, knowing we had a tiring and full day in front of us.

I suspected we would find a den. I'd been seeing signs of foxes right through the winter. Despite this, I'd never once had a flash of an eye in the light. This meant either the foxes were keeping well away from civilisation (and my ground has plenty scope for that), or they were as lamp-shy as they get. I feared the latter.

All was going well. We'd checked a couple of major cairns, and the terriers had come up with nothing but an unlucky rabbit. From there we spread out into an extended line to work right out one side of the glen. My place was at the top of the line and I had a long, very steep climb to get to my position.

Right:
Once you've found
a shooting position,
it's worth protecting it
from the elements

The steam was still coming off me when the radio crackled with the news that one of the lads had come across a fresh kill. Within yards I saw one of my terriers sniffing at something among the coarse yellow grass. On investigation, it turned out to be a scat so fresh it was nearly steaming as much as I was.

"Oh, no," I thought to myself. "Not the top warren. Anything but the top warren!" A chill ran through me that had nothing to do with the brisk north wind and the 2,000 feet of altitude. A while later the slope opened out and I watched in trepidation as two of the lads converged on the hollow where this last outpost of rabbitdom lay. Even from 200 yards away I could see their demeanour change.

"They're here," came the announcement over the airwaves. I made my way down to join them and my heart made its way down to my boots.

We tried a couple of terriers in succession down the scraped-out rabbit hole. After an initial bout of enthusiasm they quickly became bored. The vixen wasn't home. We stood back with

the guns and gave it a while, just in case. As we waited, my eyes were drawn, time and again, to the microscopic speck in the distance that was the Land Rover. It was parked at the nearest accessible point – a couple of miles and 1,200 feet away.

When my eyes weren't lingering on the Rover, they were leaving the sandhole and scanning around, searching fruitlessly for a vantage point that would give a clear view of the approaches to the den. Which was just plain daft, really – it was still the blind swine of a place it always had been.

After a couple of hours it was decided that we best move on. There was an awful lot of ground still to be checked. Furthermore, I would have to be back out at this place by early evening in an attempt to catch the vixen coming in before dark.

It was late afternoon by the time we returned to the Rover. It had been a hard day, and for most of us it was only just getting started. Unusually, we'd found another den in a cairn

175

right at the head of the glen. There would be two pairs of us heading back out onto the hill as soon as we were organised.

Gus drew the short straw and was to come to the top warren with me. We arranged to meet at the farm, and scrambled off to throw our gear into bags and food down our throats. Within a couple of hours we were trudging back out to the glen. On our backs we had rifles, binoculars, radios, sleeping bags, bivvy bags, camp mats, food and drink, spotlight, battery, head torches and any extra items of clothing we deemed necessary to survive the night.

The first half of our yomp followed the centuries-old pony path that winds its way out the floor of the glen. Despite the ease of the walking, our loads ensured we had a rosy glow about us by the time we arrived at the foot of the hill. The evening light made it look dramatic… and very, very steep.

Three quarters of an hour later we arrived at the den, our faces scarlet and bathed in sweat, blowing like a couple of old carthorses. We fell to the ground and, propped in the sitting position

by our bulging rucksacks, expressed clear opinions about the place, the foxes and, well, everything else.

With our spleens well and truly vented, we hid the spare gear in a hollow, took our rifles and went off in different directions. Gus went to cover a narrow pass that led to a corrie favoured by foxes. I lay within shot of the warren.

As I settled down I was pleased to note that it was only 6.30pm. There was a good chance that, this early in the season, the vixen would be eager to return to her cubs and come in well before dark. I cranked a bullet into the chamber, got myself really comfortable and prepared for a long, motionless vigil.

Time passed slowly and the temperature dropped quickly. By the time dusk fell I was already wearing most of my 'emergency' gear. When I could no longer trust that I would spot a fox with my naked eye, I used my binoculars. When it got too dark for them, I decided to have a shine with the lamp before I moved back to the den.

I switched the lamp on and was met with the electric shine of a pair of eyes, looking over the ridge 100 yards to my left. In an instant the fox ducked out of sight. If I had blinked I would have missed it. I got on the radio to Gus, telling him to stay put in case he scared her off on his return to

camp. Then I waited what seemed like an eternity before trying the lamp again.

To cut a long, frustrating story short, the fox didn't put another appearance in until signs of dawn were appearing on the horizon. Gus had joined me and we'd kept our vigil going through the night. We lay quietly and shone the light around every 15 minutes or so. We got up and searched about on that horrible rounded slope. We tried playing various calls – all to no avail.

When she eventually did appear, she started moving off as soon as the light hit her. She ducked into a hollow, heading left, then inexplicably appeared on top of the rim of the hollow to the right. I couldn't believe my luck as she stood broadside, looking down the hollow. I was already into the rifle and wasted no time. I placed the crosshairs behind her shoulder and took up the pressure on the trigger.

The muzzle flash obscured my vision for an instant as the shot boomed across the hillside. A fraction of a second later the distinctive 'smack' of a solid hit echoed through the blackness. When the crosshairs returned from the recoil, the fox had vanished. I cycled the bolt and watched through the scope as Gus held the beam on the place. After a few seconds the beam flicked left then right, checking that the fox wasn't sneaking off out of the beam. Nothing moved.

After a minute, I opened the bolt and replaced the spent round. With the magazine full and the breech empty, we made our way slowly up the hill. A biting wind had got up in the night and we were frozen, tired and stiff. I reckoned the range to be 150 yards; my legs told me 300. Was I ever glad when we found the fox lying where it had dropped. Too tired to speak, Gus patted me on the shoulder. We were both relieved.

As I squatted to inspect our victim, a couple of things became apparent. The first was how high in her shoulder the exit wound was. I put this down to the steep uphill shot. The second was that she was a he. The more I thought about it, the more I reckoned the pair had been there together and it was the lamp-shy vixen that had headed away through the hollow. And if she was spooky before, having her mate shot within yards of her would have her on tenterhooks now.

We lamped for the rest of the night and spied the surrounding hills through dawn. There wasn't a trace of her.

Gus and I returned the next night despite of a poor weather forecast. We sat up on that hill and were blasted by wind and sleet and obscured by mist for half the night. The wily vixen never showed once. If I hadn't had the foresight to take a tent, she would be up there picking our bones right now. ■

COSTLY FOXES

ANDY'S TOP TIP

All the equipment
in the world can't
guarantee success
when foxing

In the days of yore, it was my destiny – or so it appeared – to chat up vegetarians at parties. Oblivious, I would apply the time-honoured mix of smarm and Babycham. Time and again, my lager-fuelled efforts would prove futile.

It was inevitable that, at some stage, I would be asked: "So, what do you do for a living?" And, unsuspectingly, I would tell them. The transformation would be instantaneous.

One second they would seem as approachable as a stoat-transfixed rabbit (did I mention lager?), the next they would be looking at me like I'd just grown an extra eye in the middle of my forehead.

To their minds, gamekeepers spent their lives marching through the countryside, leaving the cute and cuddly slain in their wake. Oh, if they could see me now, I remember thinking as I trudged over the glens.

We had two foxes, working massive areas on the north of the estate, and we couldn't get to grips with them. Day after day I had watched the sun come up from my hilltop lookout post. Day after day I'd trudged back down cold, hungry and frustrated at the end of the morning. Either there would have been no show from either fox, or one will have been glimpsed before disappearing into an area of hags never to be seen again.

We'd tried various tactics. We thought maybe driving out in the quiet pre-dawn might be disturbing them. So we went out the evening before, spied until dark and spent the night in place. To no avail. We'd tried joint manoeuvres with the keepers on the neighbouring estate. Several times we've cast a huge 'net' with them. A couple of times a fox was seen. One of those times a lad was even moving in and within 400 yards when a fluke in the light morning breeze put the kibosh on proceedings. It was time to call in the big guns.

Stalking a fox on the open hill, in daylight, is the most difficult form of hunting I have ever experienced. As such, Byron Pace thought it would be a great thing to try and film for The Shooting Show. A couple of dawn vigils later and he had little more than some brief footage of a fox taken at a range of about a mile. He also had a greater appreciation of the enormity of the task, and some serious bags under his eyes!

But, if nothing else, Byron is well connected. He pledged to do some string pulling before his next visit and he was true to his word.

Between Byron's hectic schedule and some good old Scottish weather, more than a week passed before we could give it the green light. Byron had been worried that we'd clean up the foxes in the interim. Fat chance! We only got out for a couple of mornings due to mist and rain, and on both mornings had drawn a blank.

It was midnight when he next rocked up to the house. We were within a few days of midsummer so it was just getting properly dark. As he transferred a ton of kit to my Land Rover I strained to get a glimpse of the gear he'd brought with him. Eventually he came out with the star of the show – an ISS T-iV HRX thermal imaging viewer. Before I could get my eager paws on it, Byron warned me just how much it would cost to replace. I wiped my palms nervously before taking it gently from his grasp.

In the gloaming, the size of it reminded me of the massive binoculars you find bolted to structures like the Blackpool Tower. In reality, it was far lighter than I could have imagined. This

and its flimsy-feeling plastic housing gave it a toy-like feel. "Some toy," I thought to myself as Byron ran through the functions of the buttons on the top of the unit.

Looking through it, my first impressions were a little disappointing. Almost completely surrounded by trees, the only open ground showed through the eyepieces as a ghostly grey blanket. It is usually hoaching with rabbits but either they weren't there, or this was one seriously large white elephant. It was time to take it for a 'toor aboot'.

I drove us to a good vantage point in one of the main glens on the estate. The night was now as black as it was going to get. We climbed out to avoid interference from the hot Land Rover and fired the unit up.

The hillsides around us were strewn with rocks, and their residual heat had them glowing pale grey against the darker grey background. I thought this was going to confuse matters until I picked up my first 'proper' white dots. From the shape of them I could tell straight away they were deer. What really wowed me was that, knowing the ground, they must have been 800 yards away. I whistled softly and continued my scan.

The unit picked up deer, sheep and rabbits all over the place. At one point I think I even picked up a weasel partially obscured by vegetation. It vanished before we could get a spotlight on it to confirm its identity.

The more I looked, the more my brain made sense of what I was seeing. Pretty quickly it instilled in me the confidence to say that there was nothing in this area. We moved on. Over the next hour we covered a lot of ground. Despite this, we only saw one other heat signature of interest. It was long and low and very 'busy'. It was also many of hundreds of yards away.

Suspecting it was a stoat – or possibly a mink – we took off to investigate. This is when another of Byron's goodies caught my eye. This was a scope-mounted lamp made by 4Greer and I was utterly amazed by the amount of light this torch-sized unit chucked out. I was in no doubt that you could shoot out to 300 yards with it. Byron informed me that this one, with its extra battery capacity, would

last for about four hours. I thought of the miles I'd trudged carrying my old lead-plate battery and saucepan-sized lamp. Poor Byron was in serious danger of being mugged.

By the time we'd walked out, the stoat was nowhere to be seen. The night was also wearing on, so we didn't hang about. We made our way back to the Land Rover and started rattling our way to the north march.

Within the hour, we were in stealth mode and clambering the last couple of hundred feet to the top of the highest hill for miles around. To take our minds off the climb we started discussing the value of the gear we had with us. The two rifles and accessories came to £8,000; Swarovski binoculars and my Gray's telescope came to £3,000; Byron placed a value of £27,000 on the thermal imager; added to that was the film camera and tripod, stills cameras, rangefinder, and radios. As a self-confessed kit-o-phobe, I was stunned when the tally came to £40,000. And that was without taking the Land Rover into account!

Our number crunching passed into insignificance as we reached the top of the hill. We were now at 3,000 feet and a paleness was creeping onto the eastern horizon. Even in this light, the view was spectacular. On three sides, the hills and glens of the Grampians stretched into the distance. To the east we could see the hills drop away to the farmland and the North Sea beyond. We must have been able to see 50 miles.

Sitting down to spy, the thermal imager clicked into life and all was revealed. Again I was impressed at the distance it covered. I was also surprised at how readily I could identify the blobs on the screen, either by their shape or the way they moved. The unit did have the capacity to increase magnification up to 8x, but this was mostly unnecessary and we both found that after 4x the image got horribly pixellated.

Right through the morning we spied, taking a turn about with the TIV and binoculars. Every 30 minutes we moved position to scan in a different direction. As the morning warmed up, the most distant heat signatures became less distinct. Despite this, the feeling remained that nothing could escape the gaze of this unit. Yet we still drew a blank. I guess you just can't buy luck.

Checking the map, I know that I was picking up red deer at nearly three kilometres. But this unit can't see behind hills or through peat hags, and that's where the foxes must have been this morning. Locating them would have just been the first hurdle, too. Covering the distance then stalking them in terrain like that is a nightmare – and often about as productive as chatting up vegetarians. ■

DOG TIRED

On 15 April each year, I start to lose those few marbles I still possess. I go into rooms and forget what I went in for. I get tongue-tied and spout gibberish. It's all down to sleep deprivation and the anti-social hours these floody boxes keep.

It's den time and, traditionally, 15 April is when we start checking our sandholes. Any earlier than this and we might visit before the vixen has set up home. If that happens, all we do is disturb an empty hole. When she returns, she'll realise the game is up and relocate, perhaps to a place we don't know of.

Leave it too late, however, and we still won't catch her in. The cubs will be big enough that she'll be spending the day lying up away from the den. No, in an ideal world, we find her at home and the terrier bolts her to our shotguns. But the dog fox will still be at large, and that is normally where the rifle comes into play.

During the first few weeks of raising a litter, dog foxes tend to spend very little time at the den. Their visits are often confined to fleeting food-drops during the small hours. So, while I'm enjoying a daytrip to the ideal world, let's have the dog fox come to the den – and my crosshairs – at dusk.

Reality, I'm sad to say, usually bears little resemblance to this. For whatever reason, the foxes in these parts are usually super-sly. That means in practice, early in the season, our adult foxes rarely appear at the den before dark.

Despite this, we'll spend the last hours of daylight lying motionless within shot of the den. And if that act of pure optimism doesn't work, the 'stake-out' continues by lamping – right through the night, if necessary. More often than not, we'll spend a series of nights without so much as a flash of eyes. Sure, we'll know there is a fox about, we'll hear the alarm calls of grouse and curlew out in the darkness, but elusive is the key word.

If the vixen is still at large, her maternal instincts will usually get the better of her by the second or third night. If it's the dog, we can often find

ANDY'S TOP TIP

Once you've spotted your fox, don't take your eye off it

ourselves pulling the jack-plug on him after five fruitless nights. But that's not to say we've given up on him altogether. We have other tricks up our tweed sleeves.

Once we've dealt with our sandholes, our next step is to walk the ground. The places that get our attention first are the steep, rocky faces that foxes love and ankles hate. My six colleagues and I walk along these faces in a widely spaced line. We carry shotguns and let our terriers work the ground. Virtually every year this method locates a den in some small cairn or crack in a rock face that has never been known before. Furthermore, this process will often produce a solitary fox that's chosen a heathery ledge for its bed.

My favourite position in the line is right at the top. When doing this, I'll often carry both rifle and shotgun and keep well out in front. In such broken terrain, it's easy for a fox to get round a corner or along a ledge without giving the lads on the face the chance of a shot. If that happens, the rifleman suddenly finds himself drinking alone in the Last Chance Saloon. In all likelihood it will be a steep downhill shot at a moving target taken from some lofty perch. Better make that a double, bartender.

We will end up walking most of the 50,000 acres that make up this estate. Yes, there are

areas without any nooks that can be used for a den. They might not get looked over – but that doesn't mean they are overlooked. They'll certainly come under scrutiny when it comes to our third tactic: the early morning wait.

As spring progresses to summer, foxes are hit by a double whammy. Firstly, as the cubs grow they need more and more food. Secondly, the hours of darkness get less and less. By the time we reach midsummer, even those foxes without young – and those that possibly eluded us at dens – have only four hours of darkness to ply their trade.

The nub of this is that most foxes are forced into being active in the evenings and mornings. And so, therefore, are we. The theory is simplicity itself: get yourself up onto a hilltop, spy until you see a fox, and go and shoot the blighter. As ever, putting theory into practice is anything but straightforward.

We begin our early morning ambushes from the start of the season. We're out whenever we have a clear, bright morning. If we've spent the night fruitlessly staking out a den, we'll often head up to a vantage point at daybreak. From there we might just pick up our difficult customer heading off to its daytime hideaway.

Initially, these 'dawn raids' are no great hardship. We start by spying our 'in by' ground. It might only take a 20-minute hop in the Land Rover to get from vestibule to viewpoint. However, as the season progresses, daybreak gets earlier and earlier and our 'commutes' get longer and longer. Eventually, it gets to the point where we have to get up an hour before we go to bed. When we reach this stage, we'll often sleep out on the hill.

If we're going to do this, we head out well before last light. There is always the chance of picking up a fox in the evening. However, the sheer scale of the ground is often a major hurdle. Many is the keeper who has eventually arrived, panting and sweaty, at Tod's last known location only to find he's run out of light. To add injury to insult, that sweat will also make for an uncomfortable night once he's stumbled back to base.

I far prefer the mornings. Sunrise in the hills on a tranquil morning can be stunning – if you're not already stunned by your 3am alarm. But a breathtaking dawn isn't the only incentive to lumber from your slumbers. You've also got the anticipation of the most challenging form of hunting that I know – stalking a fox on the open hill in daylight.

By their nature, foxes tend to be on the move a lot. And they use every bit of cover available to them. Often when you spy for them, you pick them up at more than a mile away. Invariably, as you move in on the animal, you will drop into dead ground. You get back into sight of the place as quickly as you can, but reacquiring your target after a lapse of even 10 minutes can be a nightmare. Is he still in the hollow where you last saw him? Or is he round the back of the hill by now?

If he's still in that hollow and you are hurrying to get to a look at the next bit of ground, the chances are he'll come up to periscope depth and spot you. Then he'll be long gone and you won't even know it. Likewise, you could be painstakingly stalking the hollow while he's trotting off over some distant horizon. To counter this, we often

work in teams. Two or three of us will be on different hilltops and in radio contact. If a fox is spotted, one person will move while the others try to keep tabs on the fox. With emphasis on the 'try'.

The general rule is that if you're a 'spotter' and you pick up a fox, you don't take your eyes off it. Not for a pee, not to locate the radio, not even to stop your terrier gnawing the walnut stock on your Rigby. Even then, poor light, broken ground or distance can stymie you. Or the fox can simply disappear into an area nobody is covering.

For an estate like this, the fox tops our 'most wanted' list by a long way. The damage they can do to our grouse stocks can be devastating, especially during the breeding season. Every time I stalk a fox I'm aware of this fact. I'm also acutely aware of how many man-hours it takes to get a fox into my crosshairs. All this, along with the simple truth that the fox is the most artful, sneakiest adversary I know, means my heart is always thumping when I'm after one. I wouldn't want it any other way. ■

Below:
The terriers are sent to bolt the foxes out into the path of Andy's gun

183

GROUP MANOEUVRES

ANDY'S TOP TIP

Make use of the
intel provided by
neighbouring shooters

I can't believe it when the alarm clock goes off. There is no way my night's sleep can be over already – but it is. I stumble downstairs like I'm auditioning for *Dawn of The Living Dead* – except that dawn is still over an hour away. My preparations are made entirely on autopilot. Before I slip out the door I've just surfaced enough to mumble through my mantra. Rifle, check. Bolt, check. Bullets, check. Binoculars and telescope, check. Radio, check. Terrier, check. Flask of tea, check. Time: 2.45am.

As I step outside, my nostrils fill with that unique scent that you only get by a highland river on a summer night. It smacks of warm peat and cool air, birch woods and bog myrtle. The first flush of the pre-dawn shows a cloudless sky. There isn't a sound. It's going to be a stunning morning and I start to feel alive.

As the crow flies, I have barely five miles to go, but it still takes nearly an hour. Crows don't have to contend with gates or Land Rover tracks. This particular track climbs 1,500 feet, and the precipitous drops mean the only thing tighter than the hairpins is your bum cheeks as you negotiate them. Unsurprisingly, I'm wide awake by the time I reach my destination.

It's a fantastic vantage point overlooking a vast area. It's also near where we march with

Above:

The stars of the show: Ed the terrier, a wily ex-Charlie and the beautiful Scottish highlands

two neighbouring estates. On a morning like this, *every* keeper for miles around is out. By arrangement we've agreed to use a 'mutual' radio channel. That's a lot of keen eyes, spying many thousands of acres of hill. I just know there's going to be some action.

I've timed it well. Although the sun is still below the horizon, there is enough light to start spying the nearest hills. It seems that I barely have time to focus my binoculars before I get a call on the radio. Neighbours have spotted a fox and I might be in a position to help. I fire up the Land Rover and head towards the march.

I take the vehicle as far as I can, then leg it from there. Twenty minutes later I'm settling in just below the summit of Scotland's most easterly Munro. The sun is rising and the view would be breathtaking, if I had any breath left to take after the climb.

The latest bulletin tells me the fox has joined its mate and they are on the move. I follow their progress on the airwaves and realise they should be coming up onto a face within sight of me. It's a steep face of scree, long heather and juniper thickets. It's also a long way from where I'm sitting, and the low sun has cast it in deep shadow. I spy hard enough to make my eyes bleed but I can't pick these foxes up.

My concentration is broken by a grouse 'tukking' somewhere over to my left. I spy in that direction but it's impossible to gauge how far the sound has travelled in this deathly hush. The grouse goes quiet and I can see nothing bar a pair of hinds. I put it down to a territory dispute and focus again on the gloom of that distant hill.

Minutes later the grouse fires up again. This time I see the hinds glaring intently at some hags. I follow the line of their stares and get the briefest glimpse of a fox worming through the network of peat banks and runners. I send out an alert on the radio and sweep the hags for another glimpse.

Unfortunately, this area of hags spreads for hundreds of yards in every direction, with plenty of hidden exits. After spying for 10 minutes I'm starting to worry that this fox has given me the slip. I lower my binoculars to get the bigger picture. Ed, my terrier, is looking fixedly down the hill. Immediately I pick up the fox. He's less than 400 yards away and contouring round below me.

For the briefest of moments I consider a long shot, but this fox has a trot on and the distance is increasing with every second. I decide to gamble on getting a better chance. As the fox trots around the slope and out of my sight I'm mightily relieved to hear that Colin, next door's head keeper, has moved position and has picked it up.

From two miles off, Colin watches the fox as it works its way quickly down the hill. Then it drops into the shade of a vast bowl and he loses it. I've also been moving and can now see down to the rim of this bowl. Between us, we feel as if we should have the exits covered. Maybe. We wait, bathed in golden sunlight and nagging doubt.

We hear the other foxes have disappeared amid the junipers. We decide to try to drive the face out, but it's a big area to cover. Colin puts out a request for help and it's heartening to hear keepers responding from far and wide.

But now we have to make a decision about our fox. If we knew where it was, I could stalk it. Or if we were certain it was in there somewhere, we could walk it up with shotguns. But we're not certain and we're needed elsewhere. I agree to walk it through, despite only having the rifle with me.

I walk down to the rim of the bowl and ready myself. My radio is turned right down and placed in a breast pocket. I check the magazine has its full complement and – unusually for me – I place a fourth round in the chamber and slip the safety on. If I end up shooting a bolting fox, I might be glad of that extra bullet.

With my heart in my mouth I start off down the hill. In this hush, each footfall is placed with infinite care. Every yard I stop and scan the bed of deep heather around me, searching for the slightest tinge of red. I'm dismayed to see how many bumps and deep hollows there are in here

As I make my painstaking way down the hill, Colin keeps radio silence. Finally, I there's a barely audible "I last saw it 20 yards to your left." I turn across the steep slope, my eyes darting everywhere.

I get barely five paces when the fox explodes out of the heather up to my left. As I lift my rifle and slide the safety off, I'm all too aware that the fox only has 30 yards to go before he is on the skyline. I pick up the thin line of him visible above the heather and – as

he is going slightly left-handed – put the cross at the point of his left shoulder and pull the trigger.

There's no sound of a strike, and the fox keeps going. Somewhere in my head, among the sirens and flashing lights, a calm voice says, "He doesn't need any lead at this range, stupid." It then adds, "And you'll have to get it right this time or he's gone" – in case there wasn't enough pressure.

Somehow the loaded rifle is into my shoulder again and the crosshairs find the base of the fox's outstretched neck. He's now five yards from the skyline. This time, when the rifle kicks there is a deep 'thump' to the shot. When the crosshairs settle back from the recoil, only his motionless tail is visible above the heather. Relief washes over me.

Experience tells me to fill the magazine pronto, but this middle-aged dog is very much dead. I sit down while my pulse returns to double figures and my legs regain some substance. Nothing would be nicer than to sit there and bask in the glow – inside and out – but there's work to do.

I walk for an hour to a point where I can be picked up by Land Rover. From there it's another hour to the rendezvous point. When everyone has gathered, another hour of driving and walking sees us at the last known address for the pair of foxes.

I'm a walking gun. Halfway along the face, Ed points a juniper bush. For the second time today I kick myself at not having brought the shotgun. When the fox bolts I'm unable to shoot anyway; he tears down the hill directly in line with the next gun. Then, as only foxes can, he finds the smallest of hollows and escapes the net. The other is never seen.

When the dust has settled and the fat has been chewed, I'm taxied back up to the march. Another long trudge finds me back at my Land Rover, 13 hours after I left it. On the passenger seat is my flask of cold tea. No matter, it is drained anyway. That makes two of us. ■

AFTER DARK

ANDY LOVEL

ANDY'S TOP TIP

Be adaptable: any hunting trip should turn into a foxing one if the landowner asks for your help

I was away on one of my stalking jaunts north of Hadrian's Wall across lands once roamed by the infamous Border Reivers. This area covers 2,500 acres of forestry and moorland that runs down to a vast valley bottom predominantly grazed by sheep.

This particular weekend was really a bid to compile a census of the deer population. My fellow syndicate members and I have found the best way to achieve this annual count is with the aid of night vision combined with a number of trail cameras. However, at the time I still had the Guide IR on test. This fantastic piece of kit had more than proved its worth on the low-ground and I was keen to give it a go on the hill. That said, I was also here to do a bit of stalking, and,

as the freezer was rapidly becoming devoid of red meat, I was keen to grass a beast first. The weekend started slowly, and having stalked the south side without success, I decided to cross the river and stalk the north side during the evening.

I stopped en route to speak to the resident shepherd, who seems to be about at all hours. At 70 years old, he is as fit and keen as a man half his age. Pleasantries were exchanged and the conversation soon got round to foxes. As one would expect, he hates them with a vengeance, and was experiencing a lot of lamb losses. He asked if it would it be possible for me to do something about it. I certainly could, so I left him with a firm promise to deal with the culprit and turned about to head back to the vehicle.

It was now late afternoon as I climbed into the Hilux and made my way up the winding forest road. Pulling up, I checked two trail cams on the moor edge where the road petered out. These trail cams are dotted about the estate and help me to get an idea of numbers and sex ratio and make decisions on how best to stalk the ground. The snap shots revealed two roe does, a nice six-point buck and a fox regularly passing by. When I say regular I mean every day – the actual time recorded was rather irregular. Despite the absence of a more defined time pattern, I decided to set up an ambush.

I positioned the pick-up along the forest edge, about 100 yards from a ride exit onto the open hill. It was a warm, pleasant evening, made all the better by the relaxing sound of displaying

blackcock nearby, their behaviour no doubt brought on by the balmy weather. The buck captured on camera made a fleeting visit, but I passed him by in favour of a chance at my main quarry.

Day turned into dusk and even my top-quality optics started to struggle. It was time to attach my Archer NV unit on to the back of the Kahles scope, making it instantly usable in total darkness. Although I had now set my stall out for fox only, my original intention was for roe. I was using my .222 bull pup as in Scotland it is legal to use this calibre on roe. I have always found that this is an accurate and pleasant cartridge to shoot, and cannot understand why the law is not the same south of the border.

The Archer has been a godsend for our deer census work and is incredibly versatile as it turns any day scope into night vision using a bayonet fitting. The Guide IR thermal imager, meanwhile, is amazing, revealing wildlife activity you would never normally see. I amused myself watching the abundant vole population scurrying through the long grass. To my immediate right, the sheep I was endeavouring to protect were easily visible through the thermal imager to a fair distance. It was entertaining and interesting to observe how the sheeps' heads and legs shone brightly, yet their insulated bodies gave little heat signature away.

I could see a roe in the tree line well over 100 yards away with the Guide, but looking through the NV revealed only trees. It wasn't until it left the safety of cover that the night vision actually picked it up. For the next few hours everything was quiet apart from the occasional vocals of a male tawny owl lower down in the valley.

With another sweep of the Guide, I spotted a fox-sized blob about 300 yards into the sheep field and heading my way. Mounting the rifle, I tracked its progress across the field, making its way towards one of my trail cameras. I was determined that this lamb-killing vulpine would only get on film once more, and that would be with me holding it by the scruff of its neck.

A single squeak from me and it stopped to stare in my direction. The half second the fox took deciding its next course of action was all that I needed. The feather-light recoil of my moderated .222 allowed me to observe everything that followed. Pleasingly, the fox was standing broadside, so I aimed for the middle of its chest and pressed the bull pup's button trigger. The satisfying sound of the bullet strike saw the menace drop on the spot with legs kicking and tail flicking wildly.

It was a job well done, and one that would have been a great deal harder without the use of the thermal imager and the NV. But one of the downsides of having kit that works 24 hours a day is that my body struggles to keep up with it. As daylight wasn't far away, I had to make the decision of whether to wait for the new day and a chance at the roe buck or to retire and get some badly needed sleep. In reality it was a foregone conclusion: I decided to forgo what the body cried out for and began a new vigil for a six-point roebuck in the rapidly approaching dawn. ■

FOXING DOUBLE

ANDY'S **TOP TIP**
For the serious fox shooter, a thermal imager is a smart investment

It was the same old story: a friend rang me to ask if I would deal with a fox problem, as the smallholding next door had lost some chickens. My mate wanted the culprit brought to book post-haste as he feared the vulpine villain would soon turn its attention towards his own geese.

The field I'd be working in was 22 acres in extent, and the oversized paddock currently contained 14 ewes and my mate's two precious geese. The sheep were safe enough, but the geese had started to lay. If things went like the year before, as soon as the goose started to sit, the fox would turn its homicidal attentions towards her. We had gone through this same scenario the year before, and I had been too late to stop the then three geese turning into the present two. It was embarrassing to say the least, and a long-lasting friendship was now at stake, not to mention my reputation.

One of the discarded chicken carcases was 20 yards into the paddock. I had a good idea the culprit would be back the next night, so another pal Steve Coultas and I set up in the pick-up 120 yards downwind from the remnants of the fox's most recent crime. I was using my Archer monocular attached to the Kahles scope, effectively turning the day scope into a night vision unit. The Guide IR thermal imager would function as the spotter to locate the offending fox who would then hopefully fall to my single-shot Pfeifer bullpup in .222 Remington.

I had been smitten with the thermal imager from the first time I'd used it – and it had consistently proven its worth in the field. Unlike night vision, this sees heat, detecting animals partly hidden by trees, grass and the like. It won't see through walls but it will see through light foliage. It does, therefore, have practical daylight applications for some shooters too.

Below:
A fox that otherwise
would have escaped
if not for the
thermal imager

The Guide unit we were using was the 518b. I found it could detect hares out to 300 yards, foxes at 400 and roe deer as far as 500. Note I said detect – you would probably have to halve those distances to identify them. You would have to initially, at least, because the more you use the unit, the more proficient you become at animal identification.

Weighing in at just 500 grams, it is incredibly light and mobile, and there is a button to double the size of the image, which helps greatly with identification. Furthermore, you can switch from white hot to black hot, which helps greatly with clarity in adverse conditions.

I was regularly scanning the hedge sides with the Guide when I saw a white, fox-like shape moving towards us from behind the hedge. Switching to the rifle, I tried to locate the fox in the NV-assisted scope – but the hedge proved to be a barrier. Steve had switched role to

spotter on the Guide IR, and he immediately informed me that Charlie had fortunately come under the thorns, now at about 120 yards. I soon picked up the fox, with nose to ground, quartering towards the chicken.

Patiently I watched through the Archer as the fox stopped to stare round, completely unaware of our presence. I squeezed off the shot and it dropped on the spot to the 50-grain Sako soft point. The feisty round did the business. A closer inspection revealed an average-sized vixen; the night was still young, so we waited out for the possibility of the dog fox risking his brush.

The ewes decided to bed down and chew the cud about 20 yards in front of the pick-up. I spent the next couple of hours watching the wildlife. A barn owl floated over the paddock, and even early season bats stood out like mobile white blobs in the Guide IR viewer. Steve was now in charge of the rifle. He had accompanied me on many foxing forays, and he was ready to take his first fox.

Deploying the Mini Colibri fox caller, I let the 'hare in distress' call screech out into the night. Soon after, I saw the ewes turn as one towards the fence on our left through the Guide IR viewer. Turning my attention to this area revealed a fox trotting along the fence line. Steve was already following it with the night vision.

I cranked up the Colibri caller once more, but on a lower volume. Charlie stopped at about 80 yards and stared in our direction, captivated by the call. Steve composed himself and took the shot. The fox collapsed instantly with the rifle report, its rapidly flicking brush soon slowing to a permanent stop. As I suspected, the fallen vulpine proved to be a dog fox. I congratulated Steve and felt the geese were safe for now.

The Guide IR is an amazing bit of kit. Actually it's more than that – it's revolutionary. While I know it isn't cheap, for serious fox shooters it has to be a must-have. When the time came to return the test unit, it felt like I'd gone back to the dark ages. Maybe I can sell a kidney (not one of mine of course) and get one of my own – watch this space. ■

GIANT FOX

I had been asked to deal with a fox problem on a number of neighbouring smallholdings. The fox in question had lately favoured a small field containing an insecure run that held about 20 mixed breed chickens. Some of the bantams weren't using the coop, preferring instead to run the gauntlet and roost in the thick hawthorn hedge. The pond next-door had also once held 14 geese, but the rogue fox had reduced this number to just one.

On my initial investigation, the latest goose corpse had been almost completely devoured by the time I arrived, but despite my misgivings I chose to wait through the night for the marauder. Finding a suitable position with a favourable wind, I made myself comfortable and watched the sun both set and rise without sight of a fox. Clearly it had abandoned its kill.

Work and stalking commitments kept me away for a few days, leaving the fox with free rein to run riot. During my absence three more chickens had been killed, and two of the deceased still lay close by were they had been slain. I decided on another stakeout from the same position.

As time was on my side this visit, I had a flask and sandwiches to make the night-long vigil a little less of a hardship. My rifle was the Austrian-made Pfeifer bull pup in .222 – a very short single-shot rifle. It is a high-quality hunting arm and, unlike most bolt-action rifles, it is perfectly balanced and ideal for use from the confines of a vehicle cab or cramped ambush position. Even with a moderator fitted, the rifle is still very much shorter than a bolt-action, and is not muzzle-heavy.

As darkness descended and I was just draining the dregs of my first cup of tea, movement caught my attention. Reaching for the Archer Gen 3 night vision monocular, I could soon see a fox quartering the ground nervously. I am a big fan of the Archer, having used it for about four years now. A handy tip for its use: by securing it with a cord around your neck, you free up both hands to set up and work your rifle – simple but effective. In a fluid movement I quickly attached the Archer to my scope via the unit's

193

Above:
Andy stuck to the NV after the fox became wise to the lamp

bayonet fixings and found my target. It was still totally unaware of my presence, searching around for one of its earlier victims with nose to ground. Placing the crosshairs on its chest flash, I increased the pressure on the bull pup's button trigger. Off went the moderated shot, and my 40-grain Berger home load put an end to this small vixen's poultry killing habits.

It couldn't have been more than half an hour later when another pair of vulpine eyes made their way down the side of the boundary fence. Unfortunately this time they were at the wrong

side, and on land I did not have permission to shoot over. The eyes disappeared, and even using the Mini Colibri caller didn't make Charlie reappear. The Mini Colibri is a small but effective caller with adjustable volume and call settings that are easily accessible. These variations allow the caller to be used in a variety of situations and over a range of distances.

Over the years I have called in a lot more than just foxes with various calls. Owls being a regular visitor, usually it's a barn owl responding to the rodent in distress. However, this time it was a tawny owl who circled the caller, attracted by the rabbit squeak. My next visitor was definitely a first for me – a very noisy and agitated curlew on night-time manoeuvres dive-bombed my hare in distress call. Flushed with success and my position probably now untenable, I called it a night at 1am, having attracted just about everything in the area apart from a fox.

The following day I found the shepherd leaving the next field. He was not a happy man. Apparently the fox had turned its attentions to his lambing ewes, and when checking his stock he had found two badly mauled lambs. They were still alive, but both had been bitten badly at the backend, and had a fair amount of flesh missing. The only option was to put them out of their misery, as they could never have survived with such horrendous injuries.

Deploying the same gear, I stayed till 2am, when it started to rain heavily – but again I saw nothing. Over the next two weeks I visited the field a number of times, and although I saw it twice, both times the elusive fox evaded the rifle. On the first sighting, I was scanning with the Archer when suddenly I saw it walking among the resting sheep. This time I made the mistake of using the lamp – as soon as the field became illuminated, it instantly ran for the hedge. I tried to keep the fox on the edge of the beam, and hoped it would stop before going through the fence. But no such luck as it didn't even break stride, nipping under the sheep netting. I kicked myself for not turning the lamp off immediately and reverting to the Archer.

This was obviously a seasoned veteran that knew all about lamps and the dangers that come with them. So from now on it looked like I would have to stick with night vision only. The second time I crossed the marauder's path, it was 200 yards away with no backstop and going in the wrong direction. I was starting to believe this fox was destined to die of old age.

I went roe stalking that weekend and shot a buck. Unfortunately there was a lot of front-end damage owing to the bullet striking the scapula. Using this to my advantage, I salvaged all the meat I could and put the rest of the carcase out as bait. My plan at the moment, owing to my restricted schedule, was simply to wait until the bait got hit then put the precious time in. A good plan, I thought – but this fox obviously didn't like venison.

Meanwhile, my wife asked me to get a couple of rabbits as she wanted to try a new recipe. Just on the off-chance of catching up with my elusive Charlie, I took the .222 bull pup and went to the field in question. My theory was to head-shoot my two rabbits, thus keeping them fit for the table, and if foxy turned up, be suitably armed to deal with the larger target.

Soon after dark I left the pickup behind and slowly walked the fence, keeping the wind in my favour. Usually there were a good few bunnies in the far corner and tonight was no exception. The night vision monocular revealed about 20 scattered around this end of the field. Placing the rifle on my shooting sticks, I attached the Archer to the scope and settled the crosshair on the nearest rabbit's computer room and squeezed the button trigger. The outcome was very effective – basically, its head was vaporised. It was a quick, ethical kill. Rapidly reloading, I took the second rabbit in a similar fashion.

With the conies safely in the game bag, and my domestic chore taken care of, I had a quick scan around with the NV, revealing a fox staring in my direction. Amazingly, it was laid on its belly like a faithful old Labrador. Turning round, I lined up my rifle and attached the Archer, finding the fox still laid-up without a care in the world. Taking careful aim just below the eyes, I sent the 40-grain Berger on its way.

The green orbs instantly went out, hopefully indicating a good hit. I approached to find a dead dog fox, the bullet having entered through its mouth and destroyed the top three vertebrae. As soon as I saw it I noticed the sheer size of the fox, and lifting it confirmed that it had to be weighed. After the photos, I returned to the larder and weighed him in at a whopping 34½lb. Now that is a whole lot of fox. ∎

FOXING INITIATION

BYRON PACE

It always gives me great pleasure to bring new people into hunting. It is the only way we will survive in the long term, and the more people we can encourage to pick up a rifle, or indeed a shotgun, the brighter the future will be for shooting and country sports as a whole.

My good friend Edan has shot with me for many years, but had always been a shotgun man. After a few years of rabbiting and foxing with his gamekeeper brother and me, he eventually gave in to his desire to own a rifle and applied for an FAC.

Starting where most of us begin, he opted for a rimfire, with the intention of using his new .17 HMR for rabbits, hare and the occasional fox. It didn't take long for his now cherished rifle to rack up some impressive stats as we headed out week after week to curb the rabbit population – but he was yet to claim his first fox with a rifle. I promised him that the next time we bumped into our nemesis it would be his turn to chase Basil down with some high-velocity medicine. Little did we know that this opportunity was just around the corner.

Right:
Byron calls the foxes in using his hand

196

We had been asked to get to grips with some rabbits on the outskirts of a local town, as the farmer was beginning to see visible evidence of damage. Frustratingly for him, there was a railway line that cut through the centre of the farm, providing the perfect embankment for the coneys to call home. As with most railway lines, the ground either side was overgrown and inaccessible, making any pest control attempts difficult. The only real option was to head out with a lamp and catch them in the act.

As it wasn't a massive area, we opted for the stealthy approach and headed out on foot. I was lamp man, and Edan took up first gunner with his .17 HMR. The first couple of fields proved fruitful, with only a handful of bunnies escaping the fine shooting on display. This was a systematic search and destroy mission, and we were working well together. There is definitely a big advantage to hunting at night with the same person repeatedly, as you begin to second-guess one another. This was certainly

becoming the case with the two of us, and we were having a lot of fun.

At the far end of the farm, a rough overgrown strip dropped down into a den bordering the neighbouring estate. There was a good number of rabbits here, but a forest of dead standing dockings made clean shots difficult. It doesn't take much for the fragile, light bullet of the HMR to disintegrate, so you have to be conscious of the terrain. An inconveniently placed leaf or grass stem will be enough for a bullet connection failure. However, this does have its advantages from a safety point of view.

Unlike a .22LR, the ballistic-tipped HMR bullets don't ricochet. This is particularly important when, like us, you are hunting on the edge of a built-up area. It is definitely a safer calibre to shoot with.

We swept the light across the den. A bright flash shone back from the opposite side before vanishing promptly into the darkness. As we scanned down the line of beech trees again, a lone roe deer emerged near the top of the bank, quelling our optimism that we were about to get a chance at a fox.

When we focused the beam ahead of us, two coneys dashed from cover and paused momentarily in full view. Dropping his rifle back on the sticks, Edan nestled into the butt, when the magnesium burn of foxy eyes flashed back once again from the edge of the beam. This couldn't be a deer – it could only be Charlie boy. At about 70 yards away, it would

Below:
A night worth remembering as Edan takes his first Charlie

be a comfortable shot, and, assuming the bullet was well placed, the .17 HMR should be able to close the deal without much trouble.

Drawing aim on the skulking shadow, Edan positively identified the bushy-tailed predator. "Where should I shoot him?" he whispered to me. He was obviously worried about his small calibre, and, having not taken a fox before, was looking for a little reassurance. "Just find a spot behind his shoulder," I said, "right in the middle of his chest. You will be fine with that. Take your time."

A moment later, the muted crack of Edan's rifle broke the silence of night. The returning 'thwack' was solid. It certainly sounded like a good shot. In a frenzy, the fox turned and dashed across the stream, through a patch of nettles and over the open ground before disappearing.

Edan turned to me. "It felt good, but he ran a long way. I really hope we find him." I was confident he wouldn't be too far away, as the strike had sounded good.

Tracing the fox's path from the stream to where we lost sight, I paused to survey the ground. There were two options: he would have either headed into the narrow, rough bramble maze on our side, or tracked up the den away from us.

Selecting a search pattern, we began scouring the ground. For more than 20 minutes we hunted for the carcase, but to no avail. I was 90 per cent sure that the fox was dead, so we extended the search across a ploughed field, and higher up the den. Nothing.

Returning once more to where we lost sight, I retraced his steps, imagining where a fatally wounded fox would have run. Then I found him. He was in a shallow hollow on the edge of some overhanging dead grass – a shadow had concealed Edan's prize. The shot had been perfect, yet the fox had travelled more than 70 yards.

As I am sure you can imagine, Edan was immeasurably relieved that his shot had been a good one. ∎

FOX MARAUDERS

The small shoot I run with a couple of mates brings me a lot of joy throughout the year. We have a couple of informal rough days, which are as much about the bar and food as they are about knocking birds out of the sky. The shoot is blessed with a high density of hares, which allows each of us to take one a year, and there are also a couple of roe to fill the freezers. Our preparation starts earlier than most as I breed half the birds myself, adding another exciting but sometimes depressing dimension to the shoot. Counting the losses doesn't start from releasing birds in the pen; it begins with eggs in the incubator. But the rewards outweigh any frustrations I have with my primitive incubation system, or the added worry of disease among the very young birds (which can be devastating if not caught very quickly).

I remember one year that started well, but I suffered a complete disaster on the third and final hatch with only a tiny percentage making it out the egg. This was due to an extended storing period and is a lesson painfully learnt.

Despite this, we still had more birds to release than in previous years and only suffered a small intestinal gut problem with 20 or so birds, which was quickly rectified before they were transported to the release pens a short distance from my house. Due to our low numbers we are able to net the tops of our three pens so I could guarantee that all the birds we put in are there when the time comes to open up the sides. Or so I had thought.

The shoot has never had a serious predator problem, although we always lose a few to our sharp beaked, taloned feathery friends. But this year nature has made a concerted effort to make up for it. Two days after the first birds were lovingly set free into our brand new pen we lost two to a stoat, followed by another the night after. Despite a military operation to catch the little bugger, he eluded me in the face of more fen traps than there are landmines in Bosnia (although

I did get him a few weeks after the birds were out). After the third kill he never showed up again and I thought I had had a lucky escape. Charlie boy, on the other hand, had other ideas.

The torrential rain had made life difficult for everyone and the farmers were weeks behind in harvesting their crops. Some friends of mine, with their own syndicates, were reporting losses in the hundreds due to sickness brought on by the bad weather. This hadn't been a problem for us, but we did have a more pressing issue than the need for fresh wheat. A tour around the fringes had shown some fresh fox spoor, but the layout of the farm made lamping all but impossible until the fields were cut. I had to sit and wait, losing two birds to the fox while I could do nothing to stop it.

BYRON'S TOP TIP

Little and often is a perfectly acceptable approach to foxing

My smallest rifle, a Sako .243 shooting 100-grain handloads, would do the job adequately (I have never been wholly comfortable using my .17HMR for foxes, especially on a night with even a breath of wind). The 6x42 Schmidt & Bender scope was a bit restrictive for longer range fox shooting at night, but it was a set-up designed for deer so I would just have to keep the range down. A Petzl headlight, knife, battery pack, Lightforce spotlight, extra ammo and bipod completed the array of gear strewn across the back of my pick-up.

Below:
Byron spots and shoots off the bonnet of his pick-up

As the shadows lengthened and the subtle shimmer of light faded over the back of the Caterthuns, we set off to survey the killing fields from a hill in the middle of the farm. To our amazement we spotted a fox within two minutes of driving up the farm road. Across the first stubble field, about 150 metres away, two eyes glinted back at us as my foxing buddy Edan swept past. Engine off and lights off, I squeaked my heart out trying to get the fox to venture from the ditch where he sat just out of sight, but this fox was no fool and certainly not a cub. After a good 15 minutes, the intermittent reflection from his eyes eventually stopped and it became clear that we had lost our first chance of the night.

Shortly after the engine came to life and started carrying us across the deep ruts, Edan again spotted the distinctive bright eyes of our midnight killer. At over 300 metres he was a bit far for me, but repetitive squeaking soon had the death-dealing critter wandering slowly in our direction.

As he approached the 200 metre mark, I was preparing for a shot when the wind changed direction and gusted our scent down the hill into the nostrils of our hunting fox. With that he turned and headed straight for the woods, never to be seen again that night.

We headed back out just after one in the morning to be greeted by a fox in exactly the same place as the wily old boy we had first seen. Again he was moving just out of sight, but I wasn't banking on being able to call him in this time.

Disembarking from the vehicle with lightning speed, Edan hooked up the battery pack and we quick-stepped it to a bale some 30 metres closer to the fox. With a slight elevation I was hoping I could make out enough of the fox to take a clean shot. As Edan unleashed the piercing light, two beady eyes shone back from the underside of a bale some 130 metres away. I lined up my crosshairs just below his eyes, somewhere near the tip of his nose – not to shoot him in the head, but to drop the bullet in the centre of the chest.

The crack of my .243 shattered the silence. The muzzle blast momentarily blinded us from the result of my shot. We walked over, scanning the ground for a sprawled out fox or any sign of blood, but on approaching the bale where the fox had been there was no evidence.

Then, just as I started to replay the shot in my mind, Edan spotted Charlie boy half a dozen steps from where we were standing. Closer inspection revealed a very old dog fox bearing more than a few battle scars. The shot was slap-bang in the middle of his chest, with the bullet exiting near the back leg. It was a satisfying job well done.

The next weekend I was out again. It was fruitless, but just after 12am I decided to go have one last look. After scanning the usual places I headed to the top of the hill. The battery pack had given up the ghost and I had to spot and shoot at the same time.

I stood ready with the rifle set up on the bipod, resting expectantly in the direction of the woods by my release pen. After an hour of squeaking my mouth was dry, but I was eventually rewarded

A bold young fox, clearly from this year's litter, came trotting across the grass field. Sighting in on the fox, I shouted to make him stop, which he promptly did 100 metres from where I was standing, poised and ready. As the firing pin struck, Charlie, Jr. had no idea that it was good night forever.

After a short search I found the body in the long grass. Taking two foxes out of the equation would make a big difference to the number of pheasants left for us to shoot. I was sure there was still a vixen and a couple of cubs kicking around, but I resolved to pay them a visit as soon as I possibly could. ∎

THE CRUCIAL SHOT

BYRON'S TOP TIP

Foxing and a full-time job don't always mix, but make the most of any opportunities you have to go out with lamp and rifle

Above:
Edan scans the fields for signs of Reynard

Thinking back to 2011's foxing forays in the vicinity of our pheasant shoot still makes me wince. Having lost a substantial number of birds to my toothy adversary that year, I became determined to get ahead of the game every year as soon as the stubbles were laid bare and I could cover my ground.

One year rain had plagued the farmer's efforts in the first weeks of the harvest, but by the end of August I was free from the obscuring sea of grain-laden stalks; the fields were open for business once more. I had made a pact with myself to put what precious time I had available into fox control.

My day job limited my ability to partake in night-time vulpine quests, and left only small windows of opportunity each week to complete the task at hand. However, I had resolved to take every opportunity and not make any excuses. My right-hand man and lamping buddy Edan Annand was as anxious as I was to get out with the lamp as often as possible, but it was the same old story with work – earning a living doesn't always leave time for the things we live for. So it was imperative to make the most of the outings we had, exploring the shadows of every gully and ditch and not letting any opportunity pass.

The preceding weeks had also seen a concerted effort on the rabbit front: scouring the grazed grass fields for the twinkle of rabbits' eyes before sending 40 grains of .22LR on their way to provide food for the pot and keep the farmer 'on side'. During this time I had surprisingly failed to get much of a glimpse of Charlie. I naively thought that the neighbouring estates must have conducted an efficient den clearance and snaring campaign, leaving my small area unmolested. It was indeed as unlikely as it seemed – as the weeks went on, the fox menace increased.

It was after 10pm when the crunch of gravel outside signalled the arrival of the evening's hunting party. Edan, my usual shooting partner, was joined by a mutual friend of ours who was much newer to the whole experience. Mark had accompanied me on a single trip the previous year, but it had been a fruitless affair, and so he hoped to see more action this time. He was not to be disappointed.

A final series of checks ensured lamps, ammo, rifles and the other usual kit were accounted for, along with my trusty sandbag for shooting from the bonnet. I had originally used this not out of choice, but because my only bipod was too long to shoot comfortably from the vehicle. Now, however, I find that even though I have the appropriate benchrest size, the old-school sand bag is more comfortable. Whether taking a shot from the roof or bonnet, it just seems to nestle the rifle the way I like it.

Our first task was a quick spin around the pheasant shoot to see what we could come up with, before heading up the hill to bag some bunnies. We hoped that by showing Mark some quick action, we would re-kindle his interest in vermin control.

The initial tour of the farm produced a few glaring roe eyes and a handful of bumbling hares, but Mr Fox remained unaccounted for. The hurl up the hill was much more productive, with Mark and Edan efficiently dispatching a bagful of coneys.

With the hour hand now well past 12, we entered into the foxing zone. Almost all the foxes I had shot on this farm had been between midnight and 3am, so now was the time to focus.

Creeping up the rutted farm track, Edan swept his searchlight across the land, parting the darkness to uncover what the night tried to keep hidden. Barren stubble stretched from side to side as I drove on in the Isuzu pickup, willing the piercing, fiery glow of a fox's eyes to shine back through the darkness.

The initial loop once again showed very little, so we decided to visit a neighbouring farm, where I had been given permission to lamp earlier in the day. The short drive around allowed us to view where we had just been, along with a further two stubble fields and an expanse of potato crops. On clearing the

Below:
Byron Pace's persistence pays off in the end

horizon, Edan immediately zoned in on a dung heap 300 yards or so away, where a movement had caught his sharp eye. Sure enough, a moment later a fox stared back through the night, clearly perturbed at being disturbed from his beetle hunt. Even at this distance we could see he was a big fox, but being in the limelight was obviously not his cup of tea – he quickly made a beeline in the opposite direction, into the unharvested potatoes and out of sight. This fox had obviously seen a lamp before, and quite possibly heard the crack of a rifle to boot. We cursed our luck for not having the chance to put a bead on the scoundrel, and headed back to our pheasant shoot for a final lap of the farm.

As we neared the woods by the primary release pen, the lamp picked up distant eyes periodically flashing as another fox made his way along the periphery of the field. He didn't seem to be in any rush, stopping to mouse about and pick up the odd slug – which gave me time to dismount the driving seat and set up my battle station on the roof of the pickup.

I knew from the off that it was a long shot, but the darkness hampered my ability to accurately account for the distance. I figured it was somewhere in the region of 200 yards – well within my ability – requiring an aim point just above the centre line to drop the 70-grain bullet through the engine room. I squeezed off the shot. I succumbed to the muzzle flash thanks to the lack of a moderator; as my night vision recovered, I was able to follow the perfectly spritely-looking fox striding diagonally towards us. I had made two rookie mistakes. Firstly, as I discovered the next day, my range estimation was wrong (it was more like 300 yards). Secondly, I had picked up 100-grain bullets and not 70-grain, resulting in greater drop than expected. Both were big mistakes. I was baffled enough by the first error as my range judgement is normally pretty good. However, to pick up the wrong bullets was inexcusable, even though it is an easy mistake to make.

To our amazement, Charlie swiftly zigzagged towards us, passing around 100 yards in front

but intermittently obscured by a thick strip of long grass. Edan swept the beam right to intercept the fox's path, honing in on a safe clearing between the two gates where the fox had been headed.

With my .243 Win locked and loaded, I rotated 30 degrees and firmly fixed my crosshairs on the gap, ready to unleash the bullet the moment Charlie-boy dared to show himself once more. As he broke cover, however, his speed made it clear that he had ideas of living another day, and didn't relish the concept of having another high-velocity projectile lobbed in his direction.

Edan, on the ball as always, hollered at the fox and caused him to pause momentarily. It was all I needed. A moment later I redeemed my earlier mistake, as the crack of the rifle signalled the end of another predator hungry for poults.

I was satisfied to have ended the night with a fox in hand, although my initial miss had tarnished the proceedings. Fortunately, I was able to explain my misplacement; had that not been the case, the seeds of doubt would

be set, and I would have needed a trip to the range to restore my self-belief.

The following night – the last before the grind of work recommenced – Edan and I set out once more, this time with the right ammo packed and a conscious mental picture of the distances we were covering. I was reminded that a rangefinder should move to the top of my 'to buy' list, hopefully to prevent a repeat of the same mistake.

Unlike the previous night, the first circuit of the neighbour's field yielded a fox crossing towards the stream. While I organised my gear once more, Edan squeaked with his wigeon whistle to keep Charlie's attention, bringing him in closer as I positioned the rifle on the bonnet. With a rock-solid rest, and the distance less than 150 yards, the 70-grain ballistic tip found its mark easily and rolled the fox over to his final resting place amongst the stubble.

With two successful outings completed, I ended the weekend with a sense of achievement. My work would undoubtedly save a good number of birds from meeting a premature end. ∎

Above:
Byron's bean bag proves its worth for Edan when shooting off the bonnet

SKYE FOXES ARE THE BOMB

BYRON'S TOP TIP

Remember the saying: 'There's no bad weather, only inappropriate clothing'

I recall fondly my times on Skye foxing. The terrain is difficult – and filming for The Shooting Show equally so, but the rewards are spectacular. One occasion that sticks out saw me joining friend and hunter Scott Mackenzie. Given the limited number of roe on the island, and with the hind season well and truly over, Scott's attention was firmly placed on a search and destroy mission.

Although he had made a concerted effort over the winter months to fend off the encroaching fox population, we were now at the start of the lambing season, and this was no time to be taking stock.

It is important to understand what a massive impact the loss of one lamb can make in a crofting environment. Obviously any loss is felt by a farmer, and is a reduction of potential future revenue.

However, on the island, a crofter may only have 30-head. On this much smaller scale, one less lamb to market is a substantial proportion of the expected year's takings from crofting activities.

With this in mind, Scott gathered together a number of adjoining crofts to help provide a unified front against their vulpine thief. With unimpeded scope to cover a large area of ground, Scott could now more efficiently control problem foxes. This is a plan that has proved successful over a number of years. Of course, the good efforts and work throughout the year could mean little if the crofters suffered heavy losses during lambing. It is, after all, this time that Scott's year of foxing control comes fruition. Just one marauding killer could make it look like he had been slacking throughout previous months.

It was the end of a miserable week. The previous year had been fairly dry in the northwest, and this was noticeable as my Landy wound its way northward. Peering across to the fleeting bodies of water, the bare bones of rocky shores were obvious to see. The countryside was in need of a drink – it

Credit: Peter G Trimming

Scott's perserverance is rewarded

was just a shame the parched watercourses were only now being filled. We made do with the hand we had been dealt, and I set off with Scott for my first venture in six months across the unforgiving Skye landscape in search of Mr Fox.

Scott was armed with my Kimber .243 Win, topped with Swarovski optics and Hardy Gen 4 moderator. Loaded up a little heavy for foxes, we were running 105-grain Gecos. With time at a premium, I hadn't had a chance to zero for the 70-grain Federal Ballistic tips I would usually have for such endeavours. Scott was more than content, insisting that this was his standard ammo for foxing on Skye owing to the turbulent weather and rough, tussocky ground. All that was left now was to brave the horizontal drizzle and make a move.

Fulfilling the Scandinavian proverb, "there is no such thing as bad weather, only inappropriate clothing," we dressed for the elements. Trying to take a positive from the situation, it was likely that any foxes willing to brave the conditions would be heading for sheltered areas. To be honest, any Charlies willing to venture onto the wind-battered tops were welcome to have an undisturbed night – it was no place to be hunting, and unlikely Scott would get an accurate shot off from a distance. Fortunately, with most of the lambing underway, the livestock was concentrated on the lower, more sheltered areas, and this is where we needed to focus our attention.

Taking me to a long, hollow bowl where we had hunted previously, Scott stopped on the roadside to scan with the lamp. Brushing over the bending, dead grasses, the beam swept the landscape to no avail. Usually Scott would walk in at this point to try a spot of calling. We weren't feeling quite acclimatised just yet, so opted for a long lamp from his truck to cover all the accessible areas first, before stepping foot outside for the rest of the night.

After two hours, our chances were looking slim. It seemed that our nemesis was likely tucked up warm somewhere (arguably what we should have been doing, with a dram in hand). Not willing to be defeated, we pushed on to our fourth location.

Picking a route with only the dim light of a small, hand-held lamp to guide us, Scott positioned us on the edge of a long ledge. As I would discover once the Lightforce beam illuminated the ground below us, we now had a commanding view over a vast tract of ground. Although we were anything but sheltered from the northerly pounding, the land fell away below us to provide a relatively tranquil oasis amid the storm. After a quick flash showed nothing, Scott began to call, demonstrating to me for the first time his own-design, American-influenced caller.

Scott flashed on the light once more, immediately catching a flash back through the darkness. It was coming like a steam train towards us. Quickly, Scott got into position behind the rifle, manning the lamp with his spare hand. He was used to doing this as a one-man operation, and his slickness made this apparent. The fox broke the 150-yard mark and was still closing. As it made it to 100 yards, it paused, looking straight through us for a split second. Scott sent his projectile of death on a guided course into the engine room.

To this point, our story was much like any other foxing encounter. However, what followed the next morning added humour to our nocturnal wonderings. I received a call from my brother to let me know he was heading to Skye with the Royal Navy bomb squad. They had a call to destroy a suspect item spotted off the shore in the north part of the island. Knowing I was already on location, and with his commanding officer a keen hunter, it had been arranged for me and Scott to tag along and see the operation.

Joining the police and military convoy on the road, we followed on towards the ground we had been hunting the night before. It soon become apparent that we were following them to the exact spot we had shot the fox just 12 hours previously. Disembarking, I had a chance to speak with Darryl as he organised explosives and dive gear. Remarkably, little more than 500 metres from where we had laid down to take a shot, the suspected item lay lodged in rocks down by the sea.

Her Majesty's finest did their job, and it was soon taken care of, wrapping up an unexpected and unusual foxing trip. ■

Below:
Byron's brother Darryl after his bomb squad was called to Skye

RECOMMENDED READING

SPORTING RIFLES, PETER CARR

This newly compiled and modernised book comprises a collection of modern sporting firearms available to the British rifleman, from rimfires right through to big game calibres. From the traditional to the very recent, every type of rifle and major manufacturer is covered, with historical information, technical specifications and opinions from some of the UK's most respected rifle reviewers, including Byron Pace, Tim Pilbeam, Mike Powell and Pete Carr. This is a comprehensive, knowledgeable book, and is as close to the definitive guide to rifles as you're ever going to get.

ISBN 978-1910247037

Available at *www.virtualnewsagent.com*.

A FOXING LIFE WITH GUN AND RIFLE, MIKE POWELL

Long-standing *Sporting Rifle* contributor Mike Powell's life has, in one way or another, run parallel to that of the fox. From running a fox control business and keepering, to making a living from selling their skins, the fox has always been present.

Today, Mike is passing on his knowledge of the fox and detailing his dealings with Charlie over the course of his life in the new book: *A Foxing Life with Gun and Rifle*. The book traces Mike's early years in foxing, before delving into the various methods open to fox controllers, revealing his own hints and tips and discussing how these have evolved over his time hunting this wily predator. It's a must have resource for those who, like Mike, tangle with foxes on a regular basis, but more than a mere hunting manual, it's the story of one man's lifelong adventures with his quarry and testament to the skill required to achieve the level of hunting success Mike has in his lifetime.

ISBN 978-0954959746

Available at *www.virtualnewsagent.com*.

FOXING WITH LAMP AND RIFLE, ROBERT BUCKNELL

Foxing with Lamp and Rifle is Robert Bucknell's first book, which distills a wealth of experience into a highly readable tome. The author's knowledge of foxes and wildlife is considerable, and is complemented by his thorough knowledge of firearms and experience of being a first class shot.

With excellent photographs taken over many years, plus targets, charts and graphs that will inform and help anyone interested in 'foxing' or foxes. The second edition has been fully revised and updated.

ISBN 978-0954020613

Available at *www.virtualnewsagent.com*.

GOING FOXING, ROBERT BUCKNELL

The long-awaited follow-up to *Foxing with Lamp and Rifle* is a far more in-depth and comprehensive portrait of the lives and behaviour of foxes. The large number of colour photographs shows, in some detail, much about the natural history of this intelligent animal.

The use of firearms is covered and will allow the reader to become more effective in their use.

ISBN 978-0954020620

Available at *www.virtualnewsagent.com*.

FOXING DVD, ROBERT BUCKNELL WITH JAMES MARCHINGTON

We hope it's not too sacreligious to include a DVD in a recommended reading section, but this deserves its place. Robert Bucknell's skill, wit and expertise are perfectly suited to the visual medium and foxers of all abilities will be able to gain something from this film.

Available at *www.virtualnewsagent.com*.

FOXING WITH THE EXPERTS

ACKNOWLEDGEMENTS

Firstly I would like to give personal thanks to all the experts who are included in this book. When I took over as editor of *Sporting Rifle* magazine Mike Powell was a goldmine of information on both up to date and antiquated methods of fox control.

Soon after came Robert Bucknell, who gave me another vein of expertise to tap into. Both are long-standing contributors on their subject in the sporting press and published authors in their own right. I thank them both for their wealth of knowledge, and the unselfish way they have shared it with me over the past five years.

The same goes to the other experts featured in this book: Gary Green, Howard Heywood, Mark Nicholson, Andy Lovel, Andy Malcolm – and the silent contributor James Marchington – whose writing, and support, throughout various stages of my *Sporting Rifle* editorship has been both badly needed and valued greatly. Without their collective writings this book would have been a much tougher task.

Byron Pace never ceases to amaze me. In his short lifetime he has nearly caught me up on varied sporting experiences. His shooting tastes are as cosmopolitan as mine; he finds quarry to hunt wherever he is in the world and I'm sure he will become a successful author in his own right. He has been, and still is, one of the key players in *Sporting Rifle's* success, and long may it continue.

Nick Robbins, one of my colleagues at Blaze Publishing, has had the task of editing this book and putting right my faults. He has my gratitude and understanding for putting up with me during the compilation and structuring process that went on for longer than it should – the fault was all mine, forgive me for my conservative take on the concept of deadlines.

And to another Blaze Publishing colleague, art director Chris Sweeney, who has worked wonders designing this book in a short time frame, thanks for all your efforts, mate.

To publisher Wes Stanton for supporting this project and injecting the necessary currency to achieve its completion – I am again in your debt, a position I always seem to be in.

Finally to my wife Debra for her continued support and tolerance above and beyond the normal call of wedlock. I know if I'm not out shooting, I'm mostly writing about it. You really do deserve to sit among saints.